P9-CCO-282

Hacking
MySpace™

Hacking
MySpace™

Customizations and Mods to Make MySpace Your Space

John Pospisil

WILEY

Wiley Publishing, Inc.

Hacking MySpace™: Customizations and Mods to Make MySpace Your Space

Published by
Wiley Publishing, Inc.
10475 Crosspoint Boulevard
Indianapolis, IN 46256
www.wiley.com

Copyright © 2006 by Wiley Publishing, Inc., Indianapolis, Indiana

Published simultaneously in Canada

ISBN-13: 978-0-470-04584-8
ISBN-10: 0-470-04584-1

Manufactured in the United States of America

10 9 8 7 6 5 4 3 2 1

No part of this publication may be reproduced, stored in a retrieval system or transmitted in any form or by any means, electronic, No part of this publication may be reproduced, stored in a retrieval system or transmitted in any form or by any means, electronic, mechanical, photocopying, recording, scanning or otherwise, except as permitted under Sections 107 or 108 of the 1976 United States Copyright Act, without either the prior written permission of the Publisher, or authorization through payment of the appropriate per-copy fee to the Copyright Clearance Center, 222 Rosewood Drive, Danvers, MA 01923, (978) 750-8400, fax (978) 646-8600. Requests to the Publisher for permission should be addressed to the Legal Department, Wiley Publishing, Inc., 10475 Crosspoint Blvd., Indianapolis, IN 46256, (317) 572-3447, fax (317) 572-4355, or online at http://www.wiley.com/go/permissions.

Limit of Liability/Disclaimer of Warranty: The publisher and the author make no representations or warranties with respect to the accuracy or completeness of the contents of this work and specifically disclaim all warranties, including without limitation warranties of fitness for a particular purpose. No warranty may be created or extended by sales or promotional materials. The advice and strategies contained herein may not be suitable for every situation. This work is sold with the understanding that the publisher is not engaged in rendering legal, accounting, or other professional services. If professional assistance is required, the services of a competent professional person should be sought. Neither the publisher nor the author shall be liable for damages arising herefrom. The fact that an organization or Website is referred to in this work as a citation and/or a potential source of further information does not mean that the author or the publisher endorses the information the organization or Website may provide or recommendations it may make. Further, readers should be aware that Internet Websites listed in this work may have changed or disappeared between when this work was written and when it is read.

For general information on our other products and services or to obtain technical support, please contact our Customer Care Department within the U.S. at (800) 762-2974, outside the U.S. at (317) 572-3993 or fax (317) 572-4002.

Library of Congress Cataloging-in-Publication Data

Pospisil, John, 1971–
  Hacking MySpace : customizations and mods to make MySpace
your space / John Pospisil.
    p. cm.
  Includes index.
  ISBN-13: 978-0-470-04584-8 (paper/website)
  ISBN-10: 0-470-04584-1 (paper/website)
  1. Web sites—Design. 2. MySpace (Firm) 3. Social networks
—Computer network resources.   I. Title.
TK5105.888.P587 2006
006.7—dc22

Trademarks: Wiley, the Wiley logo, and related trade dress are trademarks or registered trademarks of John Wiley & Sons, Inc. and/or its affiliates, in the United States and other countries, and may not be used without written permission. ExtremeTech and the ExtremeTech logo are trademarks of Ziff Davis Publishing Holdings, Inc. Used under license. All rights reserved. MySpace is a trademark of MySpace, Inc. All other trademarks are the property of their respective owners. Wiley Publishing, Inc., is not associated with any product or vendor mentioned in this book.

Wiley also publishes its books in a variety of electronic formats. Some content that appears in print may not be available in electronic books.

To my wife, Rocio, and baby daughter, Grace, who in different ways
have transformed my life and made me a much better person

To my parents, Milada and Michael; my parents-in-law, Lidya and Segundo;
my sisters, Patricia and Daniela; my brothers-in-law, Carlos and Steve;
and my nieces, Marissa and baby Katie

About the Author

John Pospisil is the founder of Cogent Insights (www.cogentinsights.com), a marketing and communications consultancy specializing in new and converging media.

Originally from a journalism background, John was the product development champion and founding editor of *Computer CHOICE,* an easy-to-read computer magazine launched by the Australian Consumers' Association in 1995, and still one of Australia's most credible and independent IT titles. In 1998 he teamed up with fellow journalist Tom Crawley to launch Free Access magazine, and in 2001 they teamed with photographer Shelton Muller to launch *Total Image* magazine.

John is the author of three books, including the best-selling *How to Buy a Computer* (which went through four editions—1996, 1997, 1998, 2000), *How to Get More from Your Computer* (2000), and *How to Start a Small Business in the Real World* (2002).

John has a journalism degree from the University of Canberra, and an MBA from the University of Technology, Sydney.

Credits

Executive Editor
Chris Webb

Development Editor
Rosanne Koneval

Technical Editor
Shawn Kessel

Copy Editor
Nancy Rapoport

Editorial Manager
Mary Beth Wakefield

Production Manager
Tim Tate

Vice President and Executive Group Publisher
Richard Swadley

Vice President and Executive Publisher
Joseph B. Wikert

Compositor
Maureen Forys,
Happenstance Type-O-Rama

Proofreader
C. M. Jones

Indexer
Melanie Belkin

Cover Design
Anthony Bunyan

Acknowledgments

A lot of people have helped me with this book in one way or another, so here's my attempt to thank them.

The biggest thank you has to go my wonderful wife, Rocio, for her love and support during the ludicrously busy period when I wrote this book. Sometimes it felt as though I was working three jobs, well, actually, come to think of it...

Another big thank you has to go to my baby daughter, Grace, who was also very patient and who carefully read through each chapter. Well, the truth is, Grace tried to eat each chapter, but it's the thought that counts. Also, thank you to my mother-in-law, Lidya, who was staying with us while I was writing, and really helped to make life a lot more comfortable.

Thank you to my mother, father, and sisters, Patricia and Daniela, for their words of encouragement.

A very big thank you to Laura Lewin, my agent at StudioB, who encouraged me to pitch this project to Wiley Publishing, and a special thank you to Andrew Parsons who introduced me to Laura. A thank you to Chris Webb and Rosanne Koneval at Wiley Publishing for guiding me through the process of writing for a large publisher like Wiley. And a thank you to Shawn Kessel for being a great technical editor.

A big thank you to the following MySpace members who helped me with critical sections of the book: Ben Bledsoe, Valerie Burgess, Nate Burns, Nick Edwards, Dan Hill, Michelle Mannor, Mark McDonald, Jessica Mellott, Elda Ramirez, Michael Sabine, Jesse Smith, Willian, Kevin Turner, and the guys from rfp, Joshua's Whisper, and North of Hollywood.

Thank you to Tom Crawley for his help with the photo tips, and to Shelton Muller for assisting me with some of the photography (the nice shots, that is; the other ones were taken by me alone). Thank you to Alex Zaharov-Reutt for allowing me to draw on his expertise in the field of new media, and for his feedback on some of the later chapters.

Contents at a Glance

Part III: Design and Photography

Part IV: MySpace Music

Contents

Part I: Introducing MySpace

Part II: The Hacks

Part III: Design and Photography

Part IV: MySpace Music

Preface

With more than 80 million profiles on MySpace, how on earth do you make yours stand out? That's the question many people ask themselves when they first join MySpace.

Part of the answer is to make your profile do things that it was never intended to do — and that's where this book comes in.

While much of this book is devoted to the technical issues of helping you develop an amazing profile, some chapters are devoted to photography, design, and content to help you communicate the right message through your profile.

I've really enjoyed putting this book together, and I hope you get a lot out of it. The world of MySpace changes frequently, and I'll be providing regular updates on my web site, www.myspaceismyplace.com. If you have any comments, please don't hesitate to get in touch with me at john@myspaceismyplace.com.

While you're learning to code and customize your profile, don't forget that on the other side of all that plastic, copper, silicon, and steel that link you to the Internet and MySpace are other human beings — and that's really what MySpace is about.

Introduction

Hacking MySpace™ is designed to help you create a profile that stands out from the clutter of boring and uninspiring profiles that tend to dominate MySpace. It shows you programming tricks and techniques that will help you differentiate your profile from others, and it provides guidance on design, photography, and content to also make it interesting.

So what's the secret that allows MySpace profiles to be customized?

The creators of MySpace have allowed "codes" to be inserted into members' profiles, which means that if you know how, you can alter the standard profile, or indeed, build your own profile from scratch.

This book gives you grounding in writing code in HTML and CSS, and it takes you through a number of hacks that will allow you to modify your existing profile, or design an entirely new profile.

Because a MySpace profile is a form of publishing, I also look at design, photography, and content, all of which are just as important as the coding. In later chapters, this book helps you understand how to create amazing profiles. The masters of MySpace — MySpace members with outstanding profiles — also share some of their secrets. Those of you involved in music will find invaluable tips from up-and-coming artists on how to promote your act.

Some of the code in this book is not beautiful (by the standards of professional programmers), but such is the nature of MySpace hacking that sometimes that's just how it needs to be. My main focus is to make sure the code works on MySpace — not so much on following all conventions, although I've tried to make the code conform as much as possible.

If you come across something that doesn't seem to work, no matter how hard you try, chances are that MySpace has changed something with how the profiles work. Visit the companion web site at www.myspaceismyplace.com for an update, or leave a note in the reader forum at the same site.

Whom This Book Is For

This book is for anyone who has a MySpace profile, or who is thinking of getting one, and who wants to create an outstanding profile.

You don't need to know anything about HTML or CSS to get started — it's all covered in the book. All the concepts are carefully explained, so as long as you're open to learning new things, you should have no problems understanding what's going on.

How This Book Is Organized

It's not hard to use MySpace at a basic level, so this book does not cover the basics. It's highly likely that you already have a basic MySpace profile, and you know how to enter information about yourself, upload photos to your photo album, and so on.

The aim of this book is to take you to the next level by giving you a few technical skills and some ideas on how to use those skills so that you create a profile that stands out — in contrast to the many clichéd and downright boring profiles you'll see. To this end, the book assumes that you know nothing about coding, and begins by providing some foundation skills on coding in HTML and CSS. You continue to develop your skills and knowledge as you progress through the book.

This book consists of four parts:

- **Part I: Introducing MySpace** (Chapters 1–9) gives you the basic concepts and tools you need to "hack" MySpace. It provides the basic information you need to give you control over how your MySpace profile looks and what it contains. It also provides an introduction to HTML and CSS.

- **Part II: The Hacks** (Chapters 10–25) consists of actual hacks you can use in your profile, with the code provided and explained, ready for you to customize and place into your personal profile.

- **Part III: Design and Photography** (Chapters 26–29) looks at design and photography and how you incorporate these into your profile. It's important to remember that just because you can do something, doesn't mean you have to do it, which is why this part of the book looks at design and what you need to consider when putting together a profile that will work at an aesthetic level as well as a technical level. Good design, after all, is often quite minimalist, i.e. less equals more. Some of the best MySpace profiles are quite simple, but they have the right balance of technical innovation and good design. A big part of the impact of any profile is its photographs so you must take good photographs in the first place, and know how to use a photo editing package to correct any problems.

- **Part IV: MySpace Music** (Chapters 30 and 31) looks at how you can use MySpace to build your music career. You look at some of MySpace's music success stories, and I try to provide some tips and guidance on how to get a "break" on MySpace. The chapter also explores the future of social networking.

Depending on how deeply you want to get into developing your profile, there are two ways you can use the book:

- If all you want to do is to use the code supplied in this book to add some effects to your profile, without necessarily understanding what you're doing, you can skim through Chapters 3 and 4, which explain HyperText Markup Language (HTML), and Chapters 6 and 7, which explain cascading style sheets (CSS). Make sure however, that you read Chapter 2, which describes how to place code into your MySpace profile, and Chapter 5, which looks at the process of assembling code using a text editor.

- If you want to have a good understanding of how to write your own code so you can build on the hacks supplied, as well as develop your own, pay special attention to Chapters 3, 4, 6, and 7, which explain HTML and CSS. You'll really need to understand HTML and CSS if you want to try creating a Div overlay profile, which is covered in Chapter 25.

Conventions Used in This Book

Throughout the book, you'll find Tip icons. These are designed to provide a particular insight that is relevant to the material being discussed. You'll also come across the Caution icon when there is something you should be careful about.

A number of web links are provided in this book. If you come across a link that doesn't work, simply visit the companion web site at www.myspaceismyplace.com to find an update.

What You Need to Use This Book

Obviously, you need a computer and an Internet connection. While a PC has been used to develop the examples in the book, you should have no problem using a Mac. You also need a MySpace account, which is free.

I've made a point of not using commercial software in any exercise in this book. I did not want to alienate people who do not happen to have a particular package on their computer. All the software used in this book is open source, or shareware or freeware, and links are provided in the book (and on www.myspaceismyplace.com) so you can freely download it. Where possible, the Mac equivalents of software packages used in this book have been noted.

I've used Internet Explorer as a web browser, but feel free to use whatever browser you prefer. If you're relatively inexperienced, I recommend you stick to Internet Explorer for maximum compatibility.

What's on the Companion Web Site

You'll find a companion web site to this book at www.myspaceismyplace.com. The web site contains a number of handy resources.

All the code used in this book is available in electronic format on the site so that you don't have to retype anything. You'll also find all the links to the software used in the book, which you'll find more convenient than having to type each and every link.

As you read the book, you'll come across a number of featured profiles, and you'll find links to these as well at the site. As links are changed, they will be updated on the companion site. If you're interested in exchanging tips with other readers, or if you have a question, you'll find the reader forum a handy place to tap into the MySpace community.

MySpace is constantly being developed, which means that sometimes certain code that was once accepted is filtered out, or perhaps the way that the MySpace profile works is changed, which means that code has to be adjusted to work. When this happens, I'll post an update on the web site. If you notice something askew, please post a note on the web site and I'll find out what's going on.

Introducing MySpace

MySpace is a phenomenon in its own right. Chances are you already know what MySpace is all about, and, indeed, you may even have your own MySpace profile. This book will help you design a truly awesome profile.

The purpose of Part I is to not only give you an understanding of where MySpace fits into the greater context of the Internet but also to provide the building blocks you need to understand some of the hacks later in the book.

By the end of Part I you'll have an understanding of HyperText Markup Language (HTML) as well as of cascading style sheets (CSS). You'll also learn how to place code in your profile and how to use an HTML or text editor to compose your code. Part I also covers how to upload images to file-hosting web sites, or to your own web site, so that they can be embedded in your profile.

Making MySpace Your Space

Do you want your MySpace profile to make an impact? Do you want it to stand out from the crowd? Or maybe you just want to develop a MySpace profile that better reflects who you are as an individual? MySpace (www.myspace.com — see Figure 1-1) has more than 80 million profiles at the time of this writing, which makes it very easy for your profile to get lost in the plethora of profiles that are all competing for attention.

A profile that consists solely of programming tricks doesn't necessarily translate into a profile that is appealing — in fact, if you go overboard, such tricks can make your profile look too busy and can make it look like you're trying too hard.

To create a cool profile, you need style and good content in addition to technical prowess. While some might argue that style can't be taught, this book certainly points out some of the traps for the unwary and also provides advice on how to generate interesting content.

What Is MySpace?

Before embarking on the journey to develop a cool MySpace profile, it's worth reflecting on what MySpace is about and why it's so popular. This will help you to develop a clear idea of what you're trying to achieve.

MySpace is a "social networking" web site. There are more than 200 social networking web sites in existence, and their success can be largely attributed to the human need for connection with others. For many people, such web sites provide a way to extend their real-world circles of friends and acquaintances, or to find other people with similar interests. Some people even use a social networking site to meet romantic partners, while for others it's a way to escape the daily grind of their mundane lives — after all, almost anyone can be cool on MySpace.

Figure 1-1: MySpace has captured the imagination of millions of users.

At a fundamental level, social networking web sites are designed to mimic how people tend to make friends in real life — by meeting new people through existing friends and acquaintances.

When you first join MySpace, you create a profile where you can post pictures and provide information about yourself and your interests. You can even write a blog, which is an online journal where you share your thoughts and feelings.

Once your profile is set up, you can invite your real-world friends to join MySpace as well. They then become your MySpace "friends." They, in turn, can invite their own friends, and so on. To make a new friend, you simply get in touch with your friend's friend. A friend of a friend is in a sense endorsed by your common friend, so you can be more confident that they're not an axe murderer (though there's no guarantee about this; even axe murderers have friends). Keep in mind, however, that even your friend might not truly trust the person who is declared their "MySpace" friend. It's very easy to declare someone a friend, but not as easy to get to know them well enough for a real endorsement. In this way, you'll find that a network of friends on MySpace can mirror relationships in the real world.

Who Do You Want to Be?

"Who do you want to be?" It's worth asking yourself this question before you get too much further into the book. You might be tempted to say that you want to be yourself, as you are in your everyday life, which is a fair answer.

The problem is that people who visit your profile will know you only from the information you provide, by the design of your profile, and through your photographs. They won't actually get to see "you," only the "you" that you choose to present.

On MySpace, you have a lot of control over how other people will perceive you — in fact probably a lot more control than you do in real life.

Don't think of control in terms of deception; think of it in terms of having the opportunity to present yourself in the best possible light.

On MySpace, it's your turn of phrase, or how much effort you've put into your profile, that reflects what kind of person you are. What you choose not to reveal is as important as what you do reveal.

It's really important to differentiate yourself from everyone else. Start asking yourself what makes you different, and how you can highlight this in your profile.

Moreover, what makes MySpace exciting is that you can also search and browse MySpace's existing members outside your network and ask them to become your friend. Of course, you don't have the same safety mechanism as when you invite friends of friends to be your friend, but it is a lot more exciting, and there are a lot of cool people on MySpace for you to meet.

Why MySpace Is Cool

MySpace offers a lot of flexibility in terms of how you structure your profile, and what you put into it. Because you can put programming codes into your actual profile, you have a lot of latitude for creativity — as you'll see when you browse or search profiles. So for example, you can play music and videos in your profile, or change the background colors, change the shape of the cursor, or completely rearrange the layout of your profile. You just can't do this with many other social networking web sites.

MySpace is arguably the most popular social networking web site, with more than 80 million profiles, compared to Friendster, another well-known social networking web site, with 27 million profiles at the time of writing.

Another reason MySpace is so popular is that it gives you the freedom to express yourself without the limitations of other social networking sites, like Friendster, where there seems to be a focus on keeping things under control and nice, and users can't customize their profiles quite to the same degree as they can on MySpace. MySpace has tapped into the alternative music scene, and so has attracted a hip, young crowd with profiles that are edgier and more diverse. A quick browse of MySpace profiles demonstrates that users really are free to express themselves however they please. You'll come across everyone from musicians, to bikers, to Goths, to pagans, to plain old computer nerds, and of course everyone in between. You'll also notice that some people seem quite uninhibited online. For example, you'll find pictures of people showing off their tattoos — as you can see in Figure 1-2. With MySpace becoming a part of the News Limited media empire, the new management has made a push to clean things up, although of course MySpace is still relatively "cool."

FIGURE 1-2: "Lyttle Ravyn" showing off her tattoo

Credibility in the Music Industry

Another factor behind MySpace's success is its credibility in the music industry and the fact that it has been a launching pad for a number of emerging bands such as Hollywood Undead (www.myspace.com/hollywoodundead), West Grand (www.myspace.com/westgrand) and Fall Out Boy (www.myspace.com/falloutboy). Canadian metal band Time is the Enemy (www.myspace.com/tite) was discovered by its label INgrooves on MySpace. More than half a million bands have MySpace web pages where they provide music clips and band information, and talk to fans.

For example, if you visit the Hollywood Undead MySpace page (see Figure 1-3), not only can you find out about the band, but you can also play their music and become a "friend" or, actually, a fan (I doubt you can really be friends with a band that has thousands of "friends"). At the time of this writing, the Hollywood Undead had more than 180,000 "friends" and their songs had been played more than 7 million times.

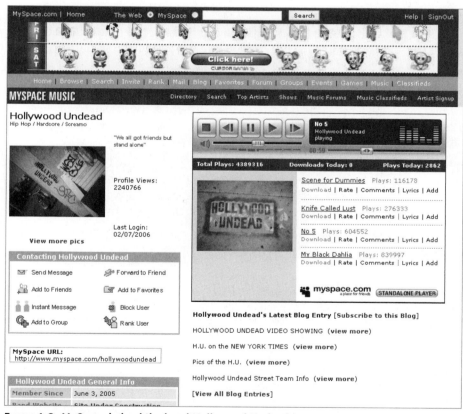

FIGURE 1-3: MySpace helped the band Hollywood Undead (www.myspace.com/hollywoodundead) break into the mainstream.

The Popular Guy Hack

The kinds of "hacks" we cover in this book are all inoffensive — they're simply designed to help you develop an amazing profile. There are, however, some mischievous hackers who take things too far, and the now famous "popular guy" hack, also known as the Samy Worm, is a great example of this.

Written by MySpace member Samy, the "popular guy" hack was actually a worm designed to make Samy the most popular guy on MySpace. Whenever someone viewed Samy's profile, that person automatically made Samy their friend — without their permission. This was interesting enough, but Samy decided to go further. He created a hack where anyone who viewed a profile where Samy was already a friend also automatically made Samy a friend on their profile. So, if ten people viewed Samy's profile, Samy would have ten new friends. If 10 people viewed the profiles of each of these new friends, Samy would have an additional 100 friends, and so on.

Ten hours after Samy placed the worm code in his profile, he had over 1,000 friends. Thirteen hours later he had almost 9,000 friends. Eighteen hours later he had almost 1,000,000 friends. Samy tried to stop the worm, but it was too late — it had a life of its own.

The exponential increase in Samy's friends meant that the MySpace servers become overloaded and had to be shut down temporarily while the worm was disabled.

The worm made the news in the mainstream media. T-shirts with "Samy is my hero" were sold online, and Samy became something of a cult hero. Luckily for Samy, MySpace chose not to take legal action.

Samy told Google Blogoscoped's Philipp Lenssen (`blog.outer-court.com`) that he believes badly designed MySpace profiles cause more damage than his work: "It is true that many people go overboard with their HTML layouts, and I believe that such 'yellow on blue' page layouts cause much more damage in the long run than my worm did."

Obviously Samy has a cheeky sense of humor, but it does give you something to think about when designing your profile.

The online popularity of the Hollywood Undead led to their being the first band signed by MySpace's record label MySpace Records, a joint venture between MySpace and music label Interscope. MySpace Records also released a compilation album, MySpace Records Volume 1, that features bands that are popular on MySpace.

And with other record labels regularly scouring MySpace for new talent, MySpace is the place to be for new and aspiring musicians. MySpace provides an opportunity for garage bands to build a profile and maybe even break into the big time.

Incidentally, it's not only new bands that use MySpace to promote their work. Established acts such as Nine Inch Nails, Black Eyed Peas, and Audio Slave have used MySpace to promote new releases. The television industry has also gotten in on the act. NBC promoted its sitcom *The Office* on MySpace (`www.myspace.com/theoffice`).

The point is that MySpace has captured the public's imagination. Whether you want to make friends, meet a girlfriend or boyfriend, tell the world what you have to say, launch a music career, or just find out what the buzz is about, the starting point is to create a distinctive profile that gets attention.

Beware the Dark Side

It's also worth pointing out that there is a dark side to MySpace, and it's not something that affects just MySpace: It's something that affects all social networking sites. Bad people are just as good at using computers as good people. In fact, the anonymity of the Internet is an attraction for all kinds of deviants and practical jokers, who use forums such as MySpace to deceive people for their own amusement or for personal gain.

Any woman who places an even slightly revealing or provocative picture of herself on MySpace will be inundated with comments from men of all ages, many of whom are not shy about expressing the kind of relationship they are looking for. So yes, there is a sleazy side to social networking sites.

You can never be absolutely sure about a stranger you meet on MySpace. It's not uncommon, for example, for married men to pretend they are single so that they can play the field. It's also not uncommon for men to pretend that they are pretty young women just to get kicks when other men start propositioning them. The giveaway is usually that the profile features pictures of an impossibly beautiful woman, with lots of suggestive innuendo in the profile itself. These types of profiles are also sometimes fronts for adult web sites — so don't get too excited if a beautiful woman (if you happen to be male) wants to be your "friend." More often than not she is not what she appears to be. Sometimes, deviants are more clever and less obvious, so in all cases it's best to be cautious.

Increasingly, MySpace profiles are being used to sell questionable products and multi-level marketing scams — don't be surprised if you get a friend request from someone who claims he can make you rich through lotto or who wants to give you a free iPod. As in real life, if it seems too good to be true, it usually is too good to be true.

Wrapping Up

With its continuing involvement in the music industry, and its cool, young membership, MySpace is an amazing world, full of possibilities and opportunities. And while it's great to embrace this exciting frontier, it's also important to be aware of the possible dangers — as I mentioned, bad guys have computers, too.

Customizing and Hacking MySpace

I n the previous chapter we looked at factors behind MySpace's popularity. One key factor is the degree of customization it offers users. Not only can you create a profile with information about yourself, but you can also change the way your profile appears.

The MySpace control panel offers a fair degree of choice, and will certainly allow you to set up a basic profile. But if you look at some of the other profiles you'll soon start to wonder how other users have managed to get their profiles to look so different.

The key to unlocking the power of MySpace lies with something called HyperText Markup Language (HTML), a special markup language that allows you to control how your profile appears, and its sister language, cascading style sheets (CSS). Both languages are covered in this book — HTML in Chapters 3 and 4, and CSS in Chapters 6 and 7.

HTML was developed in the early 1990s to allow people to have more control over how Internet-related documents appear. With HTML it's possible to control the look and structure of the page.

With many social networking web sites, it's simply not possible to insert your own code. MySpace, on the other hand, allows you to insert HTML as well as CSS. MySpace also allows you to use Dynamic HTML, which permits more interaction between the user and the web page.

Through the course of the book we'll use the terms "HTML" and "code" quite loosely — so that from a technical perspective, we may actually be talking about HTML, CSS, or even Dynamic HTML.

Getting Ready

For the benefit of going through the examples in the book, it's a good idea to set up a dummy account on MySpace, which will enable you to try things out without affecting your day-to-day account (but don't tell MySpace I told you to do this).

in this chapter

☑ Getting ready

☑ Inserting HTML

☑ MySpace editors

It's also a good idea to create a working directory for MySpace files on your computer's hard disk. This is where you can store the various files you'll be using as you work through the book. For the sake of convenience, you may want to copy the code and supporting material from the supporting web site at www.myspaceismyplace.com into your working directory. Simply download the files from the "supporting material" area of the web site into your MySpace directory on your computer.

The supporting material mainly consists of the code needed for various exercises and actual "hacks" that you'll explore as you work through the book — the goal is to save you the time it would take to retype the code. There are also a few images that you may want to use for the image-related sections of the book.

The best way to work with the code is to load it into a text editor (the one that came with your computer is fine — Notepad on the PC or TextEdit on the Mac) and then copy the code from the text editor and paste it into MySpace (as explained in the text that follows).

Inserting HTML

When you log in to your MySpace account and go to your home page, there doesn't appear to be any obvious way to start entering HTML code — so what's going on?

The answer is that basically you insert the HTML codes in the Edit profile section of your MySpace home page, usually under the Interests & Personality tab. The other tabs are for adding specific information about yourself into preset forms.

So, to demonstrate how this works, let's insert a large headline into your profile. Follow these steps:

1. Log in to your account.
2. Select Edit Profile in the Hello box in the top left of the screen (see Figure 2-1).

FIGURE 2-1: **Select Edit Profile.**

It should open the Interests & Personality window (see Figure 2-2). You'll notice text boxes labeled About Me, I'd Like to Meet, Interests, and so on.

FIGURE 2-2: The Interests & Personality window

3. Enter the following code into the About Me text box:

```
<h1>Let's get started</h1>
```

Figure 2-3 shows how your code should appear.

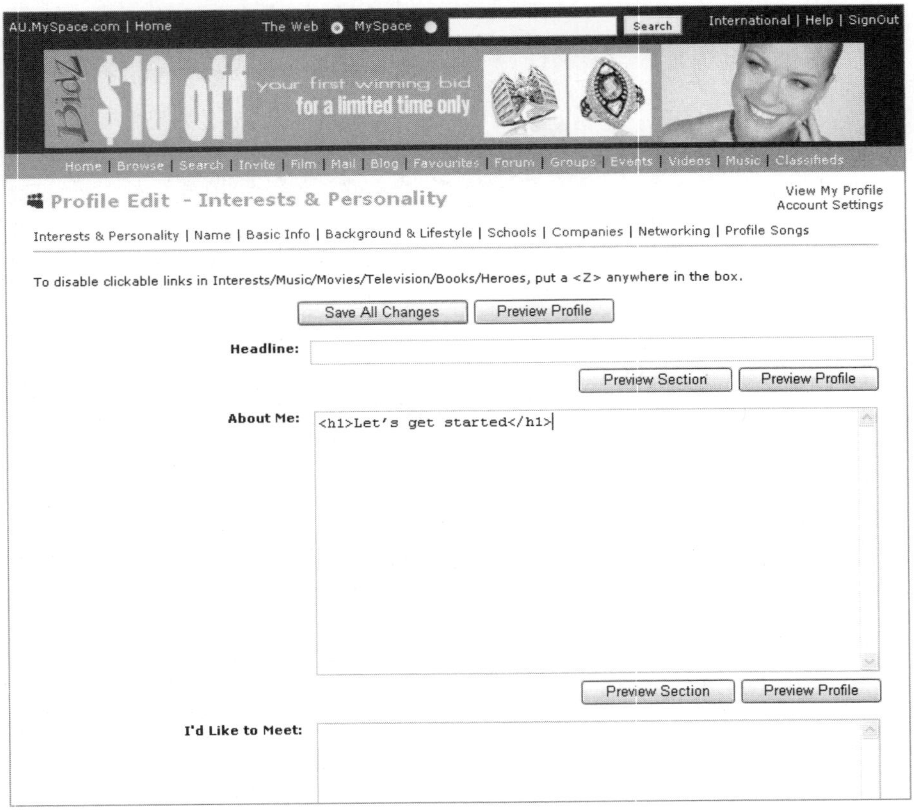

FIGURE 2-3: The About Me box with code inserted

4. From this point you have a number of options. The simplest option is simply to click the Save All Changes button at the top or bottom of the web page, and then click the View My Profile link in the top-right corner, so you can see how your actual profile has been affected by the changes made. Another option is to click the Preview Section button directly under the About Me text box. This allows you to preview how your code affects just the About Me section. You can also preview how your code affects the whole profile by clicking the Preview Profile button, directly under the About Me text box (although all the other Preview Profile buttons on this page do the same thing). Figure 2-4 shows the preview profile feature. With both Preview Section and Preview Profile, after viewing the preview you can then choose Save All Changes or Return to Edit Interests and Personality.

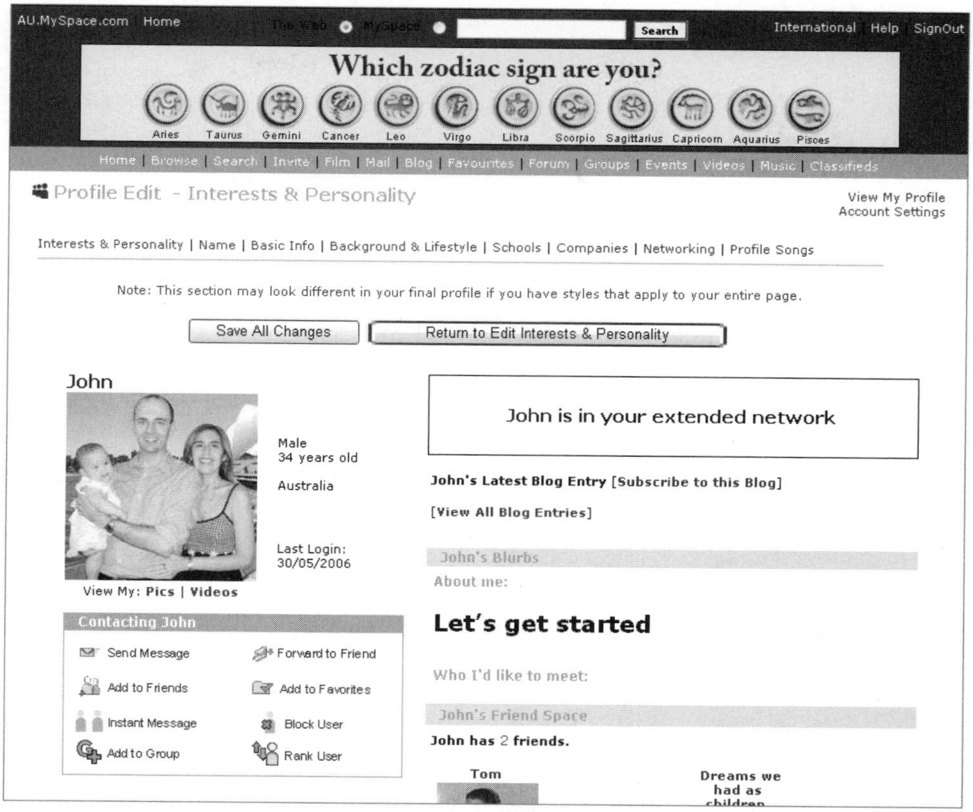

FIGURE 2-4: The Preview Profile feature shows you how your code has affected your profile.

When you view your profile you'll notice a large headline that says "Let's get started."

Tip Be aware that once you get into some of the more advanced hacks later in the book, the preview functions in Edit Profile may not work as you expect them to.

What you've done here is to create your first effect. You can enter HTML code into any of the Interests and Personality fields that you'll find on the Edit my profile page.

By using different commands you can control the way text appears in your profile, as well as apply effects to your page as a whole.

Generally the code will appear in the particular section in your profile that you've pasted it into, unless the code is CSS, in which case it may apply to other parts of the profile.

In the next chapter, you learn about particular codes that will help you specify the way that text appears in your profile.

MySpace Editors

If your eyes are beginning to glaze over at the very mention of HTML, another option is to use the MySpace Editor.

If you point your browser to www.google.com and type the words "myspace editor" you'll find countless MySpace editor web sites. These editors allow you to customize certain elements of your profile, simply by filling in certain fields on a web page. The web page then generates code that you place into your profile (as shown previously). For example, you'll find one such editor at www.myspaceeditor.org — see Figure 2-5.

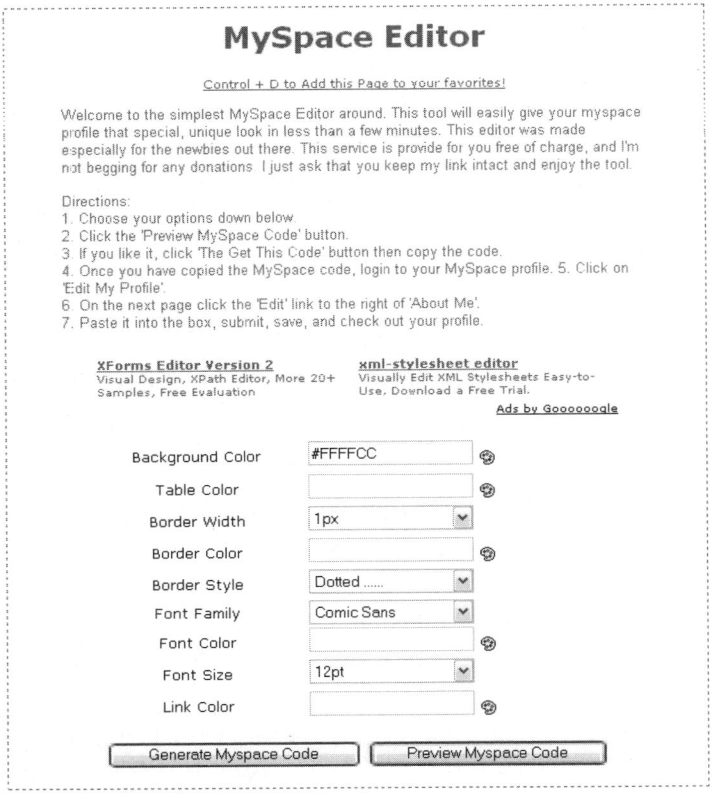

MySpace Editor

Control + D to Add this Page to your favorites!

Welcome to the simplest MySpace Editor around. This tool will easily give your myspace profile that special, unique look in less than a few minutes. This editor was made especially for the newbies out there. This service is provide for you free of charge, and I'm not begging for any donations. I just ask that you keep my link intact and enjoy the tool.

Directions:
1. Choose your options down below.
2. Click the 'Preview MySpace Code' button.
3. If you like it, click 'The Get This Code' button then copy the code.
4. Once you have copied the MySpace code, login to your MySpace profile. 5. Click on 'Edit My Profile'.
6. On the next page click the 'Edit' link to the right of 'About Me'.
7. Paste it into the box, submit, save, and check out your profile.

XForms Editor Version 2
Visual Design, XPath Editor, More 20+
Samples, Free Evaluation

xml-stylesheet editor
Visually Edit XML Stylesheets Easy-to-
Use. Download a Free Trial.

Ads by Goooooogle

Background Color	#FFFFCC
Table Color	
Border Width	1px
Border Color	
Border Style	Dotted ......
Font Family	Comic Sans
Font Color	
Font Size	12pt
Link Color	

Generate Myspace Code   Preview Myspace Code

FIGURE 2-5: The MySpace Editor at www.myspaceeditor.org

I wouldn't exactly say that using a MySpace editor is hacking, but such editors can be fun and they are a quick way to get results, which is why they're mentioned here.

You can see in Figure 2-5 that there are a number of fields in which you can enter values, including the background color, table color, border width (of each section of your profile), border style, font family, font color, font size, and link color.

Clicking the artist's palette icon to the side of fields that require a color selection brings up a palette (see Figure 2-6), which enables you to select the color you want (very convenient if you're not familiar with the color codes).

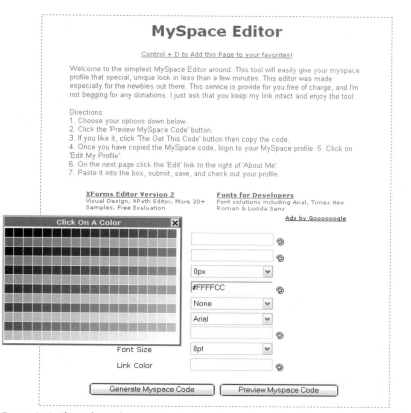

FIGURE 2-6: The color palette makes it easy to select a color scheme for your profile.

Once you've made your selections, select Preview MySpace Code and you are shown how your MySpace profile will appear (see Figure 2-7).

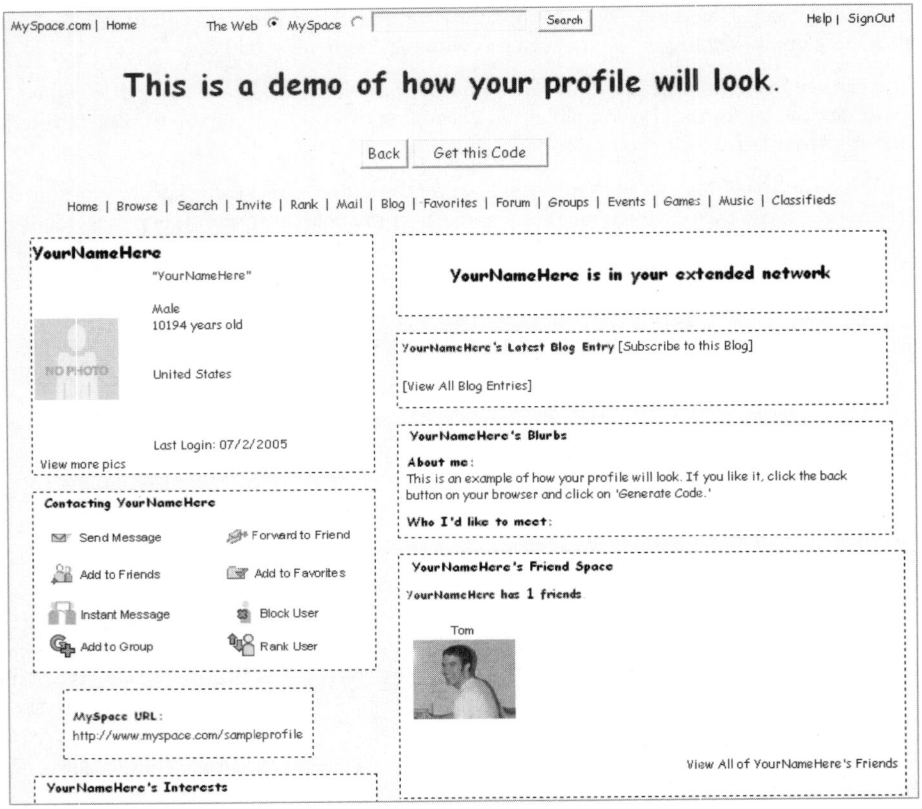

FIGURE 2-7: A preview of how your MySpace profile will appear

The final step is to click "Get this code," which brings up a screen with a text box containing the CSS code that you will need to paste into you profile (see Figure 2-8).

Now it's simply a matter of clicking on and moving your cursor over the text box, clicking your left mouse button, and copying the text by pressing Ctrl+C. Go back to the Editing Interests and Personality section of MySpace, and paste (Ctrl+V) the code into the About Me section, as described on the preceding pages.

When you view your profile you'll notice the colors, borders, and font you specified have taken effect. If you want to make changes, simply go back to www.myspaceeditor.org (or any other similar editor) and go through the process again, copying your new code over the code you've already placed in your profile.

While editors make it very easy for you to start changing the look of your profile, they do have serious limitations. The first is that you can change only certain parts of the profile. There is little leeway for you to be creative, and because everyone else has easy access to MySpace editors (in the same way that you do) you're not really going to be able to create something special.

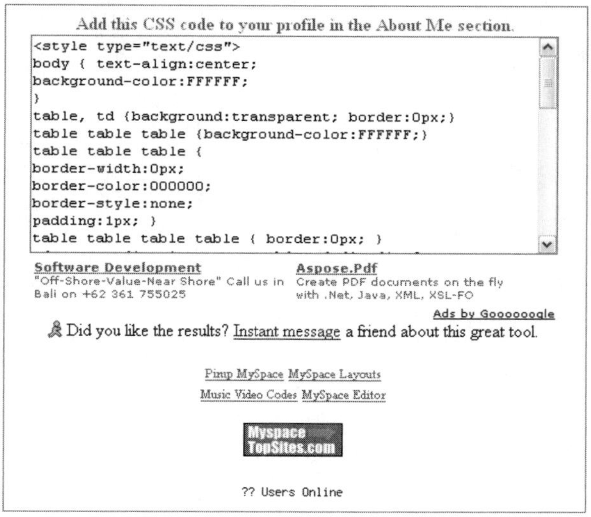

FIGURE 2-8: The actual code

Second, there's usually some kind of advertisement that comes with the code that appears in your profile. The suppliers of the editors would argue that this is a fair price to pay for the use of the editor. While this is generally very easy to remove — in the example given this is simply a matter of removing the last section of code — the advertisement is, in effect, part of the transaction. While the legal requirement for your profile to carry the advertisement is tenuous, there is certainly a moral requirement — you did use their editor after all.

MySpace editors are good for coming up with something quickly and easily, but if you want true customization, you'll need to come to grips with at least a little HTML and CSS.

Wrapping Up

While there's no obvious place to insert HTML and CSS into your MySpace profile, most HTML and CSS code will work if placed in the Interests and Personality section of your MySpace profile.

Trying out some of the MySpace editors that you'll find on the Internet is a good way to get started in MySpace customization, but you'll quickly reach their limitations and want to develop your own code.

Introduction to HyperText Markup Language

In the previous chapter you learned how to place HyperText Markup Language (HTML) code into your MySpace profile. This is, in essence, the key to "hacking" MySpace. HTML allows you to format how text appears in your profile, as well as to create other effects, such as changing colors, linking to other web sites, or displaying images. HTML text also works on regular web pages, so the commands you learn here have a broader application.

This introduction to HTML focuses on how to use HTML to format profile text. The next chapter takes a slightly more advanced look at HTML, which will come in handy for the discussion of cascading style sheets in Chapters 6 and 7. Later in the book, you look at specific examples of HTML and CSS code that allow you to perform specific tricks, such as leaving a feedback box or changing the appearance of your cursor.

You'll probably find that this is one of the most boring chapters in this entire book. There's a lot to go through, and let's face it, formatting text is not all that exciting. However, properly formatted text can really lift your profile and make it much easier to read. It's also very useful to have some understanding of HTML because later in the book as you look at specific "hacks," the more HTML you understand, the easier it will be for you to customize the hacks to your liking.

The HTML code in this chapter (and all other chapters for that matter) is provided on a support web site at www.myspaceismyplace.com so you don't need to type each example. Just load the file containing codes into your text or HTML editor (see Chapter 5 for more information) and cut and paste it from there into your profile. The important thing is that you understand what the codes are doing and how to use them.

in this chapter

- ☑ Introducing tags
- ☑ Paragraphs
- ☑ Line breaks
- ☑ Headings
- ☑ Horizontal ruled lines
- ☑ Text styles
- ☑ Alignment
- ☑ Preformatting
- ☑ Links
- ☑ Lists
- ☑ Adjusting your fonts
- ☑ Putting it all together

Introducing Tags

One of the first things you need to understand is the concept of tags. Tags allow you to place commands in your text to change certain attributes such as size, style, or color. A tag can be identified because it is enclosed by < (less than) and > (greater than) symbols.

To illustrate, the following text has no tags:

```
The early years
Born into a family of circus performers, I spent many of my
formative years on the road. These years were tough, but they
taught me a lot about life, and the importance of family.
My mother was a trapeze artist and my father was a well-known
clown. There were times when we didn't have much money, but there
was always food on the table.
```

If this text were placed in your MySpace profile, it would be quite plain. Figure 3-1 shows how it would appear in a MySpace profile.

About me:
The early years Born into a family of circus performers, I spent many of
my formative years on the road. These years were tough, but they
taught me a lot about life, and the importance of family. My mother was
a trapeze artist and my father was a well-known clown. There were
times when we didn't have much money, but there was always food on
the table.

FIGURE 3-1: Unformatted text looks plain in MySpace.

You'll notice that all the text runs into one line. Here is the same text with HTML tags:

```
The early years<br>
Born into a family of <b>circus performers</b>, I spent many of my
formative years on the road. These years were <i>tough</i>, but
they taught me a lot about life, and the importance of family. My
mother was a <u>trapeze artist</u> and my father was a well-known
clown. There were times when we didn't have much money, but there
was always food on the table.
```

Figure 3-2 shows how this text would appear in MySpace.

As you've probably already deduced, <b> means to bold whatever follows, and </b> means to stop bold. The first tag is called an *opening tag* while the second tag with the slash is called a *closing tag*. Usually an opening tag is followed by a closing tag, but this is not always the case.

About me:
The early years
Born into a family of **circus performers**, I spent many of my formative
years on the road. These years were *tough*, but they taught me a lot
about life, and the importance of family. My mother was a trapeze artist
and my father was a well-known clown. There were times when we didn't
have much money, but there was always food on the table.

FIGURE 3-2: With a few HTML tags the text is already looking much better.

Now you may be thinking that this is a laborious way of formatting text, and yes you're right — there are easier ways of doing it, such as using HTML editors (such as HTML-Kit, which is covered in Chapter 5) or web design programs such as FrontPage. However, it will be useful for you to have a basic understanding of HTML so that you can more easily understand later chapters in this book, and because sometimes it's convenient to make manual changes.

Tip

A common error is to forget the slash symbol in the closing tag, in which case the tag isn't closed, and your text will more than likely appear corrupted.

During the course of this overview of HTML you'll come across the term "attribute," which is associated with various tags. You can think of an attribute as a piece of information that tells a tag how to do its job. For example, the tag `<HR>` places a horizontal line the full width of your page. If you add an attribute — for example, `<HR width="50%">` — the line would go only half way. The attribute `width="50%"` has defined how the tag `<HR>` is rendered.

You can use both upper- and lowercase in your tags, although I recommend that you use lowercase for consistency. You should also place quotation marks around attributes — tags will generally still work if you haven't included closing tags, but it is much better to stick to this convention to ensure maximum compatibility with present and future browsers.

Document Structure

Document structure doesn't really apply to entering codes into MySpace, but it is useful to have an idea of how HTML works in a non-MySpace environment.

A regular web page is made up of two parts — the title and the body. The title contains the document's name, while the body contains the actual content of the document. Typically, an HTML document might follow this kind of structure:

```
<html>
<head><title>HTML on MySpace</title></head>
<body>This is where the body of the document would go</body>
</html>
```

In a regular web page, whatever falls between `<title>` and `</title>` would appear in the title bar at the top of the browser.

In MySpace, because you're entering HTML code into an existing web page, you don't have to worry about a title. All of the code you will be entering will relate to the body of your profile.

Now we're going to look at some specific text formatting commands that you'll be able to use in your MySpace profile.

Tip

Blank lines are ignored in HTML, so if you want to leave blank lines to make your HTML code easier to understand, that's fine. They will not appear in your profile.

Paragraphs

One of the things you'll notice in HTML is that blank lines and new lines are just ignored, unlike in a word processor where you press Enter and automatically go to the next line. In HTML, you actually need to issue a command to start a new paragraph. Let's take the example of the following text:

```
The early years
Born into a family of circus performers, I spent many of my
formative years on the road. These years were tough, but they
taught me a lot about life, and the importance of family.
My mother was a trapeze artist and my father was a well-known
clown. There were times when we didn't have much money, but there
was always food on the table.
```

You might think that because you pressed Enter after the heading "The early years" and after the first paragraph that your text might look similar in your profile. However, if you look back at Figure 3-1, which shows how this text would appear in your MySpace profile, you'll see that the text, including the heading, all runs together. The paragraph tag, <p>, allows you to indicate where paragraphs start and finish, making it much easier to read blocks of text.

Format

```
<p> paragraph text </p>
```

It is possible not to use the closing tag, but for the sake of compatibility it's better to use both an opening and closing <p> tag.

Example

This is an example of the <p> tag being used properly:

```
The early years
<p>Born into a family of circus performers, I spent many of my
formative years on the road. These years were tough, but they
taught me a lot about life, and the importance of family.</p>
<p>My mother was a trapeze artist and my father was a well-known
clown. There were times when we didn't have much money, but there
was always food on the table.</p>
```

Place the preceding code into the About Me section of your MySpace profile.

How It Will Look

Figure 3-3 shows how the text would appear in your MySpace profile with the tags included. As you can see, breaking up the text into paragraphs makes it much easier to read.

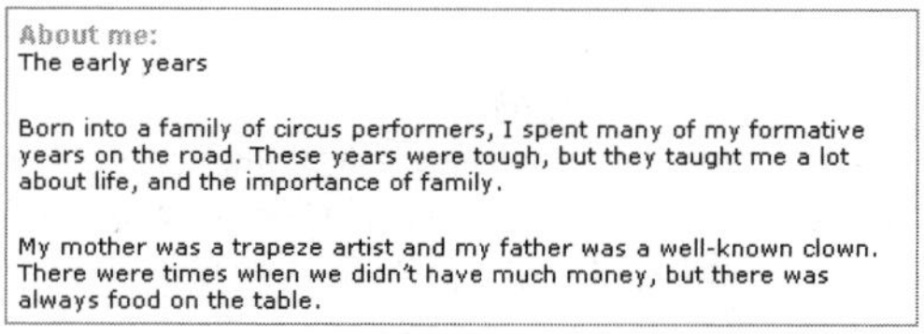

> **About me:**
> The early years
>
> Born into a family of circus performers, I spent many of my formative years on the road. These years were tough, but they taught me a lot about life, and the importance of family.
>
> My mother was a trapeze artist and my father was a well-known clown. There were times when we didn't have much money, but there was always food on the table.

FIGURE 3-3: The text is much easier to read with paragraphs marked.

Line Breaks

Sometimes instead of starting a new paragraph, you might simply want to go to the next line. That's where the <br> tag comes in handy. The main visible difference between <br> and <p> is that there is no line space added when you use <br>.

Format

```
<br>
```

Please note there is no closing tag.

Example

```
The early years<br>
Born into a family of circus performers, I spent many of my
formative years on the road. These years were tough, but they
taught me a lot about life, and the importance of family.<br>My
mother was a trapeze artist and my father was a well-known clown.
There were times when we didn't have much money, but there was
always food on the table.<br>
```

Place the preceding code into the About Me section of your MySpace profile.

How It Will Look

Figure 3-4 shows the <br> tag being used to move the text to a new line. You'll notice that there is no line space between the heading and the first paragraph, while there is a line space between the first and second paragraphs because a <p> tag was used.

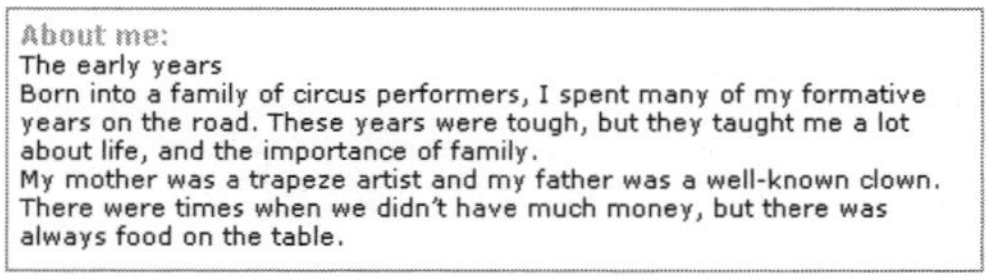

> **About me:**
> The early years
> Born into a family of circus performers, I spent many of my formative years on the road. These years were tough, but they taught me a lot about life, and the importance of family.
> My mother was a trapeze artist and my father was a well-known clown. There were times when we didn't have much money, but there was always food on the table.

FIGURE 3-4: The <br> tag moves the text to a new line without adding a line space.

Headings

Headings are usually bold and slightly larger than normal profile text. Headings allow you to introduce the beginning of a new section, or to break up different sections of your text, just as they do when you're working with a word processing document.

Format

```
<hn> Heading </hn>
```

Here, n is the size of the heading in the range 1 to 6, where 1 is the largest and 6 is the smallest. The default size is 5. You don't need to add a `<br>` or `<p>` tag after the heading, as a new paragraph is automatically started after the closing heading tag. Figure 3-5 shows how different heading sizes would appear in your MySpace profile.

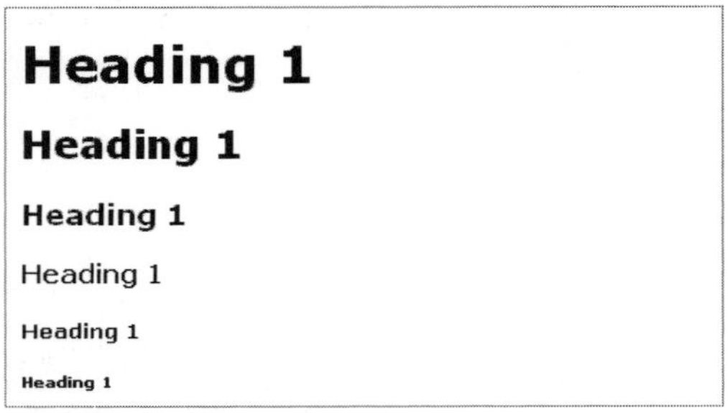

FIGURE 3-5: Different heading sizes as they appear in MySpace

Example

```
<h3>The early years</h3>
<p>Born into a family of circus performers, I spent many of my
formative years on the road. These years were tough, but they
taught me a lot about life, and the importance of family.</p>
<p>My mother was a trapeze artist and my father was a well-known
clown. There were times when we didn't have much money, but there
was always food on the table.</p>
```

Place the preceding code into the About Me section of your MySpace profile.

How It Will Look

Figure 3-6 shows how the `<h3>` heading would appear in a MySpace profile.

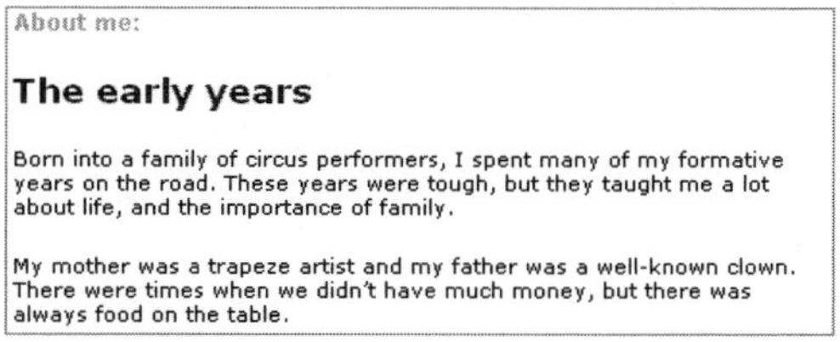

> **About me:**
>
> **The early years**
>
> Born into a family of circus performers, I spent many of my formative years on the road. These years were tough, but they taught me a lot about life, and the importance of family.
>
> My mother was a trapeze artist and my father was a well-known clown. There were times when we didn't have much money, but there was always food on the table.

FIGURE 3-6: The <h3> heading applied to the "The early years"

Horizontal Ruled Lines

Horizontal ruled lines can be used to break up sections of a web page. They're not used as much as they once were — web design has moved on a little from the days when HTML was first developed. Nevertheless, within the context of MySpace, horizontal ruled lines can be used quite effectively to break up sections of text in a profile, as you can see in Figure 3-7.

Format

```
<hr width="x" size="n" noshade>
```

Here, x is the width in pixels or a percentage of the section it's spanning, and n is the thickness of the line in pixels. The noshade attribute is used to turn off the line's shading. There is no closing tag. When no attributes are defined, the horizontal line goes the full length of the area you're working on.

Example

```
<h3>The early years</h3>
<p>Born into a family of circus performers, I spent many of my
formative years on the road. These years were tough, but they
taught me a lot about life, and the importance of family.</p>
<hr>
<p>My mother was a trapeze artist and my father was a well-known
clown. There were times when we didn't have much money, but there
was always food on the table.</p>
```

Place the preceding code into the About Me section of your MySpace profile.

How It Will Look

Figure 3-7 shows how the horizontal ruled line appears in a MySpace profile. As I mentioned, the horizontal ruled line is a little old fashioned, but there may be occasions when you may want to use it to separate blocks of text.

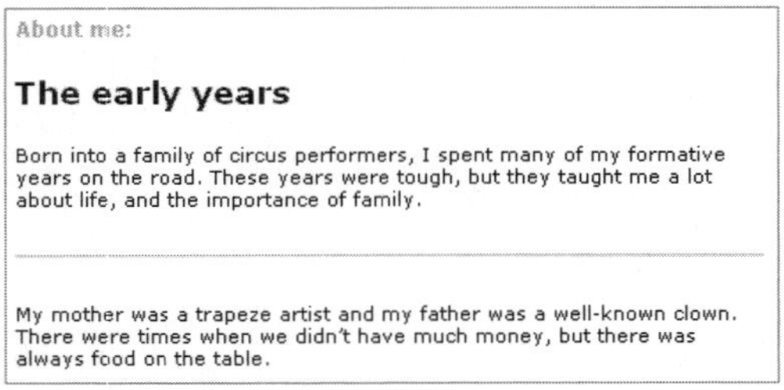

> About me:
>
> **The early years**
>
> Born into a family of circus performers, I spent many of my formative
> years on the road. These years were tough, but they taught me a lot
> about life, and the importance of family.
>
> _____
>
> My mother was a trapeze artist and my father was a well-known clown.
> There were times when we didn't have much money, but there was
> always food on the table.

FIGURE 3-7: While a little old fashioned, the horizontal
ruled line can be used to separate paragraphs.

Text Styles

Often, when you're writing a profile it may be useful to emphasize a certain word or phrase,
and just as you might in a word processor, you can apply styles such as bold, italics, and underline. The opening tag for each style is placed just before the text you want to highlight, and the
closing tag is placed just after.

Format

```
<b> </b>
<i> </i>
<u> </u>
```

<b> and </b> are used to bold text, <i> and </i> for italics, and <u> and </u> for underline.

Example

```
<h3>The early years</h3>
<p>Born into a family of <b>circus performers</b>, I spent many of
my formative years on the road. These years were tough, but they
taught me a lot about life, and the <i>importance of
family.</i></p>
<p>My mother was a trapeze artist and my father was a well-known
clown. There were times when we didn't have much money, but there
was <u>always food on the table.</u></p>
```

Place the preceding code into the About Me section of your MySpace profile.

How It Will Look

Figure 3-8 shows how the bold (<b>), italicize (<i>), and underline (<u>) tags look when
applied to text in MySpace. In practice, you wouldn't go overboard with the text styles as I have
in the example. The point of styles is to emphasize certain words, not every other word.

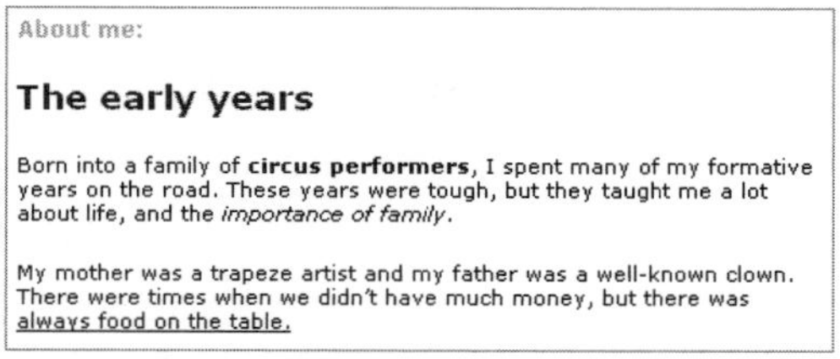

> About me:
>
> **The early years**
>
> Born into a family of **circus performers**, I spent many of my formative years on the road. These years were tough, but they taught me a lot about life, and the *importance of family*.
>
> My mother was a trapeze artist and my father was a well-known clown. There were times when we didn't have much money, but there was <u>always food on the table.</u>

FIGURE 3-8: The bold (<b>), italicize (<i>), and underline (<u>) tags are useful for highlighting words and phrases.

Alignment

Word processors allow you to left justify, center, and right justify text and pictures. HTML allows you to do exactly the same via the `align` attribute, which is placed in the opening tag. When elements are left justified, the left edge of the text is aligned, while the right edge is jagged or uneven. When it is centered, it appears in the center, and when it is right justified, the element is aligned on the right side but uneven on the left side.

The default value of the `align` attribute is always left justify.

Format

```
<tag align="alignment"> text </tag>
```

Be aware that the `align` attribute is not a tag in its own right — you need to use it in conjunction with a tag such as for a paragraph or a heading.

Here, `tag` is the tag you're using — for example, <p> or <h3>; `alignment` is left, right, or justify; and `text` is the actual text that you want to align.

<center> will also work as a standalone tag, although I recommend that you use `align="center"`: in the opening tag to ensure maximum compatibility.

Example

```
<h3 align="center">The early years</h3>
<p>Born into a family of circus performers, I spent many of my
formative years on the road. These years were tough, but they
taught me a lot about life, and the importance of family.</p>
<p>My mother was a trapeze artist and my father was a well-known
clown. There were times when we didn't have much money, but there
was always food on the table.</p>
```

Place the preceding code into the About Me section of your MySpace profile.

How It Will Look

You'll see in Figure 3-9 that the heading has been centered.

> About me:
>
> ### The early years
>
> Born into a family of circus performers, I spent many of my formative years on the road. These years were tough, but they taught me a lot about life, and the importance of family.
>
> My mother was a trapeze artist and my father was a well-known clown. There were times when we didn't have much money, but there was always food on the table.

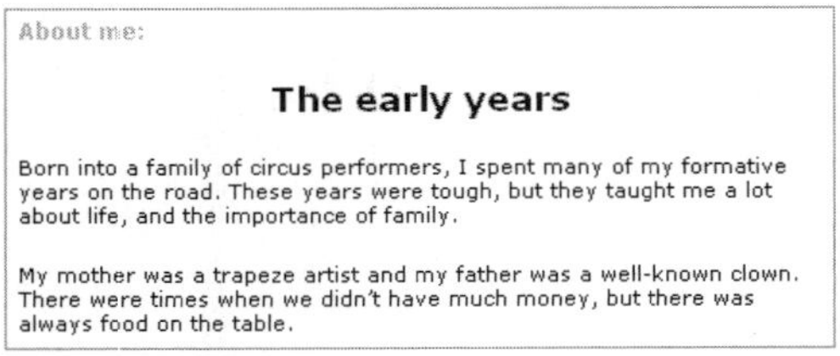

FIGURE 3-9: The heading has been centered using the align attribute.

Preformatting

The `<pre>` tag is useful for presenting text in a particular way without having to use the `<br>` command. Sometimes you may have a snippet of text that needs line returns to appear correctly in a web browser. For example, the following text:

```
H   H   IIIII
H   H     I
HHH       I
H   H     I
H   H   IIIII
```

would appear as:

```
H   H   IIIII H   H     I HHH     I H   H     I H   H     I H   H   IIIII
```

Obviously this won't make sense to anyone. In the example that follows, notice that the letters don't look perfectly aligned, even though it appears correctly in the MySpace profile. This is because the width of the letters is rendered differently on the printed page than it is in your MySpace profile. When trying to get things to align, you may need to add an extra space here and there.

Format

```
<pre> text </pre>
```

Example

```
<pre align=center>
H  H  IIIII
H  H    I
HHHH    I
H  H    I
H  H  IIIII
</pre>
```

Place the preceding code into the About Me section of your MySpace profile.

How It Will Look

In Figure 3-10, you can see that the example spells out the word HI using the characters H and I set out over five lines.

```
About me:

H  H  IIIII
H  H    I
HHHH    I
H  H    I
H  H  IIIII
```

FIGURE 3-10: The <pre> tag allows you to set out a
number of lines of text without the need for a <bw> tag.

Links

"Linking" allows you to connect your web page to other web pages, both within your web site and to external sites. Links generally appear as underlined blue text. Images can also be linked. When the cursor is run over linked text, or a linked image, it generally changes from an arrow into a hand icon. Without links, the web would be a very different place, in fact a very boring place, because you wouldn't be able to jump from link to link.

Format

```
<a href="link address">name of link</a>
```

The *link address* is a URL of the site you are linking to. *name of link* is the name of whatever it is you're trying to link to, and is often just the web address.

Example

Here's an example of a text-based link. I cover graphics links in Chapter 10.

```
For more information visit my web site <a href=http://
www.myspaceismyplace.com>www.myspaceismyplace.com</a>
```

Place the preceding code into the About Me section of your MySpace profile.

How It Will Look

Figure 3-11 shows how this would appear if you added this line to the About Me section of my MySpace profile. If you clicked the link, you would be taken to www.pospisil.com.au (which happens to be my web site).

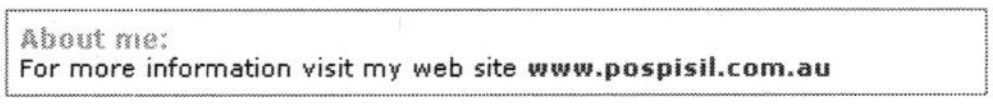

About me:
For more information visit my web site **www.pospisil.com.au**

FIGURE **3-11: Linking makes it very easy to take your visitors to web sites outside MySpace.**

The Unordered List

Sometimes you may want to present a list of information in your profile. HTML offers three types of lists — the unordered list, the ordered list, and the definition list. In the case of the unordered list, each list item is preceded with a bullet point. This is perhaps the most common type of list you'll see.

Format

```
<ul>
<li> list text </li>
</ul>
```

The list is opened by the <ul> tag and closed by the </ul> tag. Each list item is preceded by the <li> tag and closed by the </li> tag, although the </li> tag is optional.

Example

```
<h6>Career highlights </h6>
<ul>
<li> 1990 - Graduated from the Cambridge School of Circus
Performance </li>
<li> 1995 - Received an Award for Outstanding Achievement in the
Field of Excellence</li>
<li> 1998 - Won several million dollars in a lottery</li>
<li> 2003 - Founded Circus Fun with Larry Smith</li>
</ul>
```

Place the preceding code into the "About Me" section of your MySpace profile.

How It Will Look

You can see in Figure 3-12 that the unordered list is a great way to present key points in an easy-to-digest format.

About me:

Career highlights

- 1990 - Graduated from the Cambridge School of Circus Performance
- 1995 - Received an Award for Outstanding Achievement in the Field of Excellence
- 1998 – Won several million dollars in a lottery
- 2003 – Founded Circus Fun with Larry Smith

FIGURE 3-12: Unordered lists make it very easy to present lists in an easy-to-read format.

The Ordered List

The ordered list works in much the same way as the unordered list except that each item is numbered rather than preceded by a bullet point.

Format

```
<ol>
<li> list text </li>
</ol>
```

The list is opened by the `<ol>` tag and closed by the `</ol>` tag. Each list item is preceded by the `<li>` tag and closed by the `</li>` tag. The `</li>` tag is optional.

Example

```
<h6>Top career achievements </h6>
<ol>
<li> Won several million dollars in a lottery</li>
<li> Received an Award for Outstanding Achievement in the Field of
Excellence</li>
<li> Graduated from the Cambridge School of Circus Performance
</li>
<li> Founded Circus Fun with Larry Smith</li>
</ol>
```

Place the preceding code into the About Me section of your MySpace profile.

How It Will Look

Ordered lists are good for showing items in rank order, or by order of importance (see Figure 3-13).

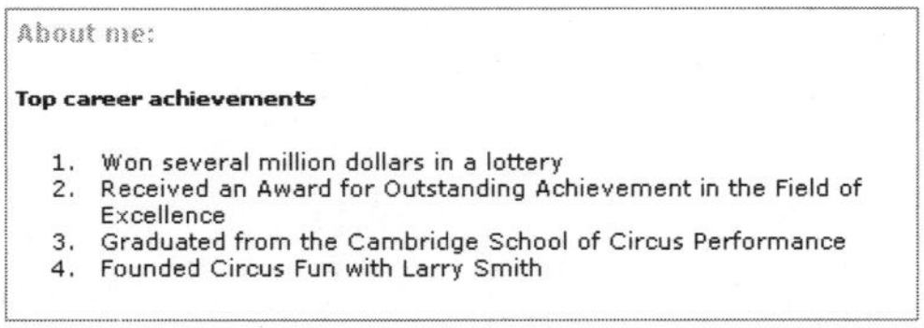

FIGURE 3-13: Ordered lists are good for showing a ranking.

The Definition List

The definition list is not used as often as the two other types of lists we have looked at. Each item is composed of two parts, the definition term and the definition.

Format

```
<dl>
<dt> defined word </dt>
<dd> definition </dd>
</dl>
```

The list is opened by the <dl> tag and closed by the </dl> tag. Each defined term item is preceded by the <dt> tag and closed by the </dt> tag. Each definition is preceded by the <dd> tag and closed by the </dd> tag. The </li> tag is optional.

Example

```
<h6>Examples of some of my better traits </h6>
<dl>
<dt> Lucky </dt>
<dd> Won several million dollars in a lottery</dd>
<dt> Committed to excellence </dt>
<dd> Received an Award for Outstanding Achievement in the Field of
Excellence</dd>
<dt> Smart </dt>
<dd> Graduated from the Cambridge School of Circus Performance
</dd>
<dt> Entrepreneurial </dt>
<dd> Founded Circus Fun with Larry Smith</dd>
</dl>
```

Place the preceding code into the About Me section of your MySpace profile.

How It Will Look

As you'll see, the definition list (see Figure 3-14) is not as neat as the unordered or ordered list but might come in handy if you're ever doing a glossary of some kind.

About me:

Examples of some of my better traits

Lucky
        Won several million dollars in a lottery
Committed to excellence
        Received an Award for Outstanding Achievement in the Field of
        Excellence
Smart
        Graduated from the Cambridge School of Circus Performance
Entrepreneurial
        Founded Circus Fun with Larry Smith

FIGURE 3-14: The definition list might come in handy for a glossary.

Adjusting Your Fonts

I'm reluctant to present the `<font>` tag because much of what it allows you to do can be done much better with cascading style sheets (CSS), which are covered in Chapter 5. The problem with the `<font>` tag is that you need to use it every time you want to change the font attributes, which can become very repetitive. However, the `<font>` tag may come in handy from time to time, particularly if you want to do something quick and dirty, and you'll probably see it when looking at other HTML code, which is why I've included it here.

Format

```
<font size=n face="font" color="color"> text </font>
```

The three attributes are `size`, `face`, and `color`.

Size

The size (the *n* value shown in the preceding line of code) can be in the range of 1 to 7, with 1 being the smallest size and 7 being the largest.

Example

```
<font size="1">This is font size 1</font><br>
<font size="2">This is font size 2</font><br>
<font size="3">This is font size 3</font><br>
<font size="4">This is font size 4</font><br>
<font size="5">This is font size 5</font><br>
<font size="6">This is font size 6</font><br>
<font size="7">This is font size 7</font><br>
```

Place the preceding code into the About Me section of your MySpace profile.

How It Will Look

Figure 3-15 shows how different font sizes appear in MySpace.

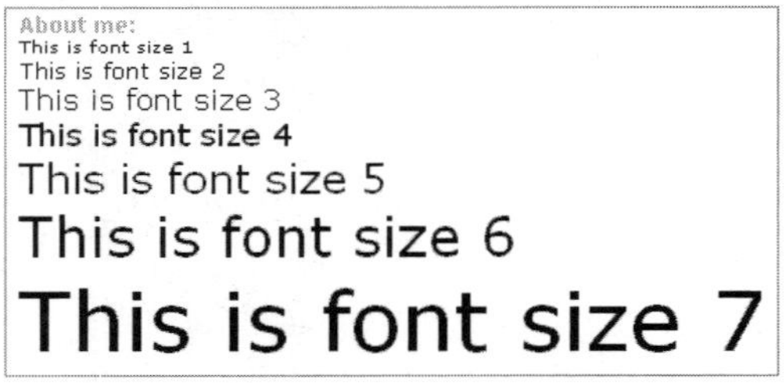

```
About me:
This is font size 1
This is font size 2
This is font size 3
This is font size 4
This is font size 5
This is font size 6
This is font size 7
```

FIGURE 3-15: Different font sizes in MySpace

Face

The face attribute allows you to change the font. Because different computers have different fonts installed, you need to make sure that you use only fonts that are likely to be installed — that is, fonts that are installed on most machines and are therefore likely to be display by most web browsers. These fonts include Arial, Arial Black, Comic Sans MS, Courier New, Impact, Times New Roman, Trebuchet MS, Verdana, and Webdings.

Example

```
<font size=6 face="arial">This is Arial</font><br>
<font size=6 face="arial black">This is Arial Black</font><br>
<font size=6 face="comic sans ms">This is Comic Sans MS</font><br>
<font size=6 face="impact">This is Impact</font><br>
<font size=6 face="times new roman">This is Times New
Roman</font><br>
<font size=6 face="trebuchet ms">This is Trebuchet MS</font><br>
<font size=6 face="verdana">This is Verdana</font><br>
<font size=6 face="webdings">This is Webdings</font><br>
```

Place the preceding code into the About Me section of your MySpace profile.

How It Will Look

Figure 3-16 shows how different font faces appear in MySpace.

Color

You can change text color using the color attribute, which can either be a name of a color or its hexadecimal (also called "hex") equivalent. There are literally thousands of different colors to choose from, and they can be defined using a unique hexadecimal code.

FIGURE 3-16: Different font faces in MySpace

For example, the color blue has a hexadecimal equivalent of #0000FF. Most browsers will allow you to put in either the color name or the hexadecimal code. Note that you don't include the hash (#) symbol in your code when specifying a hexadecimal value.

Almost all browsers will recognize the names of the 16 standard VGA colors, which are aqua, black, blue, fuchsia, gray, green, lime, maroon, navy, olive, purple, red, silver, teal, white, and yellow.

See Appendix A for a table listing all 143 colors that are recognized by newer browsers, although it's better to use the hexadecimal codes as the color attribute.

Example

```
<font size="6" face="arial">This is the default color</font><br>
<font size="6" face="arial" color="blue">This is blue</font><br>
<font size="6" face="arial" color=0000FF>This is blue as defined
by a hex code</font><br>
<font size="6" face="arial" color="yellow">This is
yellow</font><br>
<font size="6" face="arial" color="FFFF00">This is yellow as
defined by a hex code</font><br>
```

Place the preceding code into the About Me section of your MySpace profile.

How It Will Look

While you won't see color in Figure 3-17, you should see the text as different shades of gray, which reflects the different colors of the code. It should, of course, look correct onscreen.

About me:

This is the default color
This is blue
This is blue as defined by a hex code
This is yellow
This is yellow as defined by a hex code

FIGURE 3-17: The different colors will display properly onscreen, although here they appear as shades of gray.

Putting It All Together

Now that you have a basic understanding of HTML, here's an example of how you might use what you've just learned to create nicely formatted text for your profile. Take note that I haven't gone overboard with the formatting, and that I have used formatting consistently. The formatting should never be so overwhelming that it takes attention away from what you have to say.

Example

```
<font size="4" face="comic sans ms" color="red">The early
years</font>
<p>Born into a family of circus performers, I spent many of my
formative years on the road. These years were tough, but they
taught me a lot about life, and the value of family.</p><p>My
mother was a trapeze artist, while my father was a famous
clown.</p>
<font size=4 face="comic sans ms" color="red">Career highlights
</font>
<ul>
<li> <b>1990 - </b> Graduated from the Cambridge School of Circus
Performance </li>
<li> <b>1995 - </b> Received an Award for Outstanding Achievement
in the Field of Excellence</li>
<li> <b>1998 - </b> Won several million dollars in a lottery</li>
<li> <b>2003 - </b> Founded Circus Fun with Larry Smith</li>
</ul>
<font size="4" face="comic sans ms" color="red">Future
ambitions</font>
<p>Now that I have achieved so much in the field of excellence I
have decided to spend my remaining years working on my MySpace
profile. </p>
<p>For more information visit my web site <a href=http://
www.pospisil.com.au> www.pospisil.com.au </a></p>
```

Place the preceding code into the About Me section of your MySpace profile.

How It Will Look

So you can see in Figure 3-18 that what I've done is taken text that would otherwise be quite difficult to read, and formatted it to make it easier on the eye.

About me:
The early years

Born into a family of circus performers, I spent many of my formative years on the road. These years were tough, but they taught me a lot about life, and the importance of family.

My mother was a trapeze artist and my father was a well-known clown. There were times when we didn't have much money, but there was always food on the table.

Career highlights

- **1990** - Graduated from the Cambridge School of Circus Performance
- **1995** - Received an Award for Outstanding Achievement in the Field of Excellence
- **1998** - Won several million dollars in a lottery
- **2003** – Founded Circus Fun with Larry Smith

Future ambitions

Now that I have achieved so much in the field of excellence I have decided to spend my remaining years working on my MySpace profile.

For more information visit my web site **www.pospisil.com.au**

FIGURE **3-18: An example of text formatted using different tags**

Creating HTML Code (the Easy Way)

While you've learned how to style text using HTML tags in this chapter, the real purpose was to help you understand how HTML works.

You won't be surprised to learn there are much easier ways to apply HTML text. On the supporting web site at www.myspaceismyplace.com you'll find a link to a very useful utility called HTML-Kit, which is basically a text editor that allows you to apply HTML tags to text using a graphical user interface (GUI).

You'll find more information on how to use HTML-Kit in Chapter 5.

Tip Are you finding that sometimes when you enter HTML code the changes don't appear on your MySpace profile? It may be that you've forgotten to hit the Submit button when previewing your code.

Wrapping Up

Well, you've made it through HTML 101. You should know enough HTML to make some basic additions to your MySpace profile. However, what's really important is that you're starting to get a feel for how coding works, and how you can apply it to MySpace. In the next chapter you build on your basic knowledge.

More on HyperText Markup Language

In Chapter 3 you looked at how HyperText Markup Language (HTML) is used to format text in a MySpace profile. This chapter looks at some HTML tags, which in their own right might not seem very useful but become very important later in the book when you look at advanced customization.

Divisions

The division tag (`<div>`) allows you to mark out logical divisions or sections in your layout.

By itself the `<div>` tag has limited function when it comes to marking up HTML, as all it allows you to do is align the contents of each section. It also has the effect of adding a new line and a line space, which you need to watch if you are using the `<p>` tag.

The `<div>` tag might seem a bit useless, and the point of introducing you to the `<div>` tag is not for what it can do for you now, but for what it can do for you in the chapter that deals with cascading style sheets (CSS). All you really need to know at the moment is that `<div>` is a way for you to mark out a section of your HTML, and down the road it will allow you to style those sections. For now, we're just looking at it from the perspective of using it in a regular HTML page.

Format

```
<div align="alignment"> </div>
```

In the preceding line of code, `alignment` will be `left`, `center`, `right`, or `justify` to define the alignment of content within the opening and closing `<div>` tags.

Example

```
<div align="right">
<h3>The early years</h3>
<p>Born into a family of circus performers, I spent many of my
formative years on the road. These years were tough, but they
taught me a lot about life, and the importance of family.</p>
<p>My mother was a trapeze artist and my father was a well-known
clown. There were times when we didn't have much money, but there
was always food on the table.</p>
</div>
```

Place the preceding code into the About Me section of your MySpace profile.

How It Will Look

As you can see in Figure 4-1, all the text between the div tags is aligned to the right. While at this stage the practical applications of the <div> tag might seem limited, in Chapter 7 you'll see that the <div> tag can be used very effectively for styling.

FIGURE 4-1: The division tag, <div>, has little functionality in its own right but is very handy with CSS.

Spans

If you thought the <div> tag was useless, you'll think the <span> tag is worse. The <span> tag allows you to mark a section of text. Its real power comes into play when you use it with CSS, where you can use it to style text within a paragraph.

Format

```
<span> content </span>
```

Example

```
<h3>The early years</h3>
<p>Born into a family of circus performers, I spent many of my
formative years on the road. <span style="font-weight: bold;">
These years were tough,</span> but they taught me a lot about
life, and the importance of family.</p>
<p>My mother was a trapeze artist and my father was a well-known
clown. There were times when we didn't have much money, but there
was always food on the table.</p>
```

Place the preceding code into the About Me section of your MySpace profile.

How It Will Look

Figure 4-2 shows how the <span> tag is used to bold a section of text. Don't panic that you don't recognize `style="font-weight: bold">`. That's inline CSS, which we'll be looking at in Chapters 5 and 6. This is not the best way to apply CSS, as you'll learn in Chapter 6, but it does illustrate how the <span> tag works.

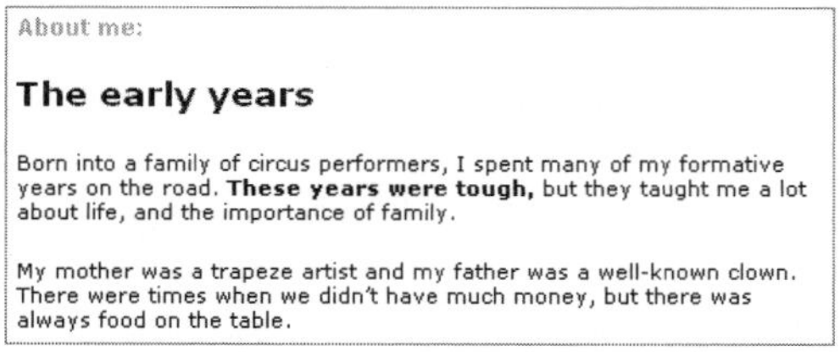

About me:

The early years

Born into a family of circus performers, I spent many of my formative years on the road. **These years were tough,** but they taught me a lot about life, and the importance of family.

My mother was a trapeze artist and my father was a well-known clown. There were times when we didn't have much money, but there was always food on the table.

FIGURE 4-2: The <span> tag being used to make a section of text bold

Tables

Tables are used in HTML to make it easier to present information or to organize the layout of a web page. For example, you might use a table to present a series of numbers in a meaningful way. Here is an example of a basic table:

Name	Game 1	Game 2
Jamie	6	8
Lynette	7	4
Sam	6	8
Tom	4	7

Each rectangle in the table is called a cell. Cells in the same line going across the table are called a row, while cells in the same line going down the page are called a column.

As you can see, it's a great way to present information that would otherwise be quite difficult to present. Tables make it very easy to keep text aligned — you can see that all the information in each column is aligned to the heading.

Tables are also used to help achieve more complex layouts. By making the borders of each cell invisible, you can place elements anywhere in the page. This is the technique MySpace uses to display profiles, and why, for reasons that will become clear later in the book, it's very useful to have an understanding of how tables work.

Format

Here is the sequence of commands you need to know in order to create a table:

- `<table>` — This tells the browser that you want to open a table.
- `<tr>` — The table row tag opens the first row of the table.
- `<td>` and `</td>` — The content of each cell is placed inside the table data `<td>` tags.
- `</tr>` — The table row is then closed with a closing table row tag.

The previous three steps are repeated to build up the contents of the table.

- `</table>` — Once the table is finished, it is closed with a closing table tag.

As you can see, the process involves building up the table row by row.

Example

For the purpose of understanding how tables work, let's put the example table into a format you can place into the About Me section of your MySpace profile.

```
<table>
<tr><td>Name</td><td>Game 1</td><td>Game 2</td></tr>
<tr><td>Jamie</td><td>6</td><td>8</td></tr>
<tr><td>Lynette</td><td>7</td><td>4</td></tr>
<tr><td>Sam</td><td>6</td><td>8</td></tr>
<tr><td>Tom</td><td>4</td><td>7</td></tr>
</table>
```

How It Will Look

Tables are not difficult, but they do require some planning to work. Figure 4-3 shows how the table will appear when placed into MySpace. While there may be instances when tables are useful in your MySpace profile, the main reason they're presented here is so that you have an understanding of tables when you look at how to redesign your MySpace profile in Chapter 25.

```
About me:
Name    Game 1 Game 2
Jamie   6       8
Lynette 7       4
Sam     6       8
Tom     4       7
```

FIGURE 4-3: A very basic table in MySpace

Specifying How a Table Appears

The `<table>` tag has a number of attributes that allow you to specify the table width, the thickness of its border, the space around the contents of each cell, the space between each cell, and the background color.

Format

```
<table width="x" border="n" cellspacing="m" cellpadding="o"
bgcolor="color">
```

Here, x is the width of your table in pixels, or as a percentage of the browser window. If you want to insert a table inside another table, as you do when you insert a table into your MySpace profile, the percentage will be taken from the section where you are placing your table.

In this code, n is the thickness of the cell and table borders. Zero (0) is invisible, while 7 is the thickest border. When the border is zero it is transparent.

Also in this code, m defines how far apart table cells are from one another in pixels, which makes a table easier to read.

Also, o defines the amount of space around the contents of each cell in pixels. This helps to avoid the contents from running together.

Finally, $color$ is the color that you would like the background of the table. You can use the hexadecimal codes or color names provided in Appendix A.

Example

```
<table border="1" bgcolor="yellow">
<tr><td>Name</td><td>Game 1</td><td>Game 2</td></tr>
<tr><td>Jamie</td><td>6</td><td>8</td></tr>
<tr><td>Lynette</td><td>7</td><td>4</td></tr>
<tr><td>Sam</td><td>6</td><td>8</td></tr>
<tr><td>Tom</td><td>4</td><td>7</td></tr>
</table>
```

How It Will Look

In Figure 4-4 you can see that the table now has a background color (which appears like a gray tint) and a border.

About me:		
Name	Game 1	Game 2
Jamie	6	8
Lynette	7	4
Sam	6	8
Tom	4	7

FIGURE 4-4: A border and background color applied to the table

Defining How a Cell Appears

The style and alignment of text are controlled by adding attributes within the table data (<tb>) tags for each cell.

Format

```
<td align="position" bgcolor="color" height="x" width="y">
```

Attributes that are recognized include:

```
align="position"
```

where the position of the text in the cell is top, bottom, center, left, right, or abs middle,

```
bgcolor="color"
```

where the background color of the cell is defined by a hexadecimal code or one of the recognized colors provided in Appendix A, and

```
height="x" width="y"
```

where x is the absolute width of the cell in pixels, and y is the height of a cell in pixels.

You can also place font styles, size, and face (discussed in Chapter 3) inside the <td> tags, but remember that the font attributes can be defined for only a particular cell, not for an entire table or row.

Example

```
<table border="1">
<tr><td><font face="impact" size="5">Name</font></td><td>Game
1</td><td>Game 2</td></tr>
```

```
<tr><td><b>Jamie</b></td><td>6</td><td
bgcolor="yellow">8</td></tr>
<tr><td>Lynette</td><td>7</td><td>4</td></tr>
<tr><td><b>Sam</b></td><td>6</td><td bgcolor="yellow">8</td></tr>
<tr><td>Tom</td><td>4</td><td>7</td></tr>
</table>
```

How It Will Look

You'll notice in Figure 4-5 that the heading is now in Impact and that two of the cells have a yellow background (which appears as a gray tint on this page).

About me:		
Name	Game 1	Game 2
Jamie	6	8
Lynette	7	4
Sam	6	8
Tom	4	7

FIGURE 4-5: Table with fonts and background cell colors

Special Characters

A number of characters are used by HTML. These include double quotes, the ampersand, and the less than (<) and greater than (>) symbols. So that the browser doesn't get confused when you want to use these symbols in your own text, use escape codes instead.

For example, instead of typing:

```
Nathan said, "Hi, how are you?"
```

you would type:

```
Nathan said, &quot;Hi, how are you?&quot;
```

Here are the escape codes for special characters:

- Double quote marks: `&quot;` `&&& I think this makes it easier to understand &&&`

- Ampersand: `&amp;`

- Greater than symbol (open angle bracket): `&gt;`

- Less than symbol (close angle bracket): `&lt;`

Opening and Closing Tags

As we now know, there are opening tags and there are closing tags. Tags should be closed in the reverse order to that which they are opened.

You can see in the following example that the `<p>` tag is followed by the `<b>` tag, but then the `</b>` tag also follows the `</p>` tag.

```
<p><b>Born into a family of circus performers, I spent many of my
formative years on the road. These years were tough, but they taught
me a lot about life, and the value of family.</p></b>
```

This is wrong and may cause errors in sensitive browsers. This is how it should look:

```
<p><b>Born into a family of circus performers, I spent many of my
formative years on the road. These years were tough, but they taught
me a lot about life, and the value of family. </b> </p>
```

Wrapping Up

If you've worked through this and the previous chapter, you should have a reasonably good understanding of HTML. Feel free to experiment with the HTML tags you've learned to get a better understanding of how they work. I've mentioned the `<div>` and `<span>` tags purely for you to have some familiarity with them when you look at how to use them with CSS.

Using a Text Editor

A text editor is like a dumbed-down word processor that is used to enter and edit code — like HTML — into your computer. Because many text editors are designed specifically for entering and editing code, they don't have all the irrelevant features you'll find in full-blown word processing programs. In fact, some text editors have become so good at editing HTML that they're better described as HTML editors.

Text editors run very efficiently with very little drain on your computer's processing ability. Often, they have features that make entering HTML code much easier. What's more, you can download many of them for free from the Internet.

In this chapter, you learn how to use a text editor to write and edit code that you can then place in your MySpace profile.

Benefits of a Text Editor

The first question you probably have is why bother with a text editor — why not enter your code directly into MySpace? You could get away with this if you were entering short, basic blocks of code. However, this approach becomes quite problematic for a variety of reasons including:

- You can't save drafts of your HTML code, so if your computer crashes, you lose all of your work.

- You can't keep different versions of your work, and sometimes it's handy to be able to refer to a previous version.

- There is little in the way of editing features and other features that can make your life easier, such as a spell checker or active preview.

- As the complexity of your code increases, you'll appreciate being able to edit and preview different sections of code in the one window, instead of having to cut code from your word processor and paste it in your MySpace profile.

Notebook is the standard text editor that comes with Windows, while TextEdit is the standard text editor that comes with the Mac. However, there are many freeware text editors that are better than these ones. To demonstrate the process of putting together HTML code for MySpace we're going to use a very good program called HTML-Kit (available from www.chami.com/html-kit/ or by following the link from www.myspaceismyplace.com), which is free to non-commercial users and has some very nice features, such as an active preview window (which allows you to see what your code will look like) and a spell checker. HTML-Kit, as the name suggests, is probably better described as an HTML editor rather than a straight text editor — you'll see why when we explore some of its features.

If you're a Mac user, there's no need to feel left out — there are a number of great text and HTML editors available for the Macintosh. Taco HTML Edit (available from www.tacosw.com or by following a link from www.myspaceismyplace.com) is a free editor that includes a spell checker and a live preview. Obviously, the operation of the program is different, but the process is similar to the one described here.

The Coding Process

Think of a text editor as a staging ground, where you can work on your code before you place it in your MySpace profile. There are three distinct steps involved in putting together code for your profile:

1. Writing, editing, and proofing the text content (if the code you're working with includes text for visitors to your profile to read)

2. Marking up the text with HTML tags or writing the code

3. Copying and pasting this marked up text/code to appropriate sections of your MySpace profile

Before we go through this process, take the time to install HTML-Kit on your PC. While you're at it, install the spell check and thesaurus plug-ins (also from www.chami.com/html-kit/proof/). Don't worry about unzipping the plug-ins — simply install the dictionary by selecting Tools ⇨ Install ⇨ Install Dictionary, and the thesaurus by selecting Tools ⇨ Install ⇨ Install Thesaurus.

Writing, Editing, and Proofing Text

In this exercise you mark up some text, although if you're writing code, you may not have very much in the way of text to mark up.

When you first start HTML-Kit, you are presented with the Open File Wizard. Select Create a New File. A new page opens. The new page will include HTML codes that you might need if you were working on a regular web page, but for MySpace, you can delete this code (just highlight it and press Delete). You can disable this feature by clicking Edit ⇨ Preferences ⇨ Startup and deselecting the "Insert following text into new documents" check box.

For the purpose of this exercise, you will mark up the following text:

```
How to start a small business
Tom and I worked together at a magazine publisher, and while our
jobs were both quite good, we wanteed to do something that was
more challenging. We'd often have lunch together and talk about
business ideas, and what we might do together in the future.
We had these kinds of conservations for about twelve months until
one day in a Chinese restaurant in Marrickville Tom said that we
should either put up or shut up. This caught me off guard. It's
one thing to talk about business ideas you might try, but it's a
very different thing to actually go out and do them.
The idea was straightforward - a free computer magazine
distributed through computer retailers. It was an ideqa that had
emerged from projects I had played with in the past. Tom was also
keen to try an idea he had for a magazine about e-commerce.
I didn't know anything about business, small or otherwise, and
neither did Tom, who was to become my business partner.
```

As you know from Chapter 3, simply placing this text into your MySpace profile would not lead to good results. The text would be all squashed together and would be difficult to read. So, you can copy and paste this raw text file (ch03-01 exercise.txt), which is available at www.myspaceismyplace.com, into HTML-Kit. Or indeed, it may be easier for you to simply load the file directly into HTML-Kit.

Once you have the text in HTML-Kit, you'll probably notice that it runs off the page. That's okay. What you need to do is to activate word wrap, which you can do by clicking Preferences ⇨ Editor and selecting the "Word wrap at column" check box. Click OK and when you return to the document you'll be able to see all of the text.

Using HTML-Kit is very simple — you can highlight text with your mouse pointer by pressing the left mouse button while you run your cursor over the text you want to highlight. Pressing the right mouse button brings up a menu where you can cut, copy, and paste among other things.

To run a spell checker, simply select Tools ⇨ Spelling. There are two typos in this text, which should be picked up by the spelling checker. There's also a place name, which will also be picked up. The spelling checker gives you some alternate spellings (see Figure 5-1). If you're ever stuck for a word, selecting Tools ⇨ Thesaurus brings up a thesaurus.

It's always a good idea to run a spell check on anything you intend to publish on the Internet, and it's a good practice to get someone else to read your work — it's amazing how easy it is to read over your own mistakes.

Tip   You can run a spell check simply by pressing F7, or check the thesaurus by pressing Shift+F7.

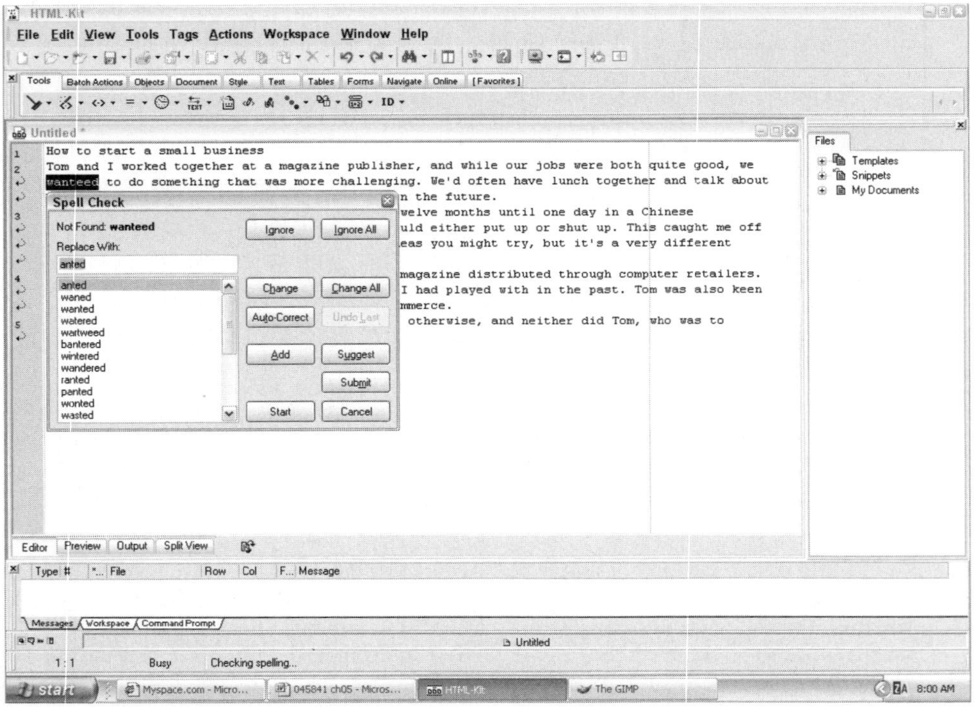

FIGURE 5-1: HTML-Kit even allows you to check spelling.

Always make sure you save your work regularly — you can do this simply by pressing Ctrl+S. Later, as we start to look at more complex code, you may find it useful to save different versions of your work, which you can do by adding v1, v2, v3, and so on to the file name.

Marking Up Text

Having edited and checked your text, you're now ready to add HTML tags. You can do this manually, as described in the previous two chapters, or you can take advantage of some of HTML's special features, which makes the whole process much easier.

But before you actually start adding tags, let's launch the active preview window by pressing Ctrl+F8. The active preview window previews what your marked up text will look like when displayed in a web browser. Resize the main document and active preview windows so that you can see them side by side (see Figure 5-2). You'll notice that without any tags, you get the same old problem of the text running together.

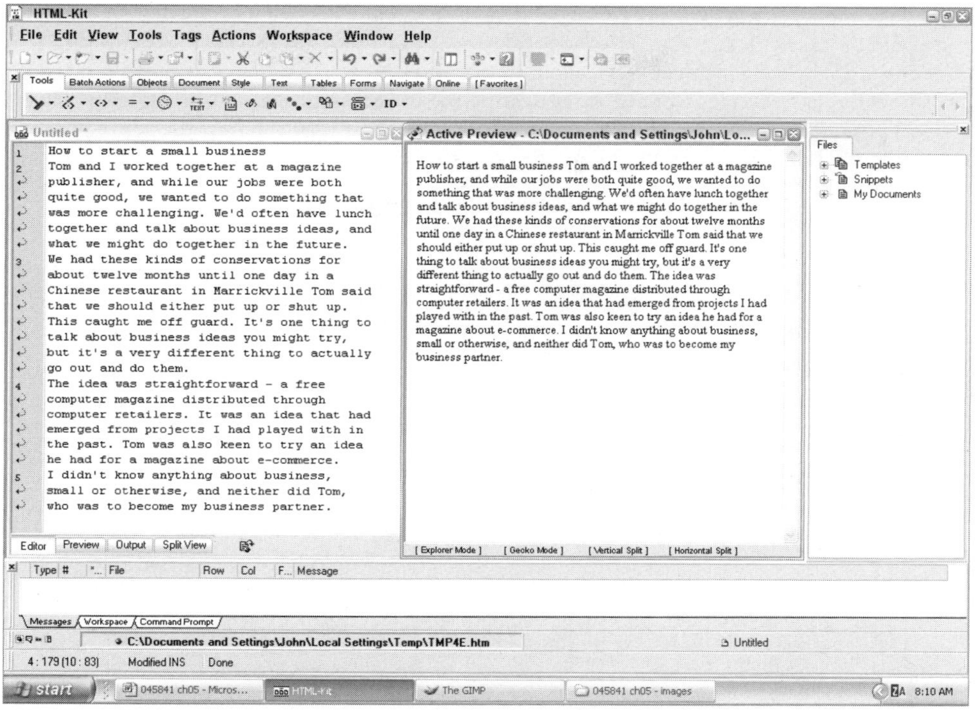

FIGURE 5-2: The Active Preview window shows you what your text will look like when it's marked up.

Select the Text tab in the toolbar at the top of the document screen, and you'll see a tool box appear with various buttons. To apply a paragraph tag to each paragraph, simply highlight a paragraph and then click the button with the paragraph symbol (first button from the left). You'll see that the opening and closing <p> tags are applied to the paragraph. You'll agree that this is much easier than applying these styles manually, and what's more, when you apply these tags, you get to see what the tags will look like in the active preview window. Please note that sometimes there may be a delay of a few seconds between when you enter a tag and when a preview appears. You can adjust the preview settings by clicking Edit ⇨ Preferences ⇨ Preview ⇨ Active Preview.

Tip

You can preview the current document in the default web browser by pressing F8.

Take some time to experiment with different tags, and you'll see just how easy it is to apply bold or italics, change fonts, and so on. There is also a tool box for creating tables and for creating CSS styles (which you learn about in the next chapter). Of course, you still need to know how the HTML tags work in order to enter the correct attributes — although you'll agree that HTML Edit makes the process a lot easier. Figure 5-3 shows you how the active preview window displays the marked up text.

And once again, don't forget to save your work regularly!

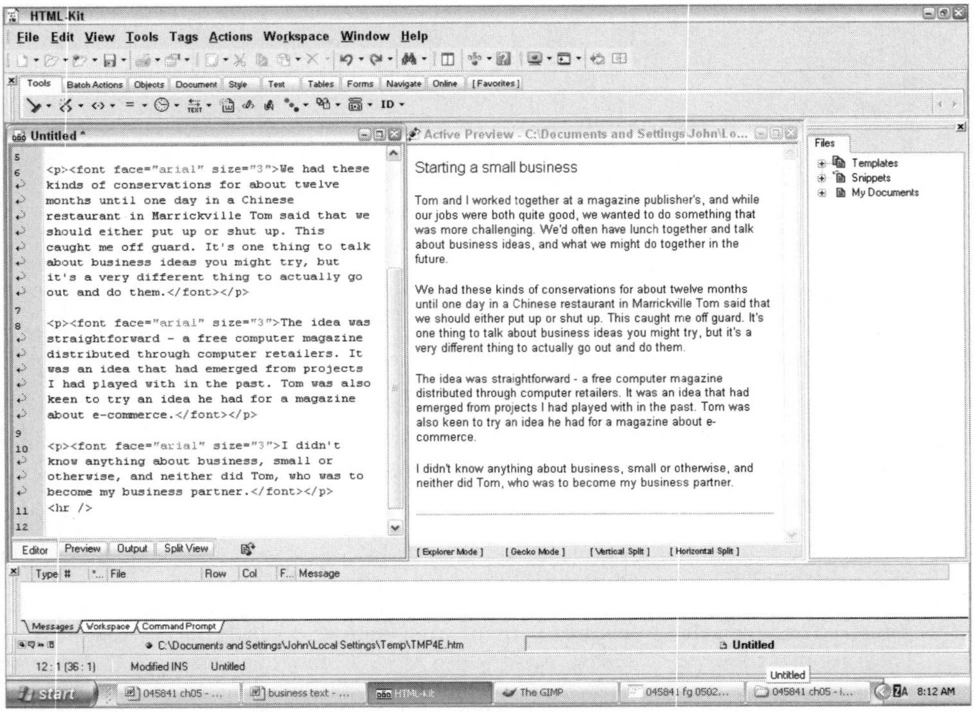

FIGURE 5-3: The Active Preview window showing a preview of marked up text

Copying Code into MySpace

Copying your marked up text/code is simply a matter of highlighting it in the main document window and pasting it into the appropriate section in your MySpace profile (as described in Chapter 2). Figure 5-4 shows how the marked up text from the example looks when placed into the About Me section of your MySpace profile. Before you quit HTML-Kit, don't forget to save the most recent version of your code.

FIGURE 5-4: This is how the marked up text appears in MySpace.

You'll notice in Figure 5-4 that I've placed the `<font>` tag inside the paragraph (`<p>`) tags — that's because MySpace has set up `<p>` tags so that in addition to marking out paragraphs, they also apply a certain font face and size. This can make applying HTML tags to text quite messy — luckily in the next chapter you look at how you can redefine the `<p>` tag, along with all other tags, so they do what you want them to do.

Wrapping Up

I hope this chapter has demonstrated that using a text editor to prepare your code can save you time and effort, and also reduce the chances of losing code should your computer crash. It can't be said too often — remember to save your code regularly.

Introduction to Cascading Style Sheets

Cascading style sheets (CSS) were developed to solve the limitations of regular HTML.

Let's say you developed a web page made up of several pages, and decided that after you finished, you wanted to change the font size. With normal HTML, you would have to go back through every page and change each tag. And then if you decided you wanted to change the font, you'd have to go back again and change each tag. As you can imagine, this process would be quite laborious.

CSS works much the same as styles in a word processing or desktop publishing program, where you define a style — let's say "body text" — and then apply that style to all the body text in your document. If you want to change the size of the body text, simply change the size in the style and the change will then apply to all body text in the document — which saves a lot of time.

While MySpace allows you to enter CSS code, there are limitations, and special ways to work around certain issues — but we'll get to that as each issue arises.

In this chapter, you learn how to use CSS in the context of the MySpace environment.

Style Sheets

The term "style sheet" simply refers to a collection of style definitions. This just means that all the styles are defined in one place. It makes it much easier to have a consistent set of web pages.

External Style Sheets

The best way to use CSS is with an external style sheet. This means you have an additional file, usually called stylesheet.css, which contains the styles and which can be referenced by different pages at your web site. This means that there is one style sheet, and if you change one style in your style sheet, all your web pages will be adjusted accordingly. Web pages also tend to load faster because the style sheet needs to be loaded only once. As you can see, this is a very handy method, but sadly won't work with MySpace because MySpace filters out the link code.

Internal Style Sheets

Fortunately, there is another way of defining styles, and that is through an internal style sheet, which MySpace does allow. Basically this means you define your styles within your web page. In the context of MySpace, this means you define the styles in one of the profile fields, and then those styles apply to all of your profile. Internal style sheets take precedence over external style sheets, and style sheets that occur later in the page override earlier ones — this is why they're called cascading style sheets.

This means that you can place style sheets in your document that supersede the original MySpace profile style sheets — a neat trick that will allow you to completely redesign your MySpace profile in Chapter 24.

Note The word "element" is often used in web design to refer to the graphics or text that makes up a web page.

Style sheets are placed inside `<style>` and `</style>` tags, which tell the browser where the CSS starts and finishes. Sometimes you'll see an opening style tag that looks like this: `<style type="text/css">`. This is basically telling the browser that the following style definitions are CSS, rather than, say, Javascript style sheets. Because MySpace accepts only CSS, you don't really need to worry about this too much.

If you forget the closing tag, your profile will appear to be blank so, for this reason, it's always a good idea to put in the closing tag as soon as you type in the opening tag, and before you've actually defined any styles.

Inline Styles

Now, of course, the whole point of CSS is to define once, use many times, but if an occasion arises where you need to define a style for an HTML tag on a one-off basis, you can do this using inline styles. Inline styles are written inside the opening tag. So for example, they might look something like this:

```
<p style="margin: 10;">
```

You can see that you've inserted a style into a standard <p> paragraph tag that you're actually placing in the body of your web page. This is the least efficient way to apply a style and should be avoided if at all possible. The best way to define styles in MySpace is to use Internal style sheets (see the preceding discussion).

Selectors

A *selector* is something to which you apply a style. There are four types of selectors to which you can apply styles: predefined HTML tags, user-defined HTML tags, IDs, and classes.

Now this may be the point where things are starting to sound complicated — don't panic! Each of these selectors simply provides a different way to define and apply styles. Let's go through each one so that you understand what they do, and to establish which ones you can use in MySpace — not all of them work!

Predefined HTML Tags

With a predefined tag you're basically adjusting the function of an existing HTML tag. In Chapters 3 and 4 you looked at HTML and were introduced to tags such as <p>, <br>, <b>, <u>, and <i>. With CSS, you can change how these existing, or predefined, tags do their jobs. The styling convention is a little different from standard HTML. Here's how you would style the <p> tag:

```
<style>
p {margin: 20px;}
</style>
```

Take note that there are no brackets around the "p", and that opening and closing brackets that contain the definition are curly brackets or "braces" that are found above the square brackets on your keyboard. The style that will apply to the <p> tag is found within these brackets. Every time the <p> tag is used, it will have a margin of 20 pixels.

User-Defined Tags

In addition to being able to style existing tags, you can also create your own new tags, which you can then use in your HTML. This might be handy if there is a particular effect that you regularly want to apply to your HTML.

```
<style>
effect {margin: 20px;}
</style>
```

Whenever you use the <effect> tag in your web page, the margin will be adjusted. Now before you get too excited about user-defined tags, the bad news is that MySpace seems to filter them out.

In any case, user-defined tags are clumsy, and a better way of applying styles is to use IDs and classes. These are style definitions that can be used with different predefined HTML tags. Basically, once you set up an ID or class, you can then use it to style different predefined HTML tags.

IDs

IDs are designed to be used once per page — for example, in a header or a footer. In order to use an ID you need to put a hash (#) sign in front of the definition. Sadly, MySpace filters out hash signs, so IDs are not an option.

Classes

Classes can be used as many times as you want in a page. They can allow you to easily change the style of a predefined tag. And the good news is that classes will work in MySpace. They are defined by putting a full stop (.) in front of your definition in your CSS rules, and look something like this.

```
<style>
.cool {color: blue;}
</style>
```

When you actually want to use that style, you reference it in your tag like this:

```
<p class="cool">
```

If you want a class to apply only to a certain predefined HTML tag, you can do it by putting the tag before the style definition. For example:

```
<style>
p.cool {color: blue;}
</style>
```

The regular <p> tag would look normal, unless you invoke the cool class. The cool class would not be available to other tags.

Defining Styles

Styles always follow this format:

```
selector { property: value; }
```

Here, the `selector` is the name of whatever it is that you're styling — such as a predefined tag or class. The `property` is the attribute you would like to change, and the `value` is how you would like to change it. So for example, if you wanted to create a class called freaky that makes all text green, it would look like this:

```
.freaky {color: green;}
```

You can also have multiple properties and values for a single selector — you just need to keep them separated by a semicolon. If you wanted freaky to indent paragraphs as well as to change the text to green, the definition would look like this:

```
.freaky {color: green; text-indent: 10px;}
```

Don't worry too much about what the properties and values mean — at this stage you're just trying to get a handle on styling conventions. You look at various properties later.

In CSS you often hear about "elements." Elements are simply the different parts of the content that make up your web page or, in the case of MySpace, the different parts that make up your profile. An element can be a paragraph or a table. The following is an example of a paragraph <p> element:

```
<p>You may look at me and think that I am a simple man, but my
interests betray just how sophisticated and worldly I really
am.</p>
```

The best way to get a handle on how to use CSS is to see it in practice, and to that end let's look at a number of different properties you can use throughout this chapter. You might think that some of the things you learn in this section are useless, but you'll find that having a good understanding of CSS will help when you're looking at some of the more complex hacks later in the book.

If you would like to try out the following exercises, clear all the code and text in your profile, or perhaps start a new profile that you can use to experiment on.

Using Safe Mode

Because you're starting with CSS, it's also worth introducing you to Safe Mode, which you'll find in the Hello box (see Figure 6-1) in the top-left corner of your screen.

FIGURE 6-1: Safe Mode is found in the Hello box.

You may find references to how important it is to use Safe Mode in older tutorials you may find on the Internet, but just as this book was being finalized, MySpace upgraded and changed the standard Edit Profile function so that it is better able to handle all kinds of code, including CSS. Safe Mode is still available, but it is no longer as important as it once was. I've kept this section in case you come across references to Safe Mode and wonder what all the fuss was about.

Safe Mode was so important because CSS gives you the power to make profound changes to the way your profile appears, and it meant that it could also completely mess up the old Edit Profile screen, which rendered a preview of each section of your profile. If this happened, you weren't able to use the Edit Profile screen to make corrections to fix problems.

The idea of Safe Mode is that it allowed you (and still does) to edit your code without rendering it, i.e. displaying it. So basically, you'll see the HTML in the Edit Profile ➪ Edit Interests & Personality of MySpace rather than a preview of how your code will appear, which is how the old Edit Profile worked. You can see this difference in Figure 6-2, which shows the old Edit Profile function, while Figure 6-3 shows Safe Mode.

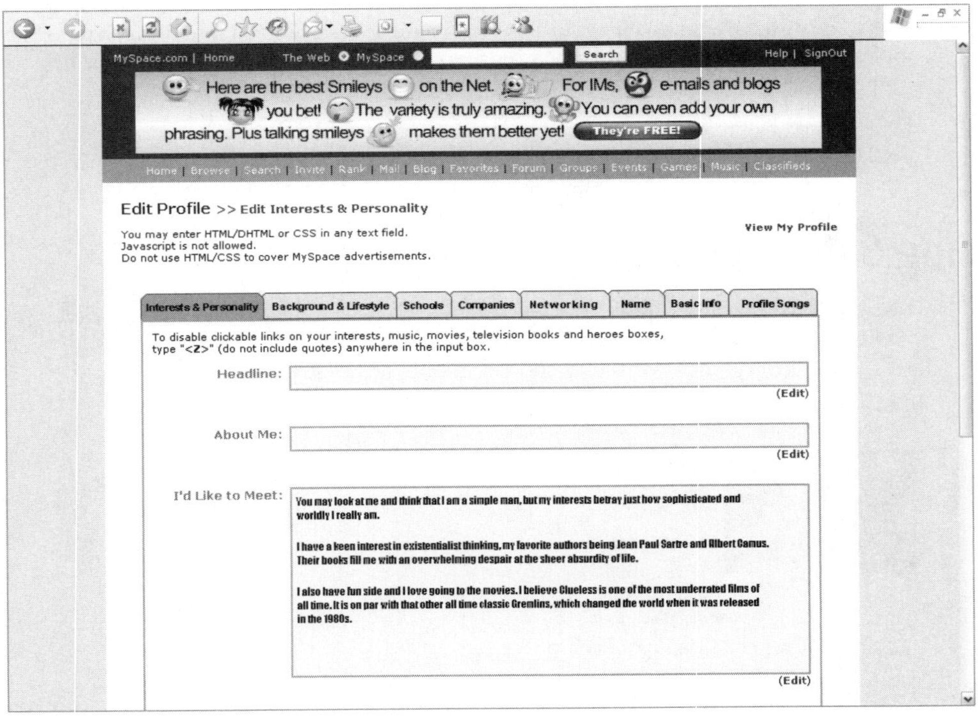

FIGURE 6-2: Normal editing mode in MySpace

In Figure 6-2, you'll notice that in the old Edit Profile, the text was rendered in the specified font and size — but you didn't see the CSS style sheets. It was technically possible that some advanced CSS code could so completely mess up this page that you wouldn't be able to correct the code to fix the problem. This doesn't seem to be a problem with the current Edit Profile function.

In fact the standard Edit Profile feature is now like Safe Mode on steroids — it allows you to see your code and preview just the sections you want, or your whole profile. Don't be surprised if some time in the future (or even by the time you read this book) Safe Mode is no longer available because it seems to be more or less redundant.

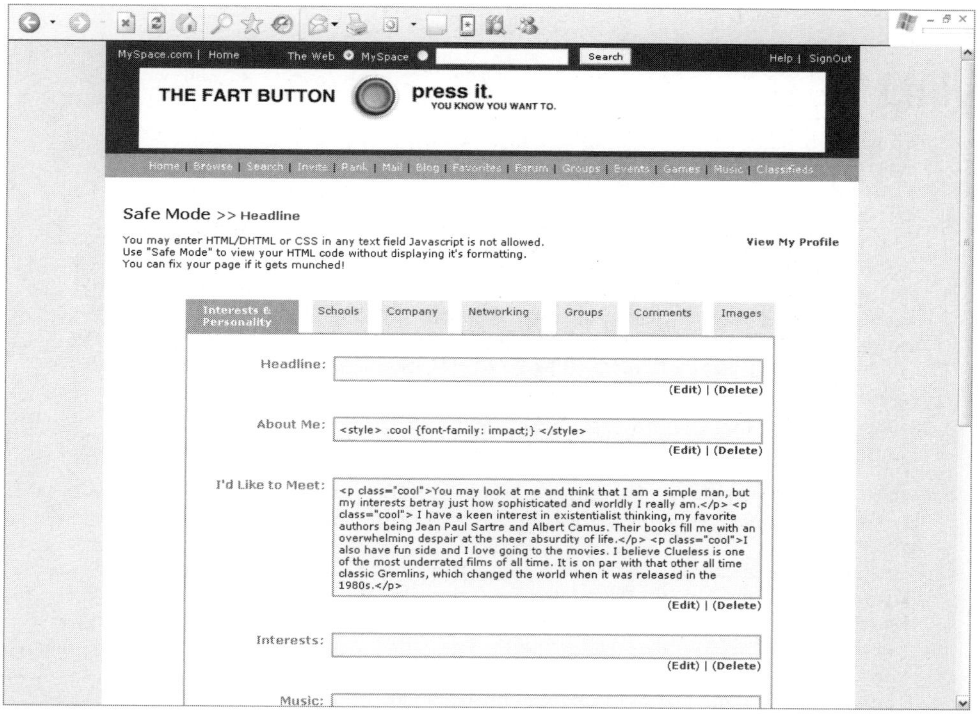

FIGURE 6-3: Safe Mode in MySpace

You actually see the HTML and CSS code when you use Safe Mode, which enables you to correct any problems that may arise. When programming in CSS, it's good practice to use Safe Mode to enter your code. This way you actually see all the code that you've entered, including style sheets, and not just code that actually displays something.

Trying the Examples

An example is provided with each concept covered. The goal of providing examples is to show you how to define style sheets and use them in practice. For this reason, it's a good idea to actually place the text into a MySpace profile so you can see for yourself how it works. You can either type in the examples — and be careful to copy them exactly — or you can copy them from the supporting web site at www.myspaceismyplace.com. It's simply a matter of loading the relevant examples into your text editor, and then copying and pasting them into your profile as directed.

Make sure that when you insert the text into sections of your profile you completely replace the existing text.

Styling Text

To learn how to use CSS to style text, you'll be using this example text:

```
You may look at me and think that I am a simple man, but my
interests betray just how sophisticated and worldly I really am.
I have a keen interest in existentialist thinking, my favorite
authors being Jean Paul Sartre and Albert Camus. Their books fill
me with an overwhelming despair at the sheer absurdity of life.
But then, I also have fun side and I love going to the movies. I
believe Clueless is one of the most underrated films of all time.
It is on par with that other all time classic Gremlins, which
changed the world when it was released in the 1980s.
```

So that the text doesn't run into itself, you need to insert some paragraph (<p>) tags:

```
<p>You may look at me and think that I am a simple man, but my
interests betray just how sophisticated and worldly I really
am.</p>
<p> I have a keen interest in existentialist thinking, my favorite
authors being Jean Paul Sartre and Albert Camus. Their books fill
me with an overwhelming despair at the sheer absurdity of
life.</p>
 <p>I also have fun side and I love going to the movies. I believe
Clueless is one of the most underrated films of all time. It is on
par with that other all time classic Gremlins, which changed the
world when it was released in the 1980s.</p>
```

However, before you place this text in the "I'd like to meet" section of our profile, you're going to apply the style "cool" to each of the paragraph tags:

```
<p class="cool">You may look at me and think that I am a simple
man, but my interests betray just how sophisticated and worldly I
really am.</p>
```

```
<p class="cool"> I have a keen interest in existentialist
thinking, my favorite authors being Jean Paul Sartre and Albert
Camus. Their books fill me with an overwhelming despair at the
sheer absurdity of life.</p>
<p class="cool">I also have fun side and I love going to the
movies. I believe Clueless is one of the most underrated films of
all time. It is on par with that other all time classic Gremlins,
which changed the world when it was released in the 1980s.</p>
```

If you place this text into the "Who I'd like to meet" section of MySpace, nothing much happens (as you see in Figure 6-4), which is fine because you haven't defined a style yet. You'll do that shortly as you look at a number of properties for styling fonts. And don't worry that the text doesn't actually talk about who I'd like to meet. You're placing the text there simply because you're going to place the style sheet in the About Me section, and at this point in time I want to demonstrate how style sheets can control elements in other sections of the profile, not just those in the same section.

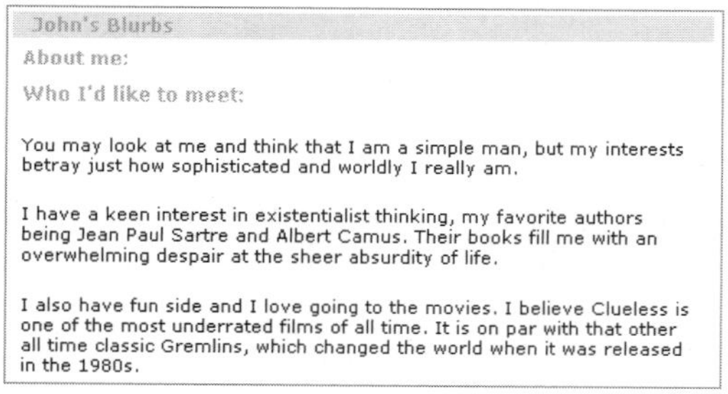

FIGURE 6-4: While styles have been applied to the text, no styles have been defined, so nothing much happens.

Now it's time for you to start playing with CSS.

Font-family

The `font-family` property allows you to change the font of text and is similar to the `<face>` tag in HTML, but it is much more flexible than its HTML equivalent.

Format

```
selector {font-family: font name;}
```

In the preceding code, the *font name* is a font installed on the user's system. To be safe, use common fonts such as Arial, Arial Black, Comic Sans MS, Courier New, Impact, Times New Roman, Trebuchet MS, Verdana, and Webdings.

Example

```
<style>
.cool {font-family: impact;}
</style>
```

Please note that throughout the course of this chapter, you'll be styling the "cool" class that you placed into the About Me section of the MySpace profile.

Place the preceding code into the About Me section of your MySpace profile. Don't forget that you will also need to have placed the example text (see "Styling Text") into the "Who I'd like to meet" section of your profile.

How It Will Look

Figure 6-5 shows how the applied code will look in your profile.

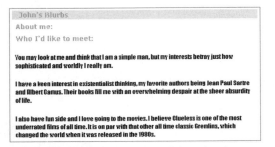

FIGURE 6-5: The font in the sample text has been changed to Impact.

Because there's a chance that a particular user might not have Impact installed on his or her computer, you can also specify backup fonts that the browser will look for in case the preferred font is not available. This is done in the following way:

```
.cool {font-family: impact, verdana, arial;}
```

If, in this example, Impact is not present on the computer, then Verdana is used, and if Verdana is absent then Arial is used, which 99 percent of computers would have.

When you click View My Profile, you'll notice right away that the font has changed in the "Who I'd like to meet" section. If you had a `<p class="cool">` attached to each paragraph in your entire profile, you can see that simply by changing the style definition of the class "cool" you can change the font of all the text in your profile — but at the same time, do so selectively (i.e., you might use a different class to apply different styles to certain paragraphs).

Also notice that although you placed the style sheet in About Me, it affected the text in the "Who I'd like to meet" box.

Color

Changing your font's color is achieved with the `color` property. Color can be specified using one of three methods:

- **Color name:** You simply type the name of the color. To be absolutely safe, you should probably limit yourself to the 16 standard VGA colors, which are aqua, black, blue, fuchsia, gray, green, lime, maroon, navy, olive, purple, red, silver, teal, white, and yellow. Newer browsers will recognize a larger palette of color names (see Appendix A for a full table), but if you use these names you can't be sure that they will work on older browsers.

- **Hexadecimal:** The color is described as a series of numbers and letters. The color table in Appendix A contains hexadecimal equivalents of the colors. This is probably the best system to use.

- **Red/Green/Blue:** Here the color is defined in terms of its red, blue, and green components. Each component can be defined as either a percentage or as a number between 0 to 255 (where 0 or 0% is no application and 255 or 100% is full application). This might be useful if you're trying to match a color from a graphics program.

Format

```
selector {color: color_value;}
```

In the preceding code, `color_value` is specified using one of the methods described in the preceding list. It can also be set to transparent.

Example

```
<style>
.cool {font-family: impact; color: gray}
</style>
```

Place the preceding code into the About Me section of your MySpace profile. Don't forget that you will also need to have placed the example text (see "Styling Text") into the "Who I'd like to meet" section of your profile.

How It Will Look

While obviously you can't see Figure 6-6 in color, you should be able to see that the color of the text has changed from black to gray.

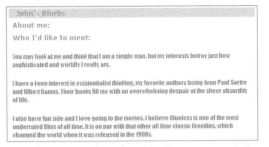

FIGURE 6-6: The color property allows you to change the color of your text.

Font Size

The `font-size` property allows you to change the size of your font. The size of a font is defined by its height — the width being a function of its height and its design. So for example, the letter *W* might be the same height as the letter *I*, but it is always going to be wider because of its inherent design.

CSS is very flexible in how you specify size values — it can understand both relative length values and absolute length values. A relative length value adjusts the size relative to the elements around it, whereas with an absolute value you just set the size — for example in inches or points. Font size can be defined in one of three ways:

- **Relative to surrounding text:** You can set the `font-size` value to be smaller or larger than the text around it.

- **A set size:** You can define the font in points (pt), the same unit used by word processing software. A point is $\frac{1}{72}$ of an inch and describes the height of the font. Fonts between 9pt and 12pt are easiest to read in body text. CSS also recognizes inches (in), centimeters (cm), or pixels (px).

- **In words:** You describe the size of the font with the following values: `xx-small`, `x-small`, `small`, `medium`, `large`, `x-large`, or `XX-large`.

See Appendix B for more information about CSS measurement units.

Format

```
selector {font-size: size;}
```

In the preceding line of code, *size* is specified using one of the methods described previously.

Example

```
<style>
.cool {font-size: medium;}
</style>
```

Place the preceding code into the About Me section of your MySpace profile. Don't forget that you will also need to have placed the example text (see "Styling Text") into the "Who I'd like to meet" section of your profile.

How It Will Look

You can see in Figure 6-7 that the font is set to medium — a little larger than it might otherwise appear.

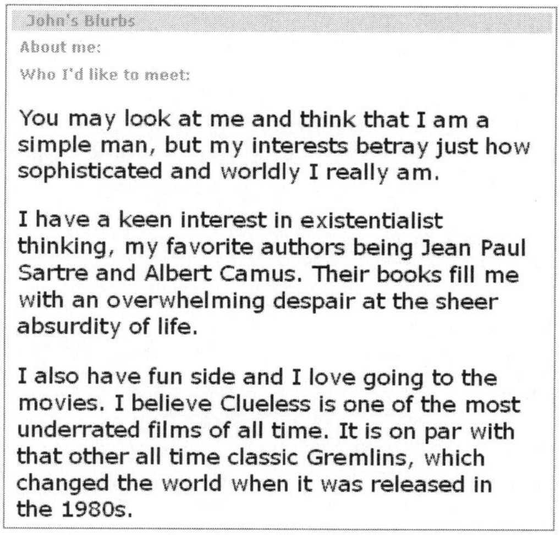

John's Blurbs

About me:

Who I'd like to meet:

You may look at me and think that I am a simple man, but my interests betray just how sophisticated and worldly I really am.

I have a keen interest in existentialist thinking, my favorite authors being Jean Paul Sartre and Albert Camus. Their books fill me with an overwhelming despair at the sheer absurdity of life.

I also have fun side and I love going to the movies. I believe Clueless is one of the most underrated films of all time. It is on par with that other all time classic Gremlins, which changed the world when it was released in the 1980s.

FIGURE 6-7: While a little too large, the text shows the font-size property in use.

Using Multiple Classes

Before moving onto the final font styles — font-style and font-weight — let's add an additional class, "hot," to the middle paragraph of our example text:

```
<p class="cool">You may look at me and think that I am a simple
man, but my interests betray just how sophisticated and worldly I
really am.</p>
```

```
<p class="hot"> I have a keen interest in existentialist thinking,
my favorite authors being Jean Paul Sartre and Albert Camus. Their
books fill me with an overwhelming despair at the sheer absurdity
of life.</p>
 <p class="cool">I also have fun side and I love going to the
movies. I believe Clueless is one of the most underrated films of
all time. It is on par with that other all time classic Gremlins,
which changed the world when it was released in the 1980s.</p>
```

You can see that we we've added a "hot" class to the <p> tag in the middle paragraph. If you paste this text into the "I'd like to meet" section of your profile, you'll find that nothing changes. In order for the changes to take effect, you need to adjust the style sheet.

For the purpose of demonstrating how to use multiple classes, insert the following text into the About Me section of your profile:

```
<style>
.cool {font-size: small; font-family: impact;}
.hot {font-size: large; font-family: times;}
</style>
```

When you view your profile (see Figure 6-8), you'll see that the middle paragraph now looks different from the first and third paragraphs. You can use as many classes as you want in your own work.

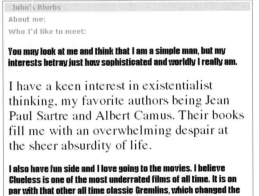

FIGURE 6-8: Here, two fonts are in use in the same document.

Font Style

The font-style property allows you apply an italic or oblique style to your text. Although the two styles look similar, there is a technical difference. Italic fonts are meant to be rendered from an italic version of the font being used, whereas with oblique, the computer simply slants the standard font. The difference is subtle, and many browsers don't differentiate between italic and oblique.

Format

```
selector {font-style: stylevalue;}
```

Here, *stylevalue* can be specified as `normal`, `italic`, or `oblique`.

Example

```
<style>
.cool {font-size: medium; font-family: arial;}
.hot {font-size: medium; font-family: arial; font-style: italic;}
</style>
```

Place the preceding code into the About Me section of your MySpace profile. Don't forget that you will also need to have placed the example text (see "Using Multiple Classes") into the "Who I'd like to meet" section of your profile.

How It Will Look

You can see the style applied in Figure 6-9.

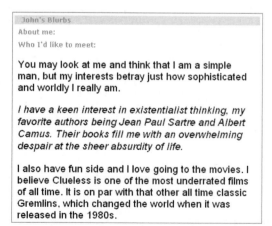

FIGURE 6-9: The middle paragraph has had an italic style applied.

Font Weight

The `font-weight` property is like the bold (`<b>`) tag in standard HTML, except that in addition to a bold value, it also has bolder and lighter values. Figure 6-10 shows how the styles look in MySpace — there's no noticeable difference between lighter and normal, and bold and bolder.

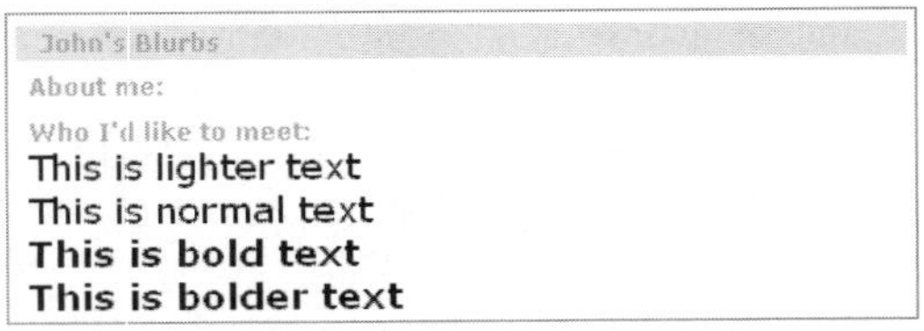

> **John's Blurbs**
>
> About me:
>
> Who I'd like to meet:
> This is lighter text
> This is normal text
> **This is bold text**
> **This is bolder text**

FIGURE 6-10: Examples of lighter, normal, bold, and bolder

Format

```
selector {font-style: weight_value;}
```

The *weight_value* can be specified as normal, bold, bolder, or lighter, or as a value between 100 to 900 in increments of 100, where 400 is the equivalent to normal and 700 is the equivalent to bold.

Example

```
<style>
.cool {font-size: medium; font-family: arial;}
.hot {font-size: medium; font-family: arial; font-weight: bold;}
</style>
```

Place the preceding code into the About Me section of your MySpace profile. Don't forget that you will also need to have placed the example text (see "Using Multiple Classes") into the "Who I'd like to meet" section of your profile.

How It Will Look

Figure 6-11 shows how the font-weight property can be used to bold text.

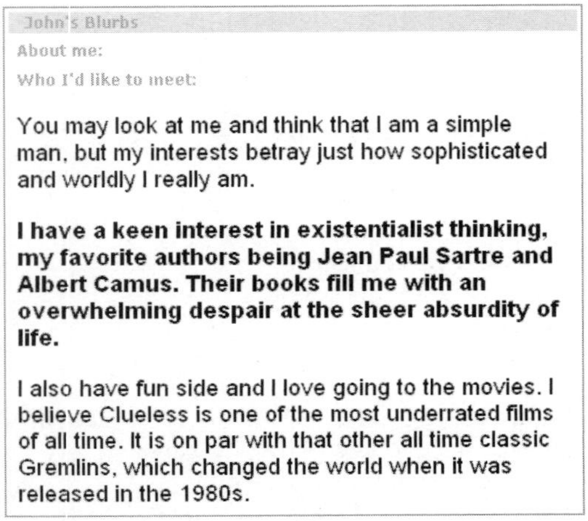

> **John's Blurbs**
>
> About me:
>
> Who I'd like to meet:
>
> You may look at me and think that I am a simple man, but my interests betray just how sophisticated and worldly I really am.
>
> **I have a keen interest in existentialist thinking, my favorite authors being Jean Paul Sartre and Albert Camus. Their books fill me with an overwhelming despair at the sheer absurdity of life.**
>
> I also have fun side and I love going to the movies. I believe Clueless is one of the most underrated films of all time. It is on par with that other all time classic Gremlins, which changed the world when it was released in the 1980s.

FIGURE 6-11: A bold style has been applied to the middle paragraph.

Line Height

Line height is the space between two lines, which is known as leading in the publishing world.

Format

```
selector {line-height: height_value;}
```

The *height_value* can be specified as either a relative length unit (%, em, ex, or px) or as an absolute value (cm, mm, in, pt, or px) — see Appendix B for more information. If it's defined as a relative unit, the value is dependent on the height of the font you're using.

Example

```
<style>
.cool {font-size: medium; font-family: arial;}
.hot {font-size: medium; font-family: arial; line-height: 150%;}
</style>
```

Place the preceding code into the About Me section of your MySpace profile. Don't forget that you will also need to have placed the example text (see "Using Multiple Classes") into the "Who I'd like to meet" section of your profile.

How It Will Look

You'll notice in Figure 6-12 that the second paragraph has one-and-a-half line spacing — not surprising since it was defined as 150 percent of the font height. If you want double spacing, simply use a value of 200 percent. If you want to use absolute values to achieve double spacing, you simply double whatever font size you are using (for example, 22pt if you had 11pt text).

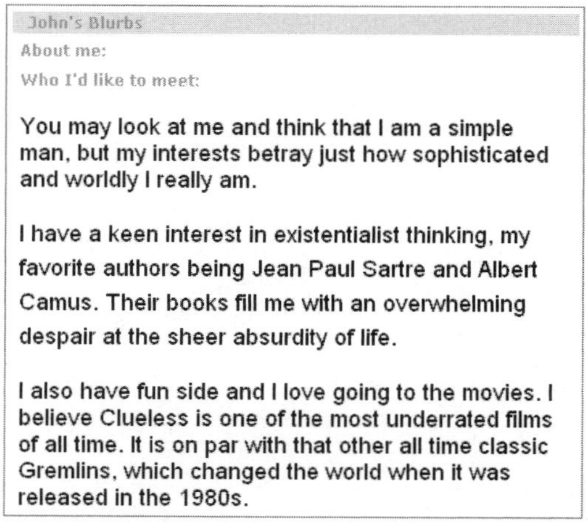

FIGURE 6-12: Line space, as the name implies, can be used to insert space between each line.

Font Variant

The `font-variant` property simply allows you to apply a small capitals style to your text — where all the text is in uppercase.

Format

```
selector {font-variant: variant_value;}
```

Here, the `variant_value` is either `normal` or `small-caps`.

Example

```
<style>
.cool {font-size: medium; font-family: arial;}
.hot {font-size: medium; font-family: arial; font-variant: small-
caps;}
</style>
```

Place the preceding code into the About Me section of your MySpace profile. Don't forget that you will also need to have placed the example text (see "Using Multiple Classes") into the "Who I'd like to meet" section of your profile.

How It Will Look

In Figure 6-13, you can see that the small capitals style has been applied to the center paragraph.

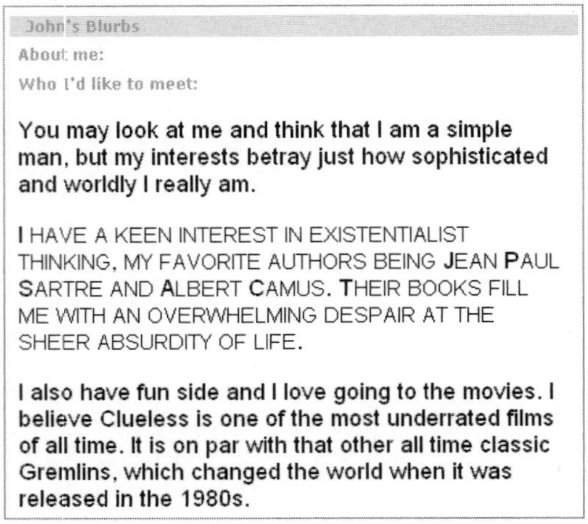

| John's Blurbs |
| About me: |
| Who I'd like to meet: |

You may look at me and think that I am a simple man, but my interests betray just how sophisticated and worldly I really am.

I HAVE A KEEN INTEREST IN EXISTENTIALIST THINKING. MY FAVORITE AUTHORS BEING JEAN PAUL SARTRE AND ALBERT CAMUS. THEIR BOOKS FILL ME WITH AN OVERWHELMING DESPAIR AT THE SHEER ABSURDITY OF LIFE.

I also have fun side and I love going to the movies. I believe Clueless is one of the most underrated films of all time. It is on par with that other all time classic Gremlins, which changed the world when it was released in the 1980s.

FIGURE 6-13: Small capitals is an interesting style.

The Combination Font Property

While all of the properties you've just looked at might come in handy, it would be a real drag if you had to use every one of them to define a style. Here's how it might look:

```
.cool {font-size: medium; font-family: arial; font-style: italic;
font-weight}
```

Obviously this is quite clumsy, and the font property is designed to make things easier by allowing you to set a number of text style values using just one property, font. The font property allows you to specify font-style, font-variant, font-weight, font-size, line-height, and font-family.

Format

```
selector {font: style_value variant_value weight_value size_value
height_value font_name }
```

Here, the *style_value* can be specified as normal, italic, or oblique, and the *variant_value* is either normal or small-caps.

The *weight_value* can be specified as normal, bold, bolder, or lighter, or it is a value between 100 to 900 in increments of 100, where 400 is the equivalent to normal and 700 is the equivalent to bold.

The *size_value* can be defined as an absolute size in words (xx-small, x-small, small, medium, large, x-large, or xx-large), as a relative size in words (larger or smaller), or in inches (in), centimeters (cm), points (pt), or pixels (px).

The *height_value* can be specified as either a relative length unit (%, em, ex, or px) or as an absolute value (cm, mm, in, pt, or pc). If it's defined as a relative unit, the value is dependent on the height of the font you're using.

The *font_name* is a font installed on the user's system. To be safe, use one of the universal fonts: Arial, Arial Black, Comic Sans MS, Courier New, Impact, Times New Roman, Trebuchet MS, Verdana, and Webdings.

Note that there is no semicolon between each value, only at the end. The first three values may appear in any order — but the last three values that define font size, line height, and font family must appear in the order listed.

Example

```
<style>
.cool {font-size: medium; font-family: arial;}
.hot {font: bold 12pt impact}
</style>
```

Place the preceding code into the About Me section of your MySpace profile. Don't forget that you will also need to have placed the example text (see "Using Multiple Classes") into the "Who I'd like to meet" section of your profile.

How It Will Look

As you can see in Figure 6-14, the central paragraph has been made bold, 9pt, and Impact using just the font property.

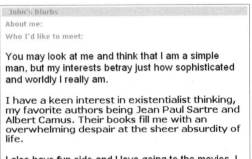

FIGURE 6-14: The font property can be used to set a number of different font attributes.

Text Indent

The text-indent property indents the first line of a paragraph. Indenting is used to make it easier to see where new paragraphs start.

Format

```
selector {text-indent: indent_value; }
```

The *indent_value* is an absolute value such as cm, mm, in, pt, or pc, or a relative value such as em, ex, px, or %. See Appendix B for more information.

Example

```
<style>
.cool {font-size: medium; font-family: arial;}
.hot { font-size: medium; font-family: arial; text-indent: 12pt;}
</style>
```

Place the preceding code into the About Me section of your MySpace profile. Don't forget that you will also need to have placed the example text (see "Using Multiple Classes") into the "Who I'd like to meet" section of your profile.

How It Will Look

The center paragraph in Figure 6-15 has a 12pt indent.

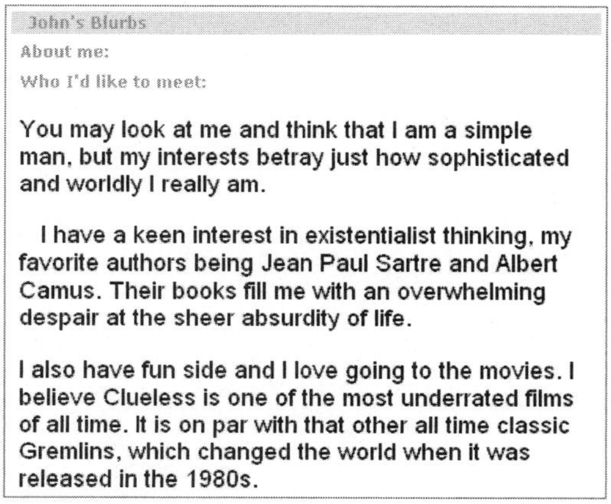

John's Blurbs

About me:

Who I'd like to meet:

You may look at me and think that I am a simple man, but my interests betray just how sophisticated and worldly I really am.

   I have a keen interest in existentialist thinking, my favorite authors being Jean Paul Sartre and Albert Camus. Their books fill me with an overwhelming despair at the sheer absurdity of life.

I also have fun side and I love going to the movies. I believe Clueless is one of the most underrated films of all time. It is on par with that other all time classic Gremlins, which changed the world when it was released in the 1980s.

FIGURE 6-15: An indent can make it easier to see where paragraphs start.

Text Align

`text-align` allows you to align your text to the left, right, or center. Or, it also allows you to justify your text, so that both left and right sides are aligned.

Format

```
selector {text-align: alignment; }
```

Here, *alignment* has one of the following values: `left` (which is also the default), `right`, `center`, or `justify`.

Example

```
<style>
.cool {font-size: medium; font-family: arial;}
.hot { font-size: medium; font-family: arial; text-align: right;}
</style>
```

Place the preceding code into the About Me section of your MySpace profile. Don't forget that you will also need to have placed the example text (see "Using Multiple Classes") into the "Who I'd like to meet" section of your profile.

How It Will Look

The middle paragraph of Figure 6-16 shows how right-aligned text would appear. Please note that the `justify` value doesn't seem to work on MySpace.

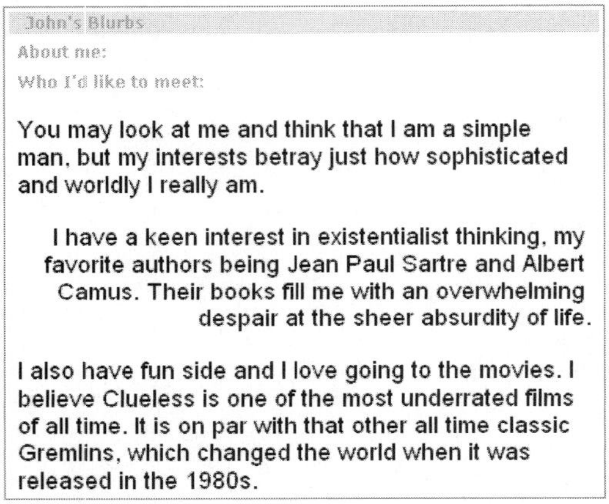

John's Blurbs
About me:
Who I'd like to meet:

You may look at me and think that I am a simple man, but my interests betray just how sophisticated and worldly I really am.

I have a keen interest in existentialist thinking, my favorite authors being Jean Paul Sartre and Albert Camus. Their books fill me with an overwhelming despair at the sheer absurdity of life.

I also have fun side and I love going to the movies. I believe Clueless is one of the most underrated films of all time. It is on par with that other all time classic Gremlins, which changed the world when it was released in the 1980s.

FIGURE 6-16: Using text-align to right justify the center paragraph

Margin

As I've discussed, CSS gives you much more control over how your elements appear in your profile, even to the extent that you can define the space around an element, even a paragraph. You can use both absolute and relative units to define the margin — see Appendix B for an overview of measurement units.

Format

```
selector {margin: top right bottom left; }
```

Here, *top* is the margin above the object, *right* is the margin to the right of the object, *bottom* is the margin below the object, and *left* is the margin to the left of the object.

Example

```
<style>
.cool {font-size: medium; font-family: arial;}
.hot { font-size: medium; font-family: arial; margin: 20px 20px
20px 20px;}
</style>
```

Place the preceding code into the About Me section of your MySpace profile. Don't forget that you will also need to have placed the example text (see "Using Multiple Classes") into the "Who I'd like to meet" section of your profile.

How It Will Look

Figure 6-17 shows the center paragraph with a margin of 5 pixels on all sides.

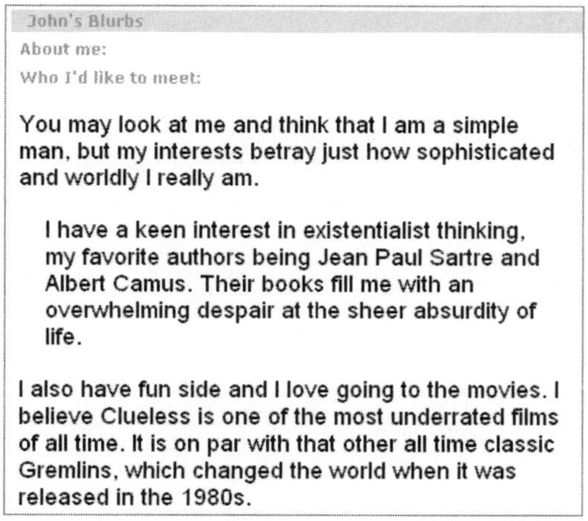

FIGURE 6-17: The center paragraph has a margin of 5 pixels on all sides.

Padding

Padding is the space between your content and the margin. This might not make any sense and you might wonder why you need padding if you can set a margin. However, if you look at the next style covered, you'll see that it is border, which allows you to specify a border for your content. Padding is the space between your content and the border, and the margin is measured from the border area — or where the padding stops. You can use both absolute and relative units to define the padding. See Appendix B for more information on measurement units.

Format

```
selector {text-align: top right bottom left; }
```

Here, *top* is the margin above the object, *right* is the margin to the right of the object, *bottom* is the margin below the object, and *left* is the margin to the left of the object.

Example

```
<style>
.cool {font-size: medium; font-family: arial;}
.hot {font-size: medium; font-family: arial; padding: 20px, 20px,
20px, 20px;}
</style>
```

Place the preceding code into the About Me section of your MySpace profile. Don't forget that you will also need to have placed the example text (see "Using Multiple Classes") into the "Who I'd like to meet" section of your profile.

How It Will Look

You'll see in Figure 6-18 that the padding looks much like a margin — it's only when you try the border style that it becomes apparent how useful margin and padding can be.

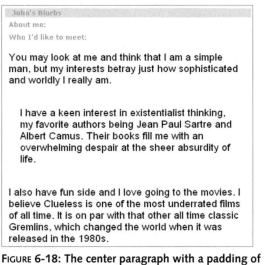

John's Blurbs

About me:

Who I'd like to meet:

You may look at me and think that I am a simple man, but my interests betray just how sophisticated and worldly I really am.

I have a keen interest in existentialist thinking, my favorite authors being Jean Paul Sartre and Albert Camus. Their books fill me with an overwhelming despair at the sheer absurdity of life.

I also have fun side and I love going to the movies. I believe Clueless is one of the most underrated films of all time. It is on par with that other all time classic Gremlins, which changed the world when it was released in the 1980s.

FIGURE 6-18: The center paragraph with a padding of 5 pixels on all sides

Border

As I've already discussed, CSS allows you to define borders around elements in your profile. The border is the line between the padding around the object and the margin. The border can be styled with three key properties — `border-width`, `border-style`, and `border-color`. However, it's much easier to simply use the combination property border, which allows you to set width, style, and color all at once.

Format

```
selector {border: width style color; }
```

The *width* is set to thin, `medium`, or `thick`, or an absolute numerical value (see Appendix B); *style* is set to none, `dashed`, `dotted`, `double`, `groove`, `ridge`, `solid`, `inset`, or `outset` (as shown in Figure 6-19); and *color* is set to a hexadecimal value, an RGB value, or a color name (as given in Appendix A).

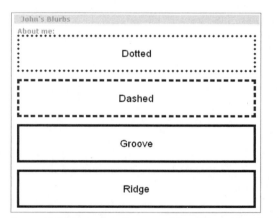

FIGURE **6-19: Samples of some of the different border styles**

Example

```
<style>
.cool {font-size: medium; font-family: arial;}
.hot {font-size: medium; font-family: arial; padding: 20px 20px 20px
20px; margin: 20px 20px 20px 20px; border: medium dashed blue;}
</style>
```

Place the preceding code into the About Me section of your MySpace profile. Don't forget that you will also need to have placed the example text (see "Using Multiple Classes") into the "Who I'd like to meet" section of your profile.

How It Will Look

In the example in Figure 6-20, I've created a blue, medium, dashed border, set 5 pixels from the text in the paragraph, with a 5 mm border.

FIGURE 6-20: The border property being used to full effect

Background Color

Just as you can set the color of an element, you can also set the background color. This is done using the `background-color` property.

Format

```
selector {background-color: color; }
```

Here, *color* is set to a hexadecimal value, an RGB value, or a color name (as given in Appendix A). It can also be set to transparent.

Example

```
<style>
.cool {font-size: medium; font-family: arial;}
.hot {font-size: medium; font-family: arial; color: white;
background-color: black;}
</style>
```

Place the preceding code into the About Me section of your MySpace profile. Don't forget that you will also need to have placed the example text (see "Using Multiple Classes") into the "Who I'd like to meet" section of your profile.

How It Will Look

In the example in Figure 6-21, I've created a black background behind the center paragraph. I've also made the text white so that you can see the text.

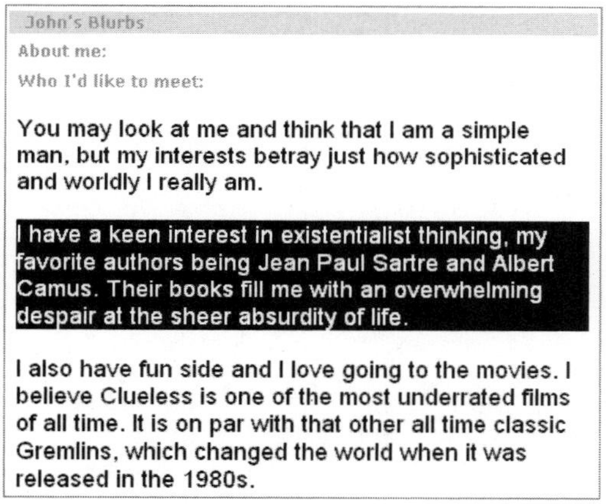

John's Blurbs

About me:

Who I'd like to meet:

You may look at me and think that I am a simple man, but my interests betray just how sophisticated and worldly I really am.

I have a keen interest in existentialist thinking, my favorite authors being Jean Paul Sartre and Albert Camus. Their books fill me with an overwhelming despair at the sheer absurdity of life.

I also have fun side and I love going to the movies. I believe Clueless is one of the most underrated films of all time. It is on par with that other all time classic Gremlins, which changed the world when it was released in the 1980s.

FIGURE 6-21: The background color of the center paragraph has been made black.

Problem Solver Checklist

It's very easy for typographic and other minor errors to mess up your CSS. Here are a few tips in case you're having problems.

- Are you using the right separator — a semicolon (;) or a colon (:) — in the right place?

- Are you using the right kind of brackets — that is, curly brackets or braces, not round brackets?

- Are you using straight quotes, not "smart quotes" when defining classes?

- Did you forget to press Submit when previewing code in MySpace?

- Has MySpace defined an existing tag, such as the `<p>` tag, that is overriding a `<div>` tag you're trying to place?

Wrapping Up

I've covered a lot of the basic CSS properties in this chapter. Already you have a lot of control over how text appears in your profile. In the next chapter, I cover some more advanced CSS concepts, which will, as you progress through the book, allow you to make some profound changes to your profile.

More on Cascading Style Sheets

I n the previous chapter you were introduced to CSS and how you can use CSS to apply styles to text. This chapter looks at some more advanced concepts of pseudo elements and classes, as well as some advanced techniques for applying styles using <span> and <div> tags, styling predefined tags, positioning, defining the order of how different elements appear on the page, and finally hiding elements.

Pseudo Elements and Classes

Before we move onto the next style, you need to understand the concept behind pseudo elements and pseudo classes. Pseudo elements and classes are designed to allow you to style parts of the document that normally can't be specified by HTML. For example, in HTML there is no way to specify the first line of a paragraph or how a link appears.

Conceptually, it's quite difficult to understand the difference between pseudo elements and pseudo classes, but let's try anyway.

As you'll recall, an "element" is any of the content that makes up a web page. Paragraphs, tables, or images are examples of elements. You can easily define how a certain paragraph appears because, as you've seen, you can apply a particular style to its corresponding <p> tag. But how would you apply a style that applies only to the first line or first letter of the paragraph because there is no way in HTML to specify these sections of a paragraph? You wouldn't be able to, which is why CSS has the pseudo elements first-letter and first-line.

You can see that pseudo elements are not really elements in themselves — hence the name pseudo elements. They're really just allowing you to specify part of an existing element.

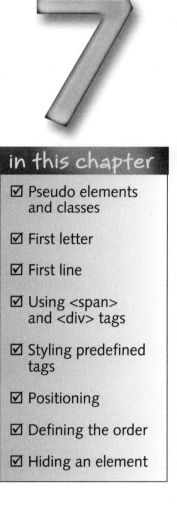

Pseudo classes allow you to specify parts of your document that aren't directly related to specific elements. So for example, you can adjust the appearance of your links, or the ways that your links behave. You can see that conceptually the way a link appears is not tied to a specific element because links can appear in a number of elements.

Pseudo classes and pseudo elements are preceded by a colon (:) rather than by a full stop (.).

Before you go through these exercises, ensure that you have placed the multiple-classes dummy text used in Chapter 6 in the "Who I'd like to meet" section of your MySpace profile.

First Letter

The `first-letter` pseudo element allows you to style just the first letter of a paragraph. It's useful for creating an initial cap or drop cap, both of which are commonly used in desktop publishing.

Format

```
selector:first-letter { property: value; }
```

Here, `property` is any applicable CSS property.

Example

```
<style>
.cool {font-size: medium; font-family: arial;}
.hot { font-size: medium; font-family: arial;}
.hot:first-letter {font-weight: bold; font-size: 200%; font-
family: times new roman;}
</style>
```

Notice the colon that precedes the `first-line` pseudo element. Don't leave a space between `.hot` and `:firstline` as it won't work.

Place the preceding code into the About Me section of your MySpace profile. Don't forget that you will also need to place the example text (see "Using Multiple Classes" in Chapter 6) into the "Who I'd like to meet" section of your profile.

How It Will Look

Figure 7-1 shows how the first letter will look.

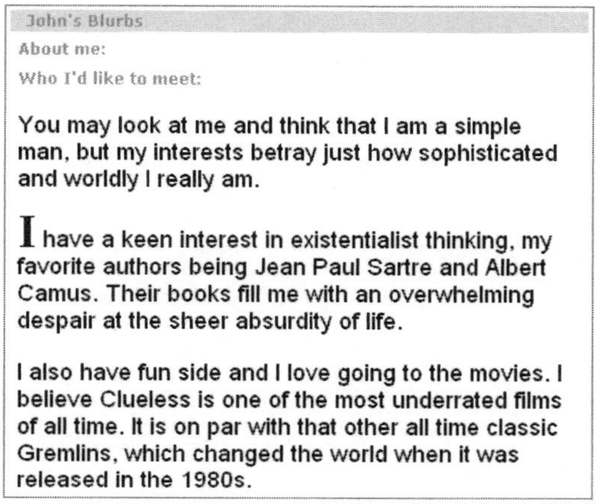

FIGURE 7-1: The first-letter pseudo element allows you to style just the first letter of a paragraph.

First Line

The first-line pseudo element allows you to style just the first line of a paragraph.

Format

```
selector:first-line { property: value; }
```

Here, *property* is any applicable CSS property.

Example

```
<style>
.cool {font-size: medium; font-family: arial;}
.hot { font-size: medium; font-family: arial;}
.hot:first-line {font-weight: bold;}
</style>
```

Notice the colon that precedes the first-line pseudo element. Don't leave a space between .hot and :firstline as it won't work.

Place the preceding code into the About Me section of your MySpace profile. Don't forget that you will also need to have placed the example text (see "Using Multiple Classes" in Chapter 6) into the "Who I'd like to meet" section of your profile.

How It Will Look

Figure 7-2 shows how the first line will look in your profile.

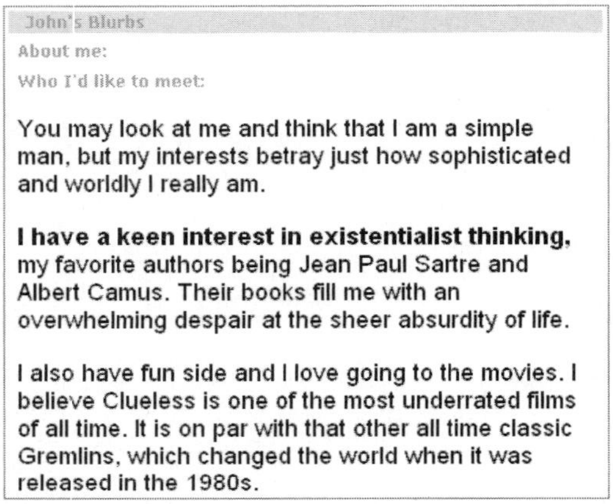

John's Blurbs

About me:

Who I'd like to meet:

You may look at me and think that I am a simple man, but my interests betray just how sophisticated and worldly I really am.

I have a keen interest in existentialist thinking, my favorite authors being Jean Paul Sartre and Albert Camus. Their books fill me with an overwhelming despair at the sheer absurdity of life.

I also have fun side and I love going to the movies. I believe Clueless is one of the most underrated films of all time. It is on par with that other all time classic Gremlins, which changed the world when it was released in the 1980s.

FIGURE **7-2: The first-line pseudo element allows you to style just the first line of a paragraph.**

Using <span> and <div> Tags

In the preceding examples and in Chapter 6, we've applied styles to paragraph (<p>) tags to demonstrate how styles work. We used the <p> tag because the concept of a paragraph is quite simple to understand, and the important thing was for you to understand how styles work, and to see that once you've embedded styles in your profile, it's very easy to change all the styles by just changing their definition.

However, this is not necessarily the most convenient way to apply styles in a document — for example, how do you apply styles to a larger area of your document that might consist of a number of paragraphs? Or how do you apply a style to just a portion of text within a paragraph? This is where the <div> and <span> tags, which I briefly mentioned in Chapter 4, become amazingly useful.

Just to recap quickly, the <div> tag allows you to mark out a logical division — or sections — in your web page, whereas <span> allows you to mark out a section of text. If you don't understand the distinction, you will once you've worked through the examples. The important thing is that they also allow you to apply a style to the sections that they've marked out. Let's try using <div> and <span> to help you understand why they're so useful. Incidentally, logical divisions are often just called *Divs*.

Place the following style definition in the About Me section of MySpace. Make sure you copy over anything you had there before.

```
<style>
.cool {font-size: medium; font-family: arial; font-weight: bold;}
.hot {font-size: medium; font-family: arial; font-style: italic;}
p {font-size: medium; font-family: arial;}
</style>
```

You'll notice that I made a point of defining the `<p>` tag so it was the same font as `.cool` and `.hot`. That's because MySpace already has a definition in place for the `<p>` tag, and you need to overwrite this if you want your `<div>` and `<span>` tags to do their job properly; otherwise the `<p>` tag takes priority.

In the "Who I'd like to meet" section of your MySpace profile, place the following code:

```
<div class="cool">
<p>You may look at me and think that I am a simple man, but my
interests betray just how sophisticated and worldly I really am.</p>
</div>
<div class="hot">
<p>I have a keen interest in existentialist thinking, my favorite
authors being Jean Paul Sartre and Albert Camus. Their books fill me
with an overwhelming despair at the sheer absurdity of life.</p>
 <p>I also have fun side and I love going to the movies. I believe
Clueless is one of the most underrated films of all time. It is on
par with that other all time classic Gremlins, which changed the
world when it was released in the 1980s.</p>
</div>
```

You'll see that we have applied the `.cool` class to the first paragraph by enclosing it with a pair of `<div>` tags — `<div class="cool">` and `</div>`, and we've applied the `.hot` class to the second and third paragraphs by enclosing them in `<div class="hot">` and `</div>`. Figure 7-3 shows how this will look in your profile.

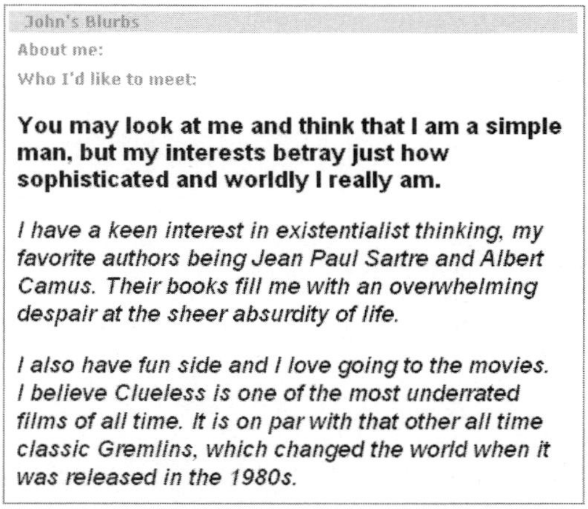

FIGURE 7-3: Here a `<div>` tag has been used to apply styles to paragraphs.

You'll see in Figure 7-3 that the `.cool` style has been applied to the first paragraph, while the `.hot` style has been applied to the second and third paragraphs. You can see that the `<div>` tag would be extremely useful for applying styles to larger areas of your profile.

Now let's take a look at how the `<span>` tag allows you to define smaller sections of text within a paragraph.

Let's keep the same styles that we used for the `<div>` example, but please insert the following code into the "Who I'd like to meet" section of your profile.

```
<div class="cool">
<p>You may look at me and think that I am a simple man, but my
interests betray just how sophisticated and worldly I really
am.</p>
<p>I have a keen interest in existentialist thinking, my favorite
authors being Jean Paul Sartre and Albert Camus. <span
class="hot">Their books fill me with an overwhelming despair at
the sheer absurdity of life.</span> </p>
 <p>I also have fun side and I love going to the movies. I believe
Clueless is one of the most underrated films of all time. It is on
par with that other all time classic Gremlins, which changed the
world when it was released in the 1980s.</p>
</div>
```

In this example, you're applying the `.cool` style to all three paragraphs (as they are enclosed by the `<div class="cool">` and `</div>` tags), and applying the `.hot` class to the second sentence of the second paragraph by enclosing it within the `<span class="hot">` and `</span>` tags. Figure 7-4 shows how this would look in MySpace.

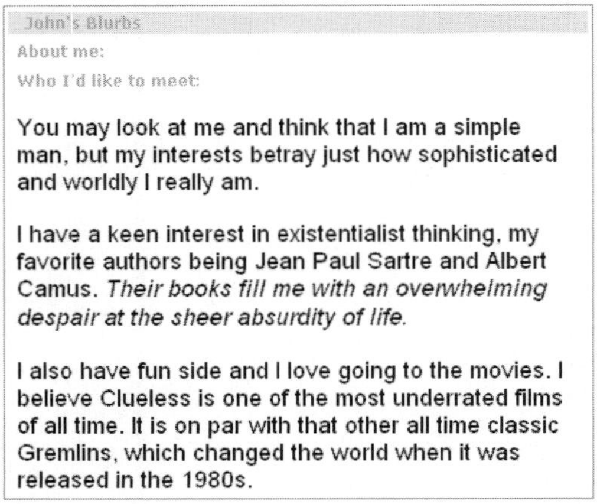

John's Blurbs

About me:

Who I'd like to meet:

You may look at me and think that I am a simple man, but my interests betray just how sophisticated and worldly I really am.

I have a keen interest in existentialist thinking, my favorite authors being Jean Paul Sartre and Albert Camus. *Their books fill me with an overwhelming despair at the sheer absurdity of life.*

I also have fun side and I love going to the movies. I believe Clueless is one of the most underrated films of all time. It is on par with that other all time classic Gremlins, which changed the world when it was released in the 1980s.

FIGURE 7-4: A <span> tag has been used to apply a style to a sentence within paragraphs.

Styling Predefined Tags

The best way to define and apply styles in MySpace is to define classes in an internal style sheet and then apply those styles to your HTML tags. However, as I discussed at the beginning of this chapter, you can also style existing HTML tags. To see how this works, place the following code in the About Me section of your profile:

```
<style>
p {font-size: medium; font-family: impact;}
</style>
```

You can see that basically what I've done is to redefine the paragraph (<p>) tag so that the font in the paragraph is medium Impact.

Now place the following code in the "Who I'd like to meet" section of your profile.

```
<p>You may look at me and think that I am a simple man, but my
interests betray just how sophisticated and worldly I really
am.</p>
<p>I have a keen interest in existentialist thinking, my favorite
authors being Jean Paul Sartre and Albert Camus. Their books fill
me with an overwhelming despair at the sheer absurdity of
life.</p>
<p>I also have fun side and I love going to the movies. I believe
Clueless is one of the most underrated films of all time. It is on
par with that other all time classic Gremlins, which changed the
world when it was released in the 1980s.</p>
```

In this code, I've removed all the classes, but as you'll see in the screenshot in Figure 7-5, because the <p> tag has been redefined, the paragraphs have still been styled.

John's Blurbs

About me:

Who I'd like to meet:

You may look at me and think that I am a simple man, but my interests betray just how sophisticated and worldly I really am.

I have a keen interest in existentialist thinking, my favorite authors being Jean Paul Sartre and Albert Camus. Their books fill me with an overwhelming despair at the sheer absurdity of life.

I also have fun side and I love going to the movies. I believe Clueless is one of the most underrated films of all time. It is on par with that other all time classic Gremlins, which changed the world when it was released in the 1980s.

FIGURE 7-5: By styling the <p> tag you can change the way paragraphs appear in your profile.

Styling existing HTML tags can be useful if you're willing to sacrifice future versatility in exchange for speed. Styling existing tags will also come in handy when you're making adjustments to the standard MySpace template, which you'll be doing in Chapter 18.

Positioning

One of the most powerful things about CSS is its ability to position elements anywhere on the web page. In the old days before CSS, web designers had to use tables to position elements, and the results were sometimes unreliable — depending on which browser was being used to view the table.

The position property allows you to determine where an element — such as an image or a block of text — will appear in your profile. You can either position an element relative to where it would have appeared normally, or you can plot its position from the top-left corner of the screen (absolute).

However, there is a problem with the absolute method for positioning your image in your MySpace profile because where your image appears is dependent on how wide the browser window is — and you have no control over how visitors to your profile set up their browser. There is a very clever workaround for this, which I discuss shortly.

As you'll see later in the book, the position property allows you to radically alter how your MySpace profile appears. For now, it's a neat trick that allows you to move elements — such as paragraphs or Divs — to anywhere on the page.

Format

```
selector { position: positioning_system; }
```

In the preceding line of code, positioning_system can have the following values:

- absolute: The position is specified with the top, bottom, left, and right properties (usually using two properties such as left or right and top or bottom), calculated from the top-left corner of the screen. So the position specified by {position: absolute; left: 100px; top: 100px} would be 100 pixels to the right of the top-left corner and 100 pixels down from the top-left corner. This might seem counterintuitive, but what you're actually saying is that you're moving the element 100 pixels from its left edge, and 100 pixels from the top edge.

- relative: The position is specified with the top, bottom, left and right properties (usually using two properties like left or right and top or bottom), calculated relative to where it would have otherwise appeared. As with "absolute" positioning, relative positioning seems counter intuitive. So the position specified by {position: absolute; right: 100px; bottom: 100px} would be 100 pixels above the place where the image would have otherwise appeared and 100 pixels up from the top-left corner of where the image would have appeared.

- `static`: This is the default value and simply means that the image appears where it would normally appear.

- `fixed`: The image stays in the one position even if the page is scrolled and where the position is specified with the top, bottom, left, and right properties (usually using two properties such as left or right and top or bottom).

Example

First, let's try placing the relative positioning system. Place the following code into the "Who I'd like to meet" section of your profile:

```
<div class="divposition">
<p>You may look at me and think that I am a simple man, but my
interests betray just how sophisticated and worldly I really
am.</p>
<p>I have a keen interest in existentialist thinking, my favorite
authors being Jean Paul Sartre and Albert Camus. Their books fill
me with an overwhelming despair at the sheer absurdity of
life.</p>
 <p>I also have fun side and I love going to the movies. I believe
Clueless is one of the most underrated films of all time. It is on
par with that other all time classic Gremlins, which changed the
world when it was released in the 1980s.</p>
</div>
```

Place this code into the About Me section of your profile:

```
<style>
.divposition {position: relative; right: 330px; bottom: 186px;}
</style>
```

How It Will Look

You'll see in Figure 7-6 that the paragraphs have been moved to the left edge of the profile, down below the contacts table. You'll also notice that the paragraphs appear over the top of the existing profile.

Working with Absolute Positioning

Relatively positioning is relatively simple, but as discussed, absolute positioning is a little more complex because the position of the horizontal coordinate depends on the width of the browser window (which you have no control over). This makes it difficult to position elements so that they appear in the right place relative to the MySpace profile. However, there is a workaround, and here's how you could position the paragraphs in the relative positioning example using absolute positioning.

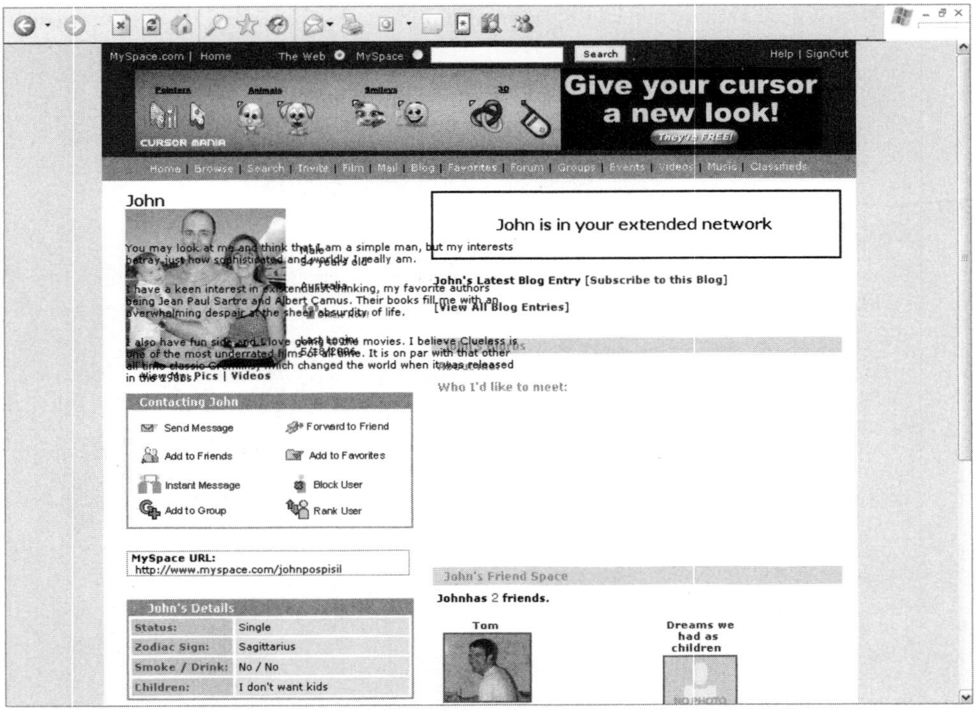

FIGURE 7-6: The sample paragraphs have been moved to the top-left area of the profile.

Place this code in the About Me section of your MySpace profile:

```
<style>
.divposition {position: absolute; left: 50%; top: 300px; margin-
left: -400px;}
</style>
```

You can see in the preceding code that the Y or vertical coordinate is specified using the top property and is simply the number of pixels that the paragraphs are from the top of the profile. The `.divposition` class contains the property `top: 300px`, which simply means that the paragraphs will be 300 pixels from the top of the page.

That's easy. But the Y or horizontal coordinate is not so straightforward, and this is basically because whereas the top of a web page is always fixed, the edge of the left and right sides of a web page can vary depending on the size of the browser window.

To get around this problem, this code uses the `left` property to place the section in the center of the page — `left: 50%;` is always the center of the page. Then the `margin-left` property is used to position the element relative to the center of the page.

Because the standard MySpace profile is about 800 pixels wide, if you place something in the middle (using `left: 50%;`) and then move it 400 pixels to the left of that centered position (using `margin-left: -400pixels`), you'll be able to roughly line up the element to the left side of the profile. If you want to place the element to the right of the center, simply use a positive value in the `margin-left` property. This is quite a nifty workaround, and once you understand this principle, it's actually quite simple.

How It Will Look

You can see in Figure 7-7 that we've again moved the paragraphs to the right of the profile, but this time there's no gap in the About Me section where the paragraphs would have otherwise appeared.

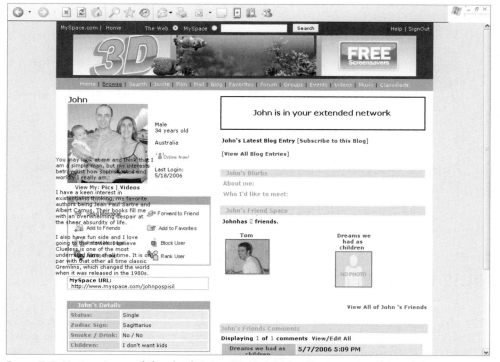

FIGURE 7-7: Here we've used the absolute positioning system to reposition the sample paragraphs.

Defining the Order

If you're positioning a number of elements on a profile, chances are that some of them might overlap, so how do you specify which elements appear on the top, and which ones appear beneath? This is where the z-index property comes to the rescue.

Format

```
Selector {z-index: value;}
```

Here, `value` specifies the order in which an element is displayed. Elements with higher z-index values are shown on top of elements with lower values. Please note that z-index works only with elements that have been positioned.

Example

Leave the code you placed in the "Who I'd like to meet" section of your MySpace profile for the positioning example (see above), and place the following code in the About Me section:

```
<style>
.divposition {position: absolute; left: 50%; top: 300px; margin-
left: -400px; z-index: -1;}
</style>
```

How It Will Look

In Figure 7-8, it looks as though our paragraphs have disappeared. They're there all right, but they're behind the existing elements in the profile because the z-index value has been set to −1, and the existing elements have a nominal value of 0. To place the paragraphs over the top of the existing elements, set the z-index value to 1.

Hiding an Element

Sometimes it's convenient to be able to hide an element, which is when the visibility and display properties come in handy. Chapter 18, for example, looks at how you can restyle the standard MySpace profile. Using the visibility or display property, you can also hide elements of the existing profile, which you can use, for example, to hide your details — or to take it to the extreme, hide the whole profile.

Format

```
Selector {visibility: value;}
```

Here, the `value` is either `visible`, so that the element is shown, or `hidden`, so that the element is not shown.

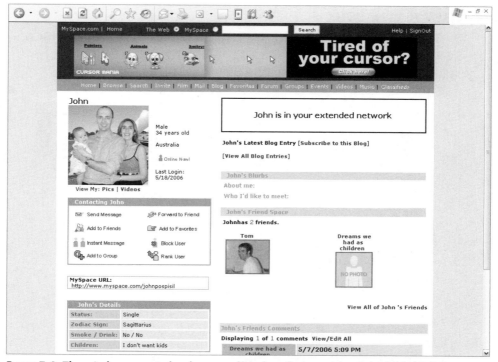

FIGURE 7-8: The z-index property has been used to place the sample paragraphs behind the existing profile elements — which is why you can't see them.

You can also use the display property to hide elements:

```
Selector   {display: none;}
```

While a number of different values work with the display property, we're interested only in none, which specifies that the element will not be displayed.

Example

Leave the code you placed in the "Who I'd like to meet" section of your MySpace profile for the positioning example (see above), and place the following code in the About Me section:

```
<style>
.divposition {visibility: hidden;}
</style>
```

How It Will Look

You'll see a blank space where the sample paragraphs should be under "Who I'd like to meet" (as in Figure 7-9) — the paragraphs are there, but they're not visible.

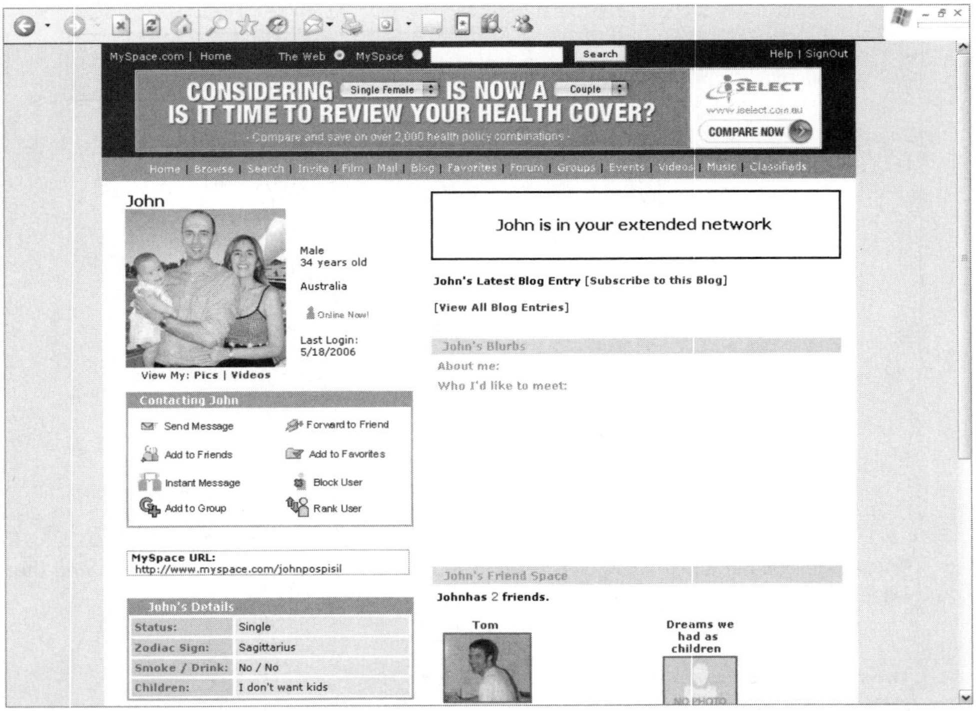

FIGURE 7-9: The sample paragraphs have been rendered invisible using the visibility property.

Now try placing this code in the About Me section:

```
<style>
.divposition {display: none;}
</style>
```

As Figure 7-10 shows, you can't see the sample paragraphs, and the space for them is also gone. This is the main difference between using the visibility property and the display property to hide elements.

FIGURE 7-10: Using display: none; eliminates any trace of the element.

Additional HTML and CSS Resources

In the chapters covering HTML and CSS you've looked at only a few of the tags and properties that are available to you. If you want to learn more, you'll find that the World Wide Web Consortium (w3c), which develops web standards, offers a lot of useful information at its web site at www.w3.org. The Microsoft Library (msdn.microsoft.com/library) also offers some very useful information — click Web Development in the index to access the material on CSS and HTML.

You might also find the tutorials offered by W3 Schools (www.w3schools.com/css) useful for building up your HTML and CSS skills. Keep in mind that because MySpace filters the code before it is sent to the browser, not everything will work in the way you might expect.

By building up your knowledge of HTML and CSS, you'll find that you'll soon be developing your own original hacks.

Wrapping Up

If you've gotten through this chapter and understood Divs, and positioning and hiding elements, you're already well on the way to understanding some of the more advanced concepts later in the book. If you've found it a little hard going, give it a break for now, and then reread this chapter before you start Chapter 25, where I cover Div overlays.

Using MySpace with Image Hosting Web Sites

While MySpace allows you to upload images to a gallery so you can share photos with your MySpace friends, if you want to embed images — or other audiovisual content such as videos or music — in other sections of your profile you'll need to store your content somewhere on the Internet where you can link to it from your profile. (Don't worry if this sounds complicated; it's covered in detail in Chapter 10.)

If you have your own web site — whether you've set up your own domain or if you have some free space given to you by your Internet service provider — you can store the images on your own site (this is covered in Chapter 9). If you don't, there's another very easy option — you can use an image hosting web site.

Image hosting web sites are designed to help you share your photo collections, but many of them also offer direct linking, which means you can link and display an image on your MySpace profile that is actually stored on the image host's web site. Most image hosting web sites offer both free and paid accounts, which cost around $25 per year. The paid accounts offer more storage, faster speed, and less intrusive advertising.

The process of uploading images is relatively straightforward. It involves the following:

- Editing the images you want to upload to make sure they fit within the specifications set by the image hosting company. This is also a good opportunity to fix any imperfections.

- Uploading your images to the hosting web site.

- Obtaining the link code that will allow you to embed the image in your MySpace profile.

Introducing Photobucket

To demonstrate the process of uploading images, I'll use www.photobucket.com, a popular image hosting service that offers both free and paid accounts. Before you continue on with this chapter, go to www.photobucket.com and open a free account (you can always upgrade later if you decide it's worthwhile).

Photobucket limits the types of images you can upload, especially if you have a free account, where images must be less than 512KB and be in JPG, GIF, PNG, BMP, TIFF, or SWF format. Even if there were no restrictions on file sizes, it's always a good idea to keep image sizes to a minimum. The smaller your image, the less time it will take to appear when someone visits your profile.

Enter the GIMP

In order to prepare your images for uploading, you're going to need an image editing program. If you already own a program such as Paint Shop Pro or Photoshop Elements, you can go ahead and use it to resize your images and save them in JPG format. If you don't have an image editing program, don't panic. For this book, I'm using an open source image editing program called GNU Image Manipulation Program (GIMP), which you can download for free from gimp-win.sourceforge.net, or you can access it via a link at this book's site, www.myspaceismyplace.com. The version used in this book is 2.2.10. Despite the unfortunate name, the program is very good and offers many advanced features. GIMP is more than powerful enough for the photo editing you're doing here and in Chapter 29 (where I cover photo enhancement). The other good news is that a Macintosh version is available and can be downloaded from gimp-app.sourceforge.net.

In order for GIMP to work on a PC, you'll first need to install GTK +2 Runtime environment — version 2.8.9 for Windows 2000 and XP or version 2.2.10 for older versions of Windows (available from gimp-win.sourceforge.net).

In order for GIMP to work on a Mac, you'll need to install Apple's X11 package, which is an optional install on your OS X install CD, or you can download it from www.apple.com/support/downloads/x11formacosx.html.

It's also worth knowing that many tutorials, plug-ins, and other resources are available on the Internet — a good starting point to find out more is www.gimp.org.

Once you have GIMP installed on your computer, you're ready to get started.

Editing the Image

You can use your own image in the following tutorial, or you can use the sample JPG file available from my web site at www.myspaceismyplace.com. This is a picture of my wife, Rocio, taken with a Nikon D100. (Thanks to Shelton Muller for taking this photo.) The image is 2,000 pixels wide by 3,008 pixels high, and is more than 3MB in size. (It's a JPG format with little compression.) Obviously, it's way too big to upload to Photobucket, and it's also way too big to fit into the About Me section of my MySpace profile, which is only 435 pixels wide.

1. Load the image into GIMP. Click File ⇨ Open in the Gimp tool box. Your image should appear onscreen, as in Figure 8-1.

FIGURE 8-1: An image loaded in the GIMP

2. Click Image in the top menu bar of the window displaying the image, and select Scale Image. A Scale Image dialog box appears (see Figure 8-2).

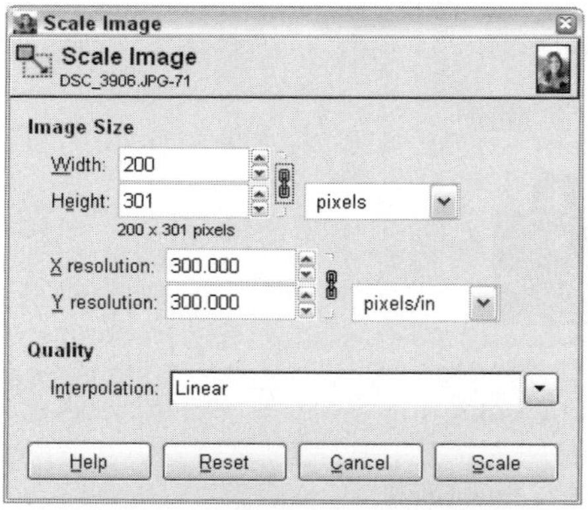

FIGURE 8-2: The Scale Image dialog box

3. In the box that says 2000, type **200**. The image will be resized accordingly.

4. Click View ⇨ Zoom ⇨ 1:1 100% to view the image at its actual size.

5. Click File ⇨ Save As and save the file in your MySpace working directory (the one you made up on your computer's hard disk) with the filename ch08-image-r.jpg — the *r* represents resized. Before GIMP saves the file, another dialog box appears, allowing you to adjust the quality by setting a value between 0 and 100. The lower the number, the lower the quality. Set the value to 40, which should result in a 16KB file that still looks quite good onscreen.

When you've done this you'll notice two GIMP image windows onscreen. Close both windows without saving the images (because you already saved the resized image and you don't want to copy over the original image).

Uploading the Image

Go to www.photobucket.com and log in with your account, which should take you to a screen where you can "Add Pictures" to your photo album.

Click the Browse button, and navigate to your MySpace working directory where you saved the resized image. Select ch08-image-r.jpg and click Submit. It may take a few moments to upload the image to Photobucket. When it's finished, a thumbnail will appear below the Add Pictures section (see Figure 8-3).

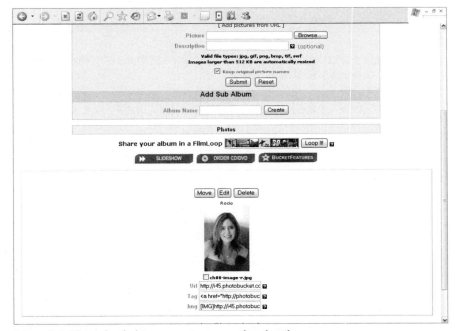

FIGURE 8-3: The uploaded image appears as a thumbnail.

Obtaining the Link Code

If you look below the thumbnail of the image, you'll see there is a text box labeled URL. Click the text box and press Ctrl+C. The link you've just copied will look something like this:

```
http://i45.photobucket.com/albums/f93/pospisil/ch08-image-r.jpg
```

Paste this into a blank text file (perhaps using HTML-Kit) and save the text file in your MySpace working area — call the file linkcode.txt. You will need this link for Chapter 10 when you learn how to embed graphics into your MySpace profile.

Tip Photobucket allows you to create different types of slide shows, such as BucketStrip, BucketStamp, and BucketShow (you can access these features by clicking the Bucket Features button in your main album page). What happens is that you select the images you want in the slide show, and Photobucket generates the link code that you then place into your profile. This is a very easy way to create some very cool effects that can really make your profile stand out. Other image hosting web sites offer similar features.

Other Image Hosting Web Sites

In this chapter, I've used Photobucket to demonstrate the process of uploading images to an image hosting web site, but a number of other services are just as good. Here's a selection of other image hosting services for you to consider, and a little about the free services they offer (at the time of this writing):

- Image Venue (www.imagevenue.com): Accepts JPG files up to 1.5MB.

- ImageShack (www.imageshack.us): Offers unlimited uploads as long as guidelines are followed.

- XS TO (xs.to): Accepts JPG, GIF, BMP, and TIFF files up to 1.5MB, maximum 500 images.

- Flickr (www.flickr.com): Limited to 20MB of uploads per month.

- Forum Sigs (www.forumsigs.com): Accepts JPG, GIF, TIFF, BMP, and SWF files up to 256KB, maximum 15 images.

- Mooload.com (www.mooload.com): Accepts most file formats up to 500MB in size.

- Village Photos (www.villagephotos.com): Up to 250KB per image, maximum 25 images.

- TinyPic (www.tinypic.com): No signup required, accepts files up to 250KB per image. JPG, PNG, TIFF, and GIF accepted.

- PicPlace (www.picplace.com): Accepts JPG, JPEG, PNG, GIF, and BMP files up to 1.5MB in size. No login required.

Wrapping Up

Images are an important part of a profile, and after reading this chapter you should be comfortable preparing and uploading your images to an image hosting site. I suggest you try out some of the special effects offered by many of these hosting sites. These special effects are an easy way to make your profile stand out with very little effort. In Chapter 10 you look at how to embed images in your profile.

Using MySpace with Your Own Web Site

C hapter 8 looked at using an image hosting web site to store images that you want to embed in your MySpace profile. If you've got your own web site, whether it's a web site with your own domain name or a free web site issued by your Internet service provider, you can also store your images there. There are a number of advantages to this approach:

- There are no limitations as to what files you can upload — so in addition to image files, you may upload audio and video files.

- The size of the file you can upload is limited only by the size of your web site account.

- Your web hosting company is less likely to shut down than many of the smaller image hosting companies, meaning there's a better chance of long-term continuity.

On the other hand, you may be tying up the resources of your web site unnecessarily when you could be using a free service. Only you can decide what is more convenient for you.

File Transfer Protocol

File transfer protocol (FTP) was developed in the 1970s and is one of the oldest protocols still in everyday use — all current browsers support FTP. A protocol is simply an agreed way of doing something. The purpose of FTP is to allow the efficient and reliable transfer of files from one computer connected to the Internet to another.

Why You Need an FTP Client

To actually use FTP, you need an FTP client — which is simply a piece of software that allows you to transfer files using FTP. One of the best FTP clients for the PC is a program called FileZilla (`filezilla.sourceforge.net`). If you're a Mac user, you may want to try Cyberduck (`cyberduck.ch`).

If you haven't already, go ahead and install FileZilla on your computer.

FTP Address, User Name, and Password

In order to be able to actually upload files to a server you'll need the following information:

- **FTP host name:** This may look something like the following: `ftp.domainname.com` (where *domainname* is a the name of the web site) or if you're using hosting supplied as part of an Internet access account it may look more like `ftp.ispname.com/~username` (where the *ispname* is the name of your Internet service provider and your *username* is the user name you use to log into your Internet service). Sometimes instead of an FTP host name, you might be given an IP address by your service provider, which might look something like this: 83.223.107.15.

- **User name:** This is generally the same user name that you use to access your account.

- **Password:** Again this is generally the same password that you use to access your account.

This information is provided to you in the initial documentation (whether electronic or paper based) that you received when you first signed up with your web hosting company, or if you're using space provided by your Internet service provider when you originally signed up. If you don't have it, get in touch with your provider, and they should be able to help.

Editing Your Photo

Whenever you upload images that you plan to embed in your profile it's important to make sure that the image is the right size (in terms of width and height) and is also small enough, so that it doesn't slow down the loading of your profile. This was covered in Chapter 8. For the purpose of this exercise, if you haven't already done so, go back to Chapter 8 and prepare a graphics file that you can upload to your FTP server. Save the file in your MySpace directory.

Using Your FTP Client

Start FileZilla, and the program should appear much like Figure 9-1. You'll see a window on the left showing the local hard disks (i.e., the hard disks physically connected to your computer). The top half of this window displays the directory tree, while the bottom half displays the files in the selected directory. Navigate to the image file you saved in your MySpace directory. This is simply a matter of double-clicking the left mouse buttons on the directories until you get to the file you saved. You may have some problem finding My Documents, but you will be able to get to it by clicking Documents and Settings in your main drive (usually c:) and then clicking your user name and then My Documents. As you see in Figure 9-1, the path to the file was C:\Documents and Settings\John\My Documents\MYSPACE\.

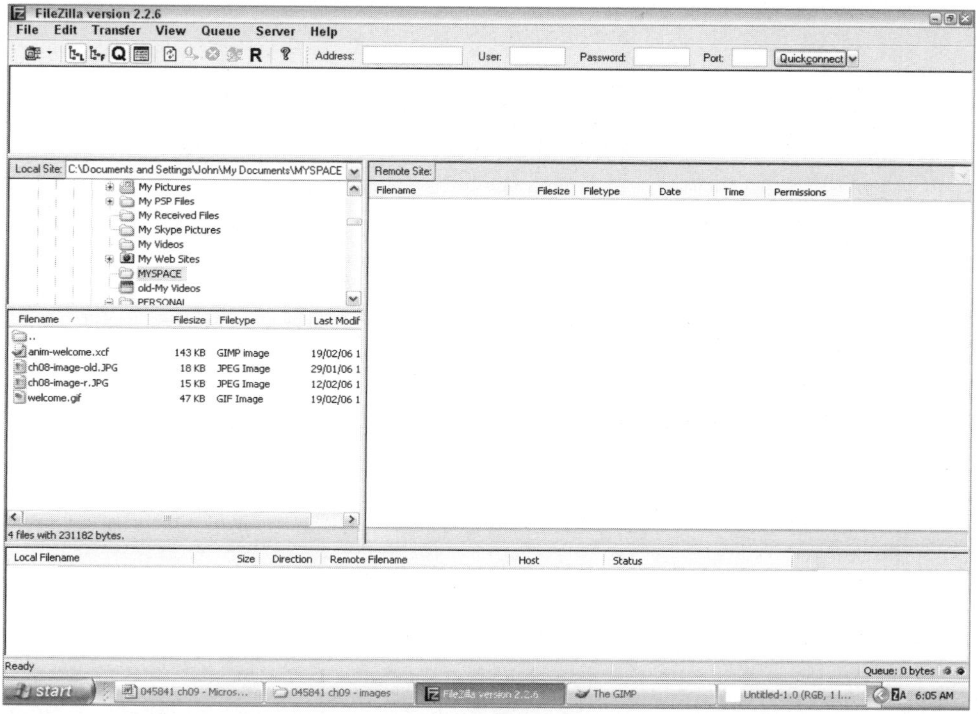

FIGURE 9-1: The initial screen when you first launch FileZilla

Now select File ⇨ Site Manager. A window appears that allows you to enter and manage FTP sites that you may want to connect to on a regular basis. While it is possible to enter your FTP details every time you want to upload or download files, it's much more convenient to enter your FTP details into the File Site Manager and access your sites from there, without having to re-enter this information every time you want to connect.

Left-click the New Site button, which enables you to enter a name for the site (it can be anything that you will easily recognize — even just the name of the site is fine), and then:

1. In the section marked host details, enter the FTP host name.

2. In the section labeled Logon Type, select "normal."

3. You'll now be able to enter your user name in the box labeled user and your password into the box labeled Password.

4. Uncheck the "Don't save password" box if it happens to be checked.

Figure 9-2 shows what the File Site Manager should look like after you've filled in the details (obviously you'll enter the FTP details for your web site).

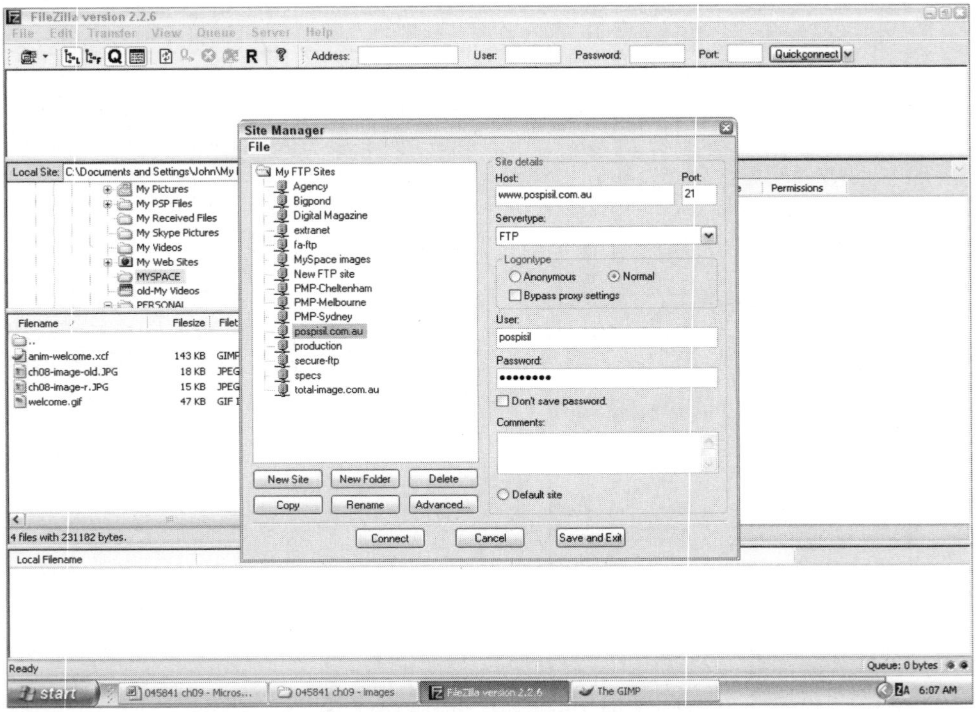

FIGURE 9-2: The File Site Manager window with details for an FTP site

Now click the Connect button. If all goes well, the welcome message from the FTP site appears in the message log (the area just under the menu and toolbar at the top of the screen. The message may look something like this:

```
Status:      Connecting to ftp.pospisil.com.au ...
Status:      Connected with ftp.pospisil.com.au. Waiting for
welcome message...
Response:    220---------- Welcome to Pure-FTPd [TLS]----------
Response:    220-You are user number 1 of 50 allowed.
Response:    220-Local time is now 10:09. Server port: 21.
```

```
Response:       220-This is a private system - No anonymous login
Response:       220 You will be disconnected after 15 minutes of
inactivity.
Command:        USER pospisil
Response:       331 User pospisil OK. Password required
Command:        PASS ********
Response:       230-User pospisil has group access to:  pospisil
Response:       230 OK. Current restricted directory is /
```

If you have a problem connecting, make sure that all the details — host name, user name, and password — are correct and try again. If you still can't connect, check with the provider that the server is up and running. In the main window you'll see an area labeled Remote Site. If you've connected successfully you should see a listing of the directory on the FTP server you've connected to (see Figure 9-3).

Depending on the setup of your provider, the first directory you see may be the root (main) directory of your web site, or the root directory of the server, in which case you will have to click a directory that may look something like this: /public_html/.

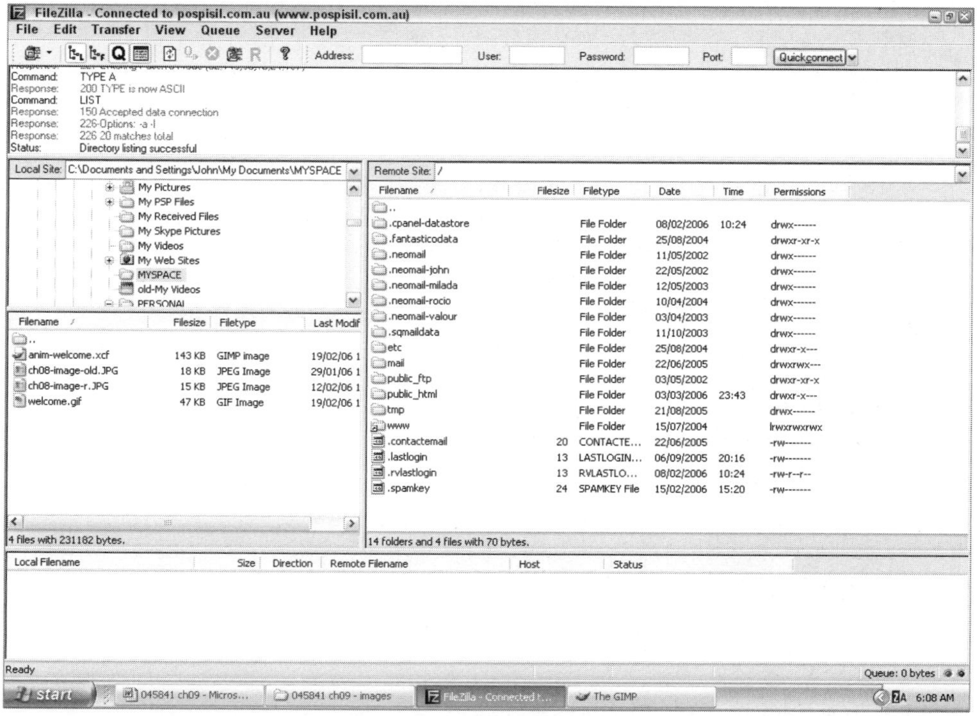

FIGURE 9-3: The first thing you see on your remote server may be a collection of unfamiliar directories.

You're going to store the images in the same directory as our web site, rather than on your FTP site (if you have one), because you want the files to be easily accessible through a web link.

Now you need to create a MySpace directory on the remote site that you can use to store images for MySpace. Place the mouse pointer over the remote site window and click the right mouse button so that context-sensitive menu appears. Select Create Directory and enter the new directory name — let's call the directory myspace — into the highlighted text. Click OK and your new directory is created. Double–left-click the new directory name. The contents of your new myspace directory will appear — which at the moment should contain nothing.

Go back to the local site window and select the image file ch08-image-r.JPG (or whatever the name is of the file you're going to transfer) and hold down the left mouse button and drag it to your myspace directory on the remote site.

Depending on your Internet connection speed, it will take only a few moments to transfer. To work out the URL of your image is quite simple. It consists of three parts:

> *web site domain + myspace (the directory you just created) + the file name of what you've just transferred*

The preceding example would look something like this:

```
www.pospisil.com.au/myspace/ch08-image-r.JPG
```

To test whether you've successfully transferred your image, open up your web browser and enter the URL of the image you've just transferred. It should appear in your web browser, as shown in Figure 9-4.

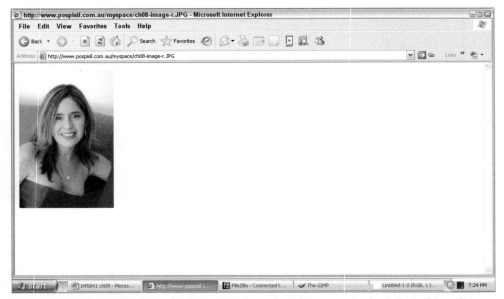

FIGURE 9-4: Just paste the URL of your image into your web browser to check that all is well.

Protecting Your Directory

You'll find that by typing `http://`*`yourwebsitedomain`*`/myspace`, all the contents of that directory will be displayed, which makes it easy for others to see what you've got stored there. In order to provide some level of privacy and security, you can do two things:

- Put an index page — a file with the name index.htm — in your remote myspace directory so that if someone tries to view the contents of the directory, the index file will be loaded instead. It's very easy to create a blank index page. In HTML-Kit, select File ➪ New from the top menu bar. Left-click the General tab, and double–left-click Blank HTML Page. A new document appears in the main window with some basic HTML code. Select File ➪ Save As and save this document as index.htm in your working myspace directory on your computer's hard disk. Using the process outlined in this chapter, transfer these files to your remote myspace directory. Now when someone tries to view your remote myspace directory, all they'll see is a blank page.

- Stop search engine bots from cataloguing your remote myspace directory. Even if you place an index.htm file in your remote myspace directory, search bots from various search engines may try to catalogue your directory. Before most search engine bots start examining a web site, they look for a file called Robots.txt in the root (main) directory of your web site to see whether anything is off-limits on your web site. To create a Robots.txt file that will block search engines from cataloguing the files in your myspace directory, start HTML-Kit and select File ➪ New from the top menu bar. Left-click the Other tab, and double–left-click "Robot exclusion file." A new document will appear in the main window with some text. You'll see two lines that look like this:

```
#User-agent: *
#Disallow: /cgi-bin/
```

Edit these lines so that they look like this:

```
User-agent: *
Disallow: /myspace/
```

Basically what you have done is removed the hashes and changed cgi-bin to myspace. The first line specifies that the following instructions apply to all search engine bots, and the second line specifies that the bot should not catalogue the specified directory, in this case, your myspace directory. Now select File ➪ Save As and save this document as Robots.txt in your working myspace directory on your computer's hard disk. Using the process outlined in this chapter, transfer these files to the root (main) directory of the web site that contains your myspace directory — this should be the directory that contains your myspace directory.

Wrapping Up

Having your own web site to store your files is truly the most flexible way of hosting photographs and other multimedia files.

After reading this chapter, you should know how to upload files — including video and audio, as well as photographs — to a web site, and how to work out the URL so that you can access those files from your MySpace profile. The next chapter covers how to embed photos in your profile.

The Hacks

part

II

In Part II, you really start to get your hands dirty, looking at a range of hacks designed to help you customize your profile.

Even if you don't intend on implementing each and every hack, it's still worth reading through each chapter to get a sense of how the code works, and also to learn about as many tags and properties as possible.

Chapter 25 deals with the Holy Grail of MySpace customization — the Div overlay. The Div overlay technique allows you to create almost any kind of profile you want, and it also allows you to integrate Flash movies. To really get the most from this chapter you'll need to have read and understood the chapters on HTML and CSS in Part I.

Embedding Images

They say a picture is worth a thousand words, and some nice images embedded in your MySpace profile can help attract attention. This chapter looks at how to actually link to an image from your profile. Before you upload an image you may want to edit and enhance that image so that it is presentable. Editing images is discussed and implemented in Chapter 29.

Preparation

If you haven't already, please read through Chapters 8 and 9 to familiarize yourself with how to upload an image to a web hosting service or to a web site. Before you can embed an image into your MySpace profile, or place a graphic directly into your profile (rather than just your photo album), you will need to have your image stored somewhere online, and you will need to know the link for your image. For the discussion of how to embed a graphic, I'll assume that you've uploaded an image with the file name ch08-image-r.JPG (as described in Chapters 8 and 9) and that you know its URL, which will look something like:

- `http://www.pospisil.com.au/myspace/ch08-image-r.JPG` — If you've uploaded the image to your web site

- `http://i45.photobucket.com/albums/f93/pospisil/ch08-image-r.jpg` — If you've uploaded the image to a photo hosting web site

Sourcing Images

There are all kinds of images that you might want to place in your profile. In this example, you place a photograph in the About Me section, but the same technique can be used to insert smilies, cartoons, and other illustrations directly into your profile.

You can source images from a number of different places. It's most likely that you would use photographs that you've taken with a digital camera, but you might also use images that you've found on the Internet, although of course you need to be careful that you're not infringing on anyone's copyright.

Caution

IThe easy access to images on the Internet makes it seem that images are free for the taking — which is far from the truth. Unless it's explicitly stated that an image is free of copyright or that copying and reposting is allowed, you have to assume that the material is copyrighted. If you want to use such an image, you'll need to obtain the permission of the copyright owner. And, it's not always easy to work out who this is!

If you type "images myspace" into Google, you can even find web sites that offer corny cartoons that you might consider using in your profile. In fact, the web site in Figure 10-1 even provides you with the codes you need to embed the image in your web site, and also hosts the images.

Here are some web sites you might want to visit for cartoon images:

- www.myspace-images.com
- www.myspacedirect.com
- www.myspacearena.com
- www.myspacenow.com

Be warned that when you visit these sites you may be inundated with pop-ups and other advertising.

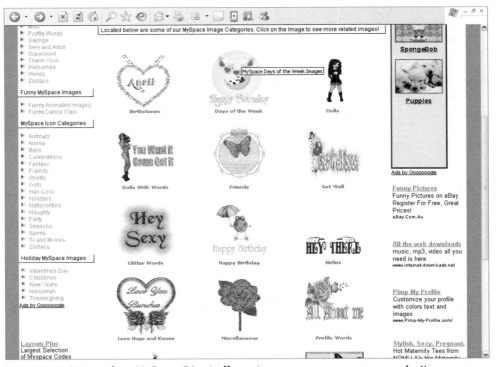

FIGURE 10-1: Sites such as MySpace Direct offer cartoons you can use on your web site.

Public Domain Images

There are also many public domain images available on the Internet. Simply type "public domain images" into Google and you'll find plenty to choose from. Here are some good sites to get you started:

- Wikipedia list of images (`en.wikipedia.org/wiki/Wikipedia:List_of_images`): Wikipedia's public domain images

- The Open Photo Project (`openphoto.net`): A site that offers images on the basis of the Creative Commons licensing system

- Flickr's Creative Commons library (`www.flickr.com/creativecommons`): Flickr's collection of images available through Creative Commons' licensing

 Tip If you want to save a picture that appears in a web page, and you're using a PC, simply position the mouse pointer over the image, press the right mouse button, and select Save Picture As.

Inline Images

In order to embed an image, you need to use an HTML tag that loads and displays the image from wherever you've stored it. As discussed and demonstrated in Chapter 8, the smaller the image the faster it will load.

Format

```
<img src="image" width="x" height="y" alt="description">
```

Here, *image* is your image's URL including the http:// prefix, and *x* is the width of the image in pixels or as a percentage. You don't need to specify the width, but it does help the browser present the picture correctly. The browser will resize the image if you enter a width and height (see the following code example) that is different from the actual width and height of the image. In this way you can resize images.

Also in the preceding code, *y* is the height of the image in pixels or as a percentage. You don't need to specify the width, but it does help the browser present the picture correctly. The browser will resize the image if your enter a width that is different from the actual width of the image.

Finally, *description* is a short description of the image. This name will appear while the image is loading or if the person viewing your profile has a text-only browser.

There is no closing tag.

Example

```
<img src="http://i45.photobucket.com/albums/f93/pospisil/ch08-
image-r.jpg" width="200" height="300" alt="Rocio">
<h1>Rocio</h1>
```

Place the preceding code in the About Me section of your profile.

Notice that the width and height have been set to the same width and height of the original image.

Don't forget to replace the URL provided (`http://i45.photobucket.com/albums/f93/pospisil/ch08-image-r.jpg`) with the URL of the image you've uploaded. If you're using your own image rather than the sample, don't forget to adjust the width and height accordingly. You may also want to come up with a more appropriate alt name.

How It Will look

As you see in Figure 10-2, the image has been loaded into the About Me section of your profile. Of course, you can place it in any section you like.

FIGURE 10-2: How the image will look when embedded in your profile

Tip You can resize your image by adjusting the width and height attributes. Keep in mind that for efficient loading it's better that you adjust your image in a graphics program to the size you want it to appear.

Linking Your Images

There may be occasions when you would like to make your image a link so that when someone clicks it, they are taken to another web site. This is actually quite straightforward and involves putting an `<img>` tag inside of an `<a href>` tag. This was covered in detail in Chapter 3.

Format

```
<a href="http://url"><img src="image" width="x" height="y"
alt="description"></a>
```

Here, x is the width of the image in pixels or as a percentage, y is the height of the image in pixels or as a percentage, `description` is a short description of the image, and `url` is the site address of the web page you would like to link to with the http:// prefix.

Example

```
<a href="http://www.pospisil.com.au"><img src="
http://i45.photobucket.com/albums/f93/pospisil/ch08-image-r.jpg"
width="200" height="301" alt="Rocio"></a>
=
<h1>Click on the picture of Rocio to visit my web site</h1>
```

Place the preceding code in the About Me section of your profile.

Don't forget to replace the URL provided (`http://i45.photobucket.com/albums/f93/ pospisil/ch08-image-r.jpg`) with the URL of the image you've uploaded. If you're using your very own image, rather than the sample, don't forget to adjust the width and height accordingly. You may also want to come up with a more appropriate alt name.

How It Will Look

Figure 10-3 looks very similar to Figure 10-2 except that when you right-click the image you are taken to another web page.

FIGURE 10-3: Linking makes it easier to send your visitors to other web sites.

Aligning Your Images

The `align` attribute we covered in Chapter 3 works with the `<img>` tag. This gives you some control over where your image appears within a particular section, and also allows text to flow around the image. CSS offers some more powerful ways of controlling where your image appears, but the `align` attribute is handy if you want to do something quickly. The align attribute doesn't support the center position. If you want to center an image, simply place the image code between `<center>` and `</center>` tags. I should also point out that this approach to alignment is now outdated, although browsers should still understand this code for the sake of backwards compatibility.

Format

```
<a href="http://url"><img src="image" width="x" height="y"
align="alignment" alt="description"></a>
```

Here, *alignment* is left or right.

Example

```
<a href="http://www.pospisil.com.au"><img src="
http://i45.photobucket.com/albums/f93/pospisil/ch08-image-r.jpg"
width="200" height="301" align="right" alt="Rocio"></a>
Here's a picture of my wife, Rocio, on the day that my sister was
married. She looks very pretty, and you would probably never guess
that she was five months pregnant with our daughter, Grace.
```

Don't forget to replace the URL provided (`http://i45.photobucket.com/albums/ f93/pospisil/ch08-image-r.jpg`) with the URL of the image you've uploaded. If you're using your very own image, rather than the sample, don't forget to adjust the width and height accordingly. You may also want to come up with a more appropriate alt name.

How It Will Look

Figure 10-4 shows the image aligned to the right with the text to the left. You could also use the `<div>` tag with the `align` attribute to position an image. For example, if you placed the image code (*sans* `align` attribute) between `<div align="center">` and `</div>` you would center the image. The `<div>` `align` attribute understands `left`, `right`, and `center`. The only problem is that the text would not flow as nicely as it does when using the `<img>` tag's `align` attribute.

FIGURE 10-4: The image is aligned to the right with the text flowing down the left side.

Applying Styles to Your Images

In Chapters 6 and 7, you looked at cascading style sheets and how they can be applied to text. The good news is that they can also be applied to images. To apply a style called "msimage" to an image, you need to insert `class="msimage"` into the `<img>` tag. Here's how it would look when applied to the example code:

```
<img class="msimage" src="http://i45.photobucket.com/albums/f93/
pospisil/ch08-image-r.jpg" width="200" height="301" alt="Rocio">
<h4>Rocio</h4>
```

Let's place this code into the "I'd like to meet" section of MySpace. As you'll recall from the chapters on CSS, all you need to do to change the style is to define the msimage class.

Don't forget to replace the URL provided (`http://i45.photobucket.com/albums/f93/pospisil/ch08-image-r.jpg`) with the URL of the image you've uploaded. If you're using your own image rather than the sample, don't forget to adjust the width and height accordingly. You may also want to come up with a more appropriate alt name.

Creating a Border Around Your Image

Now you're ready to create a style called "msimage." Place the following code in the About Me section of your profile:

```
<style>
.msimage {border: medium dashed blue; }
</style>
```

What you've done here is to create a very simple style that applies a medium blue dashed border to anything, including images. (See Chapter 6 for more information on defining borders.) Figure 10-5 shows how an image would look.

Positioning Your Image

With the absolute positioning technique you learned in Chapter 7, it's possible to place your image anywhere in your profile. Place the following code into the About Me section of your profile:

```
<style>
.msimage {position: absolute; left: 50%; margin-left: -400px; top:
184px;}
</style>
```

You'll see in Figure 10-6 that the sample image has been moved to the left edge of the profile and the top edge where the profile starts. You'll also notice that it appears over the top of the existing profile.

FIGURE 10-5: The sample image with a border around it

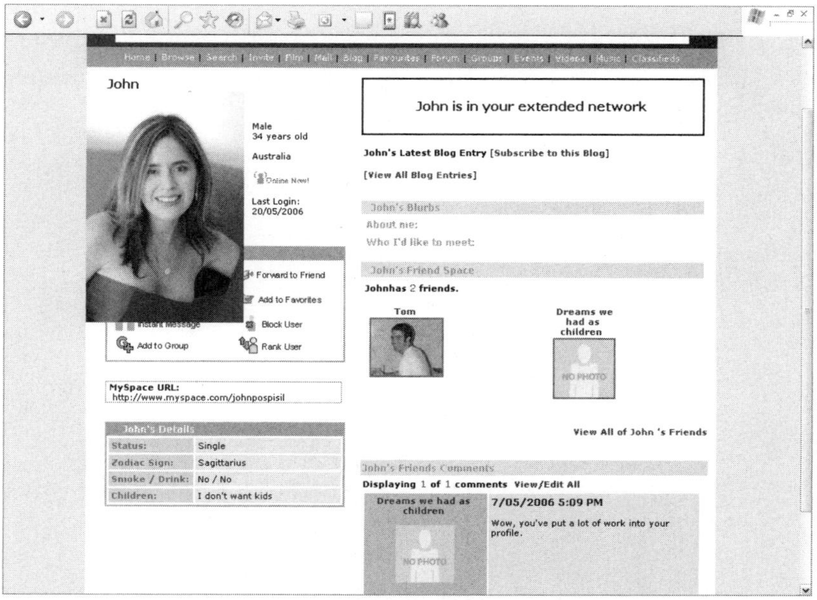

FIGURE 10-6: The sample image has been moved to the top-left area of the profile.

Advanced Concept — Using the <div> Tag for Positioning

Advanced positioning is discussed in Chapter 25, but it's worth taking a quick look now at how Div tags can be used for positioning. In the preceding example, you used the position property to position an image, but what if you wanted to position a related group of elements, such as a picture and its caption? As I discussed in Chapter 7, the <div> tag marks out logical divisions in a web page, and so gives you a means of grouping elements together.

To see how this might work in practice, place the following code into the "Who I'd like to meet" section of your MySpace profile:

```
<div class="msimage">
<img src="http://i45.photobucket.com/albums/f93/pospisil/ch08-
image-r.jpg" width="200" height="301" alt="Rocio">
<h4>Rocio</h4>
</div>
```

In Figure 10-7, you can see that not only has the sample image been repositioned, but so has the caption. With this technique, it is possible to use <div> tags to place your content anywhere in your MySpace profile. Of course, work also needs to be done to hide and reposition the existing elements for this to be useful, but I cover that in Chapter 25.

FIGURE 10-7: Both the sample image and the caption have been repositioned using the <div> tag.

Wrapping Up

At this point in the book, you should feel like you're making real progress because not only can you place an image in your profile, but you can actually place it in any position and even add a border. You've also been exposed to using <div> tags to position content. If you have some understanding of what you did in this chapter with the <div> tag, you're well on the way to understanding one of the key concepts of Div overlays, which I cover in Chapter 25.

Using Filters

A filter is a quick way of applying a special effect to an element on your profile — for example, you can make your text glow, or you can blur an image.

Many coders frown on the use of filters because they slow down your profile, which means that it will take longer for your profile to load, and not all browsers will display all the effects. If you want to be able to view all of these effects, you need to use Internet Explorer. In order for these effects to work with all browsers, you can recreate many of these effects in a graphics program. This chapter examines the various types of filters available and how to use them in your MySpace profile.

Applying Filters to Images and Text

To see how these filters work, place the following code in the "Who I'd like to meet" section of your profile:

```
.<img class="ieffect" src="http://i45.photobucket.com/
albums/f93/pospisil/ch08-image-r.jpg" width=200
height=300>
<p class="teffect"> This is a demonstration of filters
applied to both an image and text.</p>
```

Don't forget to replace the URL `http://i45.photobucket.com/` `albums/f93/pospisil/ch08-image-r.jpg` with the URL of the actual image you uploaded in Chapter 8 or 9, or you might not see an image.

You'll see that I've applied an `ieffect` style to the image (which you learned how to do in Chapter 6) and the `effect` style to the text. If you don't define the `effect` style, the image and text will appear quite plain (as in Figure 11-1).

The format of the `filter` property is as follows:

```
Selector {filter: filter_effect(attributes);}
```

Here, `filter_effect` is the filter you want to apply and may include any of the filters described in the following pages.

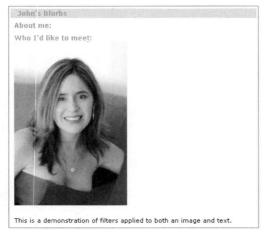

FIGURE 11-1: The image and text as they appear without filters applied

The Filters

When applying filters it's always good to specify the width of the element, and if you're working with text, the text height. Doing this helps to ensure that the filters will work as expected. As discussed, these filters will work only with Microsoft's Internet Explorer.

Alpha

The Alpha filter allows you to set the opacity of an element. Because this filter can have quite a few settings, and because it does work with most browsers, it has its own section.

Its attributes are:

- `enabled`: Can be `true` or `false` to indicate whether the filter is enabled
- `opacity`: Sets the opacity level at the start of the opacity gradient
- `finishOpacity`: Sets the opacity level at the end of the opacity gradient
- `startx`: Sets the horizontal point at which the opacity gradient starts
- `starty`: Sets the vertical point at which the opacity gradient starts
- `finishx`: Sets the horizontal point at which the opacity gradient ends
- `finishy`: Sets the vertical point at which the opacity gradient ends

- `style`: Sets the shape characteristics of the opacity gradient
    - 1 is a transparency that goes from one corner to the diagonally opposite corner.
    - 2 is a transparency that goes from the outside to the inside in a circular motion.
    - 3 is a transparency that goes from the outside to the inside in a rectangular motion.

Example

Place the following code into the About Me section of your MySpace profile. This contains the definition of the `ieffect` and `teffect` styles that will apply the Alpha filter to the text and image.

```
<style>
.ieffect {filter: blur alpha(opacity=50); width: 200px;}
.teffect {filter: blur alpha(opacity=50); width: 200px; font-size:
10pt;}
</style>
```

Note how the attributes for the Alpha filter (and for that matter all filters) are placed in round brackets.

How It Will Look

As you'll see in Figure 11-2, the preceding code creates a uniform opacity transparency effect over the whole image. You can actually create some interesting effects with the Alpha filter by playing with some of the attributes.

FIGURE 11-2: The transparency effect applied uniformly to the test image

To create a vignette effect, try placing this code in the About Me section of your MySpace profile:

```
<style>
.ieffect {filter: alpha (opacity=50,  finishOpacity=0,  style=2,
startX=0,  startY=0,  finishX=20,  finishY=20);}
</style>
```

Blur

This filter blurs the element so that it appears out of focus in a specified direction at a specified strength. Its attributes are:

- `add`: Can be `true` or `false`; adds the original image to the blurred image.
- `direction`: The direction of the blur in degrees clockwise from 0.
- `strength`: How many pixels the blur will extend.

Example

```
<style>
.ieffect {filter: blur (add=0, direction=225, strength=10); width:
200px;}
.teffect {filter: blur (add=0, direction=225, strength=10); width:
200px; font-size: 10pt;}
</style>
```

How It Will Look

Figure 11-3 shows the Blur filter applied to the sample image.

FIGURE 11-3: The transparency effect applied uniformly to the sample image and text

Dropshadow

This filter creates a shadow effect and works well with text. Its attributes are:

- `color`: The color of the shadow.
- `offx`: The horizontal offset of the shadow.
- `offy`: The vertical offset of the shadow.
- `positive`: Set to `true` or `false`. If `true`, all the opaque or "filled in" pixels have a drop shadow; if `false`, all the transparent pixels have the drop shadow.

Example

```
<style>
.ieffect {filter:dropshadow(color=ff0000, offx=5, offy=5,
positive=true); width: 200px;}
.teffect {filter:dropshadow(color=ff0000, offx=5, offy=5,
positive=true); width: 200px; font-size: 10pt;}
</style>
```

How It Will Look

Figure 11-4 shows the Dropshadow filter applied to the sample image.

FIGURE 11-4: The Dropshadow effect applied to the image — note that it works with the image only, not the text.

Fliph

The Fliph filter flips the element horizontally. It has no attributes.

Example

```
<style>
.ieffect {filter:fliph; width: 200px;}
.teffect {filter:fliph; width: 200px; font-size: 10pt;}
</style>
```

How It Will Look

Figure 11-5 shows the Fliph filter applied to the sample image.

FIGURE **11-5: The image and text have been flipped horizontally.**

Flipv

This filter flips the element vertically. It has no attributes.

Example

```
<style>
.ieffect {filter:flipv; width: 200px;}
.teffect {filter:flipv; width: 200px; font-size: 10pt;}
</style>
```

How It Will Look

Figure 11-6 shows the Flipv filter being applied to the sample image.

FIGURE 11-6: The image and text have been flipped vertically.

Glow

This filter applies a glow around the element and is particularly effective with text. Its attributes are:

- `color`: The color of the glow effect
- `strength`: The intensity of the glow effect

Example

```
<style>
.ieffect {filter:glow(color=#ff0000, strength=5); width: 200px;}
.teffect {filter:glow(color=#ff0000, strength=5); width: 200px;
font-size: 10pt;}
</style>
```

How It Will Look

Figure 11-7 shows the Glow filter applied to the sample image.

FIGURE 11-7: The Glow filter applied to both the text and image

Gray

This filter transforms the element into black and white. It has no attributes.

Example

```
<style>
.ieffect {filter:gray; width: 200px;}
.teffect {filter:gray; width: 200px; font-size: 10pt;}
</style>
```

How It Will Look

Figure 11-8 shows the Gray filter applied to the sample image.

Invert

This filter reverses the color and brightness values of the element.

Example

```
<style>
.ieffect {filter:invert; width: 200px;}
.teffect {filter:invert; width: 200px; font-size: 10pt;}
</style>
```

How It Will Look

Figure 11-9 shows the Invert filter applied to the sample image.

FIGURE 11-8: You can't see it in this screenshot, but the image has been made black-and-white.

FIGURE 11-9: The invert effect creates some interesting effects.

Shadow

This filter creates a shadow behind the element. Its attributes are:

- `color`: The color of the shadow
- `direction`: The direction of the shadow as degrees clockwise from vertical, so that 0 is top, 45 is top right, 90 is right, and so on

Example

```
<style>
.ieffect {filter:shadow(color=ff0000, direction=90); width: 200px;}
.teffect {filter:shadow(color=ff0000, direction=90); width: 200px;
font-size: 10pt;}
</style>
```

How It Will Look

Figure 11-10 shows the Shadow filter applied to the sample image.

FIGURE **11-10: The Shadow effect works with text only.**

Wave

This filter applies a wave or ripple effect to an image. Its attributes are:

- `add`: If set to 1, the original image is added to the waved image.
- `freq`: The number of waves.
- `lightstrength`: The strength of the light applied to the wave as a value 0 to 100.
- `phrase`: The degree of the starting point of the sine wave as a value from 0 to 100.
- `strength`: Intensity of the wave effect.

Example

```
<style>
.ieffect { filter:wave(add=0, freq=1, lightstrength=20, phase=50,
strength=8); width: 200px; }
.teffect { filter:wave(add=0, freq=1, lightstrength=20, phase=50,
strength=8); width: 200px; font-size: 10pt; }
</style>
```

How It Will Look

Figure 11-11 shows the Wave filter applied to the sample image.

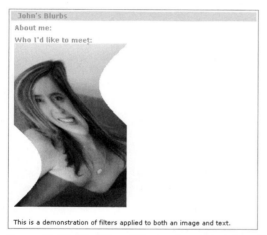

FIGURE 11-11: The Wave filter creates some interesting effects.

X-ray

This filter creates an X-ray effect by rendering the element in black and white and reversing the brightness and color effects. It has no attributes.

Example

```
<style>
.ieffect { filter: xray; width: 200px; }
.teffect { filter: filter: xray; width: 200px; font-size: 10pt; }
</style>
```

How It Will Look

Figure 11-12 shows the X-ray filter applied to the sample image.

FIGURE 11-12: The X-ray filter — interesting, but not attractive

Wrapping Up

Styles are a quick way to apply effects to your images. Just be aware that they really work only with Internet Explorer, and many coders frown on their use.

Creating Animated GIFs

A n animated GIF is a short animated image usually consisting of two to five frames. You'll often see them in banner ads, or as cute animated cartoons that are often used in MySpace profiles. They can be quite good for getting attention.

Creating an animated GIF can be a little tricky. While many tools are out there to help you create animated GIFs, almost all of them cost money. It's fortunate that the amazingly versatile GIMP, which you first came across in Chapter 8, can be used to create animated GIF files. If you haven't already installed GIMP, do so now — refer to Chapter 8 on how to do this.

Using GIMP to Create Animated GIFs

An animated GIF is basically made up of a sequence of still frames, which are displayed one after another to create an animated effect. Animated GIFs are created in GIMP using layers. Each layer contains one frame of the animation.

For those who are new to graphics programs, here's a quick explanation of what layers are. In the old days, graphics programs were very much like a traditional oil painting; it was very hard to make a correction if you made a mistake. If you drew a big X across your image, that big X actually became part of your image. Layers were developed to get around this problem. Think of a layer as a transparent canvas placed over the top of the original canvas. You can make as many changes as you like to the layer and the underlying canvas stays the same.

Creating Layers and Animation Frames

To create GIF animations in GIMP, you basically create each frame in its own layer and then save all the layers as an animated GIF. If all of this sounds too confusing, the following example will clear things up.

Here's how you can create a GIMP animation:

1. Start GIMP. Select File ⇨ New. Enter **200** into the width option and **125** into the height option.

2. A new window appears with a blank 200 × 125–pixel canvas.

3. Select File ⇨ Save and save the blank image as anim-welcome.xcf in your MySpace working directory. Select the text tool in the GIMP tool box and left-click in the center of the blank canvas.

4. Type **Welcome** into the text dialog box. Click the Close button.

5. From the image window's drop-down menu bar, select Dialogs ⇨ Tool Options. A Tool Options window should appear that will allow you to adjust the font size and font (if the Tool Options window shows something else, make sure you have the text tool selected). You can also access this menu by pressing Shift+Ctrl+T. Clicking the Aa button allows you to change the font, while changing the font size in the Size text box allows you to directly adjust the size of the font (see Figure 12-1).

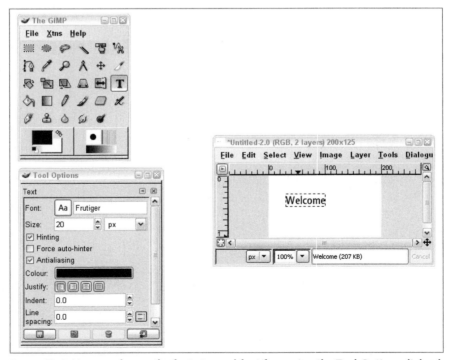

FIGURE **12-1: You can change the font size and font face using the Tool Options dialog box.**

6. Select a font you like and set a size that means it fills the width of the canvas (around 40 px). In my example, I've used the font Gi Gi, which you may or may not have on your computer (see Figure 12-2).

FIGURE 12-2: The first frame of your animated GIF

7. Select Dialogs ➪ Layers. The Layers window will appear (you can also reach this window by pressing Ctrl+L). You'll notice that there's a background layer and a text layer. Both layers should have an eye icon next to them, which indicates that they are visible (see Figure 12-3).

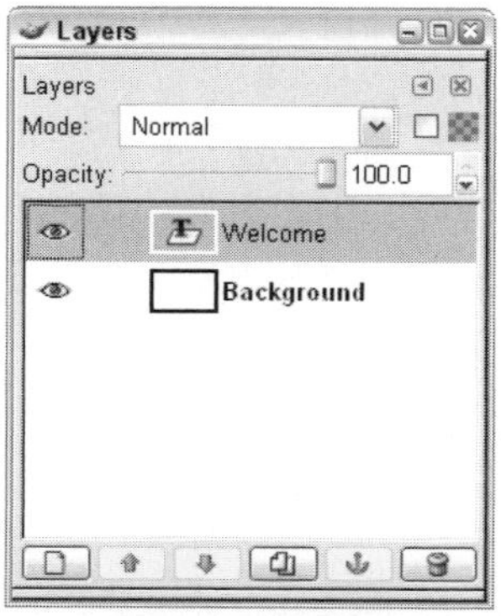

FIGURE 12-3: The Layers window

8. Select the text layer by right-clicking it and then selecting Layers ⇨ Merge Down. This combines the text and background into one layer, or for your purposes, you can think of it as one frame.

9. Right-click the background layer, and select Duplicate Layer. A new layer called Background copy should appear in the layer palette. Do this again and a new layer called Background copy#1 appears.

10. Rename the layer called Background to "frame 1 (500ms)" by double-clicking its name in the Layers window. Rename the second and third layers frame 2 (500ms) and frame 3 (500ms). The 500ms basically means that each frame will appear for 500 milliseconds or half a second — 500 being half of 1,000.

    You'll notice in the Layer window that there's an eye icon next to each layer. Left-clicking the eye icon effectively turns off the corresponding layer so that it is not shown. Turn off all the icons and you'll see that your image window becomes blank.

    You need to select a layer in order to be able to make changes to it, and you need to be able to see it to know what you're doing. Select the layer called "frame 1 (500ms)" (by left-clicking it) and left-click the space where the eye icon should be so that eye icon and the corresponding layer is displayed.

11. Now select Filters ⇨ Light Effects ⇨ SuperNova. A dialog box appears (see Figure 12-4) that allows you to adjust the settings of the SuperNova effect, which you will use to create a basic animation effect.

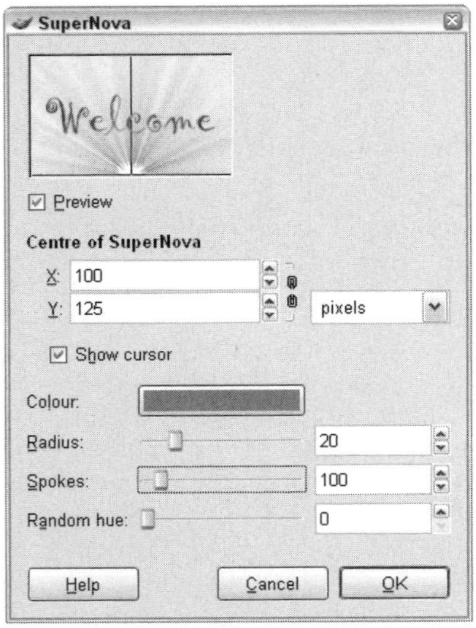

FIGURE 12-4: The SuperNova dialog box

12. Enter the following settings into the SuperNova dialog box:

- **X:** 100
- **Y:** 125
- **Color:** Blue
- **Radius:** 20
- **Spokes:** 100
- **Random hue:** 0

Remember that this setting will apply only to the first frame (currently selected). Left click OK and you'll see that the SuperNova filter will be applied to frame 1. Now go to the Layers window and left click the eye icon next to the layer called frame 1. The image window should now look blank.

13. Now left-click the eye icon (or rather the space where it was earlier) next to the frame 2 layer. "Welcome" should appear in the image window, but you'll notice that it's the original without the SuperNova effect you just applied to frame 1. Make sure frame 2 is selected in the Layers window and select Filters ➪ Light Effects ➪ SuperNova. This time make sure the following settings are entered:

- **X:** 100
- **Y:** 125
- **Color:** Blue
- **Radius:** 40
- **Spokes:** 120
- **Random hue:** 0

14. Left-click OK and you'll see that the SuperNova filter has been applied to frame 2. Now go to the Layers window and left-click the eye icon next to the layer called frame 2. The image window should now look blank. Now apply the SuperNova effect to the third and final frame by left-clicking the eye icon next to the frame 3 layer. The original "Welcome" should appear in the image window. Make sure frame 3 is selected in the Layers window and select Filters ➪ Light Effects ➪ SuperNova. This time make sure the following settings are entered:

- **X:** 100
- **Y:** 125
- **Color:** Blue
- **Radius:** 60
- **Spokes:** 130
- **Random hue:** 0

Left-click OK. What you've done is to create three frames, each with a slightly different effect, to create a very basic animation. To see how your animation might look, select Filters ⇨ Animation ⇨ Playback and press the Play/Stop button (see Figure 12-5).

FIGURE 12-5: You can preview your GIF in the Animation Playback window.

Animating the Image

Now to actually create the GIF animation file, do the following:

1. Select File ⇨ Save as, and enter the file name, making sure it has a .gif extension (let's just call this animation welcome.gif). Click the Save button, and the Export File window appears.

2. Select "Save as animation" and "Convert to indexed," and then left-click the Export button. The Save as GIF window will now appear. Use the default settings, but make sure that "Loop forever" is checked. Click OK.

To check whether you've successfully created an animated GIF, simply load the image into your web browser. In Explorer, simply select File ⇨ Open ⇨ Browse and navigate to your newly created GIF file (you may need to select GIF in the Files of type drop-down menu). Select the file and click OK, and then OK again. The animated GIF should now play back in your browser window.

Wrapping Up

While, among other things, you've learned how to apply the Supernova filter, the aim of this chapter was to show you how to use GIMP's layer feature to animate a number of single-frame images. How you create those single frames is really only limited by your imagination.

You can now use the techniques you learned in Chapters 8, 9, and 10 to embed your animated GIF in your MySpace profile.

Backgrounds

chapter

13

The background is what appears behind your profile. It can simply be a color, or it can be an image. Changing the background of your MySpace profile is one of the easiest ways to dramatically change the appearance of your profile with minimal work.

Finding and Selecting a Background

There's no shortage of background images on the Internet. Simply type "background image" (without the quote marks) into Google and you'll be presented with an extensive list of sites that offer background images. If you type "myspace background image" into Google you'll be presented with an even more targeted list, some of which will also have codes for you to copy and paste directly into your profile. You need to be aware of a few things when looking for a background image:

- A background image shouldn't be too dominant; otherwise you won't be able to read the text sitting on top of it. It's also better if there's no subject in the background, and for this reason photographs are usually not good background images. If the background takes attention away from the overlying profile, look for something else. Good backgrounds tend to be textures or wallpaper designs that don't have any subject (and hence no central point of focus), and at the same time don't reduce the readability of the type that is sitting over the top.

- A background needs to fill up the whole web page; otherwise, the background will *tile*, or repeat, which can be quite ugly if the background image isn't designed for tiling. These days, most people set their screens to at least 1,024 × 768, so make sure any background you use to fill up the whole screen is at least this size.

- Some background images are designed to "tile," which simply means that each edge of the background is designed to blend with the opposite edge. When laid out next to each other, the tiled images appear to be a continuous, repetitive image. These can work very well.

Creating Your Own Background

While there are plenty of background images on the Internet for you to choose from, there's nothing stopping you from designing your own. Most graphics programs have gradient tools, which are very useful for creating backgrounds. Here's a quick tutorial to show you how you can use GIMP to create a background.

1. Open a new image of at least 1024 × 768 if you want a full-screen background.

2. Left–double-click the Gradient tool (the box icon with the green gradient fill) in the main GIMP tool box to open up the Tool Options window. Make sure the mode is set to Difference by selecting Difference in the Mode drop-down menu (see Figure 13-1).

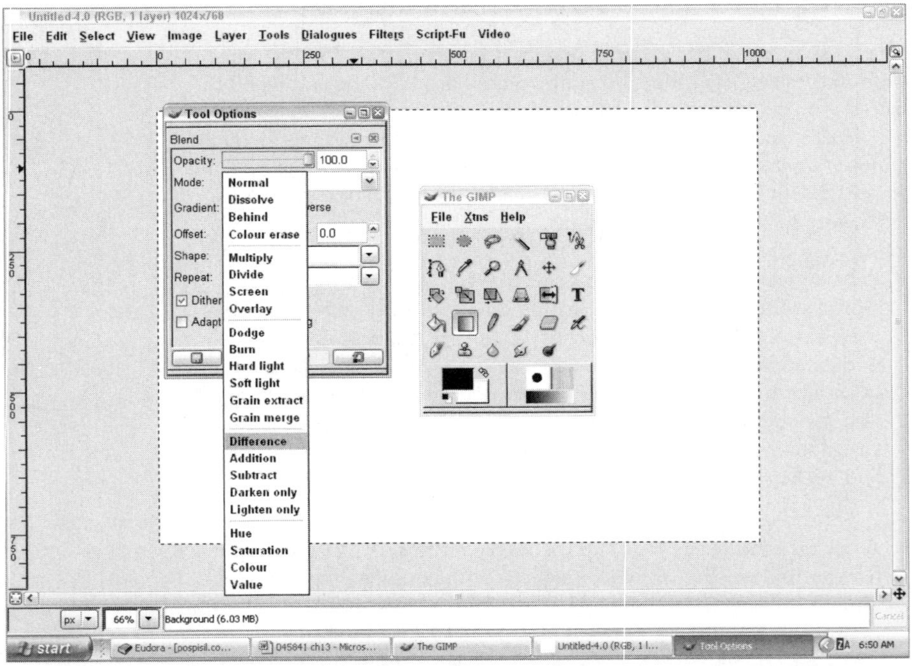

FIGURE 13-1: The GIMP Tool Options window with the Mode drop-down menu showing

3. Apply the Gradient tool to the canvas by moving the mouse pointer around the canvas while holding down the left mouse button. You might try different gradient shapes by selecting a different option from the Shape drop-down menu. You can also select different starting and finishing gradient colors by selecting different foreground and background colors — simply double–left-click each of the two color swatches in the

bottom-left corner of the main GIMP tool box. With some experimentation you'll find it relatively easy to create pleasing effects (see Figure 13-2).

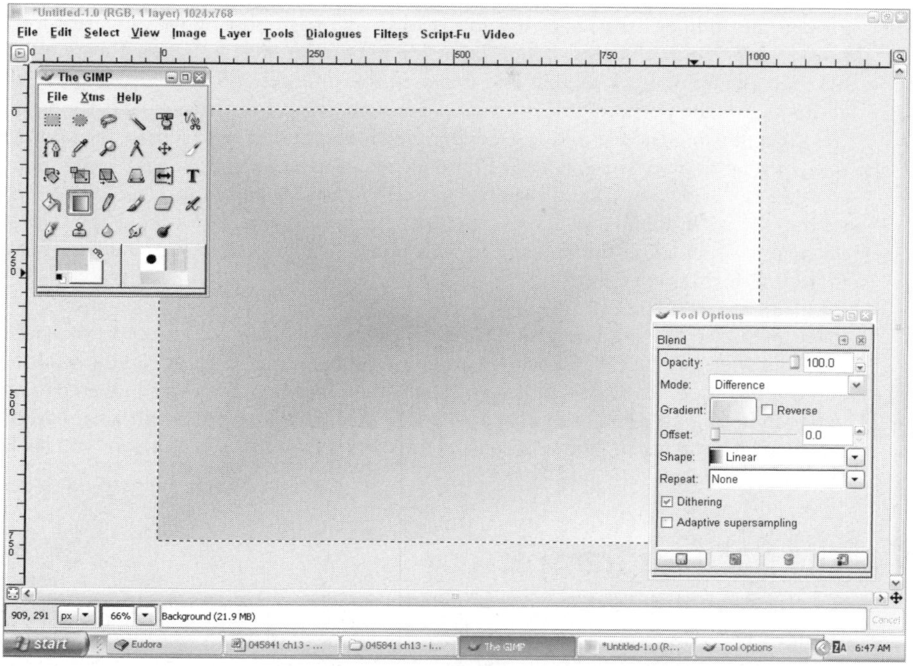

FIGURE 13-2: In just a few minutes you can create pleasing backgrounds.

4. Now select Layers ➪ Colors ➪ Color Balance. First, adjust the midtones (central color range), which you can do by ensuring the Midtones checkbox is checked and by playing with the Cyan, Magenta, and Yellow sliders. Click OK when you are happy with the results. In a similar way, adjust the highlights and shadows. To make the background image lighter (and less obtrusive) go to Layers ➪ Colors ➪ Brightness-contrast and move the Brightness Slider to the right.

5. When you're happy with your image, select File ➪ Save to save your image. Make sure you add a .jpg extension to your file name so that your image is saved as a JPEG file.

GIMP offers a lot of latitude for you to try other filters and paintbrushes to create other kinds of effects. Creating backgrounds that repeat is far more complicated and is beyond the scope of this book because you need to make sure each edge will blend with the opposite edge. In any case, there are plenty of repeating background images on the web for you to work with.

Because of the size of the image you need to create — 1,024 × 768 — it's a good idea to save the image in JPEG format with medium to high compression.

Uploading Your Background to the Internet

Like any other image you show on your MySpace profile, you'll need to upload your background image to either your own web site or to an image hosting web site. Just follow the same process as given in Chapters 8 and 9. For the remainder of this chapter I'll assume that you have already uploaded a background image to the Internet and that you know its URL (web address). For the purpose of this exercise, I have uploaded the image background.jpg, which was created using the technique described previously and is provided on the book's web site at www.myspaceismyplace.com, to Photobucket. Its URL is http://i45.photobucket.com/albums/f93/pospisil/background.jpg. Please don't use this URL when trying this exercise, as it's unlikely to still be active. Instead, upload a background image (either your own, or the one supplied on the web site for this book) to Photobucket or your own server and use that URL for this exercise.

Tip   Some web sites offering background images will actually give you the code you need to enter into your MySpace profile. These sites also host the background image. If you want to go ahead and use this code, that's fine, although usually there's some advertising in the code provided. If you read through the rest of this chapter, you should be able to figure out what part of the code displays the background, and what part of the code is the ad — which means you could strip out the ad.

The Need for Transparency

Your MySpace profile is a table floating in the middle of a web page. If you were simply to change the background color or to insert a background image, you wouldn't see the background because your profile would be sitting over the top.

It's fortunate that CSS allows you to redefine the tags that are used to lay out the MySpace profile table. Using CSS, you can make the tags transparent.

As you may recall, the great thing about CSS is that it allows you to redefine elements that have already been set. The following line of code makes all the tags that make up the profile transparent:

```
a, body, input, table, td, textarea,{background-color:
transparent; border: none; border-width:0;}
```

Add this line to your style sheet. Or if you're not ready for that yet, simply cut and paste the following code into the About Me" section of your MySpace profile:

```
<style>
a, body, input, table, td, textarea{background-color: transparent;
border: none; border-width: 0;}
</style>
```

If you view your MySpace profile, you'll notice that it's now transparent — well actually, it'll look light green, which is the underlying background color.

Inserting a Background Image

A number of CSS properties allow you to insert an image and control how it appears.

Format

```
a, body, input, table, td, textarea{background-color: transparent;
border: none; border-width: 0;}
body{background-image: url (address);
background-attachment: attachment_value;
background-repeat: repeat_value;
background-position: position_value;
```

The first line simply makes the existing profile transparent.

The *address* is the Web address of the background image.

The *attachment_value* is either fixed, so the image is static if you scroll the page, or scroll, so the image scrolls if you scroll the web page.

The *repeat_value* specifies whether the image appears once or is repeated; it can have the following values:

- repeat: The image is repeated both vertically and horizontally.

- repeat-x: The image is repeated horizontally.

- repeat-y: The image is repeated vertically.

- no-repeat: The image does not repeat and is displayed only once.

The *position_value* specifies the position of the image on the web page. The position can be specified in three ways:

- Using a two-word description — the first word describing the vertical location of top, center, or bottom, and the second word describing the horizontal location left, center, or right.

- As a percentage of the viewing window in the form *x% y%* where the top-left corner is 0% 0% and the bottom-right corner is 100% 100%.

- As horizontal and vertical coordinates in pixels (px) or in other recognized CSS units.

Example

If you simply want to insert a background, insert the following code into your MySpace style sheet. Make sure that you change the URL http://i45.photobucket.com/albums/f93/pospisil/background.jpg to the URL of your background — you can put it in the About Me section of your MySpace profile.

```
<style>
a, body, input, table, td, textarea{background-color: transparent;
border: none; border-width: 0;}
body{background-image:
url(http://i45.photobucket.com/albums/f93/pospisil/background.jpg)
;
background-attachment: scroll;
background-repeat: repeat;
background-position: center center;}
</style>
```

How It Will Look

As you can see in Figure 13-3, the background image I created in GIMP is in the center of the page. It is large enough to fill the whole screen but blends quite nicely when it does repeat. Incidentally you can use the background-image property with any element — not just the body. So if you wanted to, you could define the background of just a paragraph (<p>) or a logical division (<div>) in your web page.

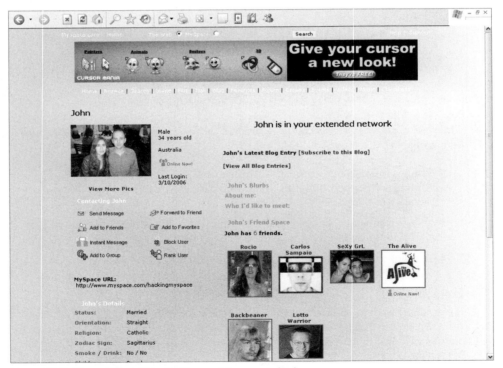

FIGURE 13-3: The profile with a background image applied

Changing the Background Color

If you can't be bothered changing the background image, you can very easily just change the background color of your profile. This does not require that you upload a background image.

Format

The following code would be placed in your style sheet:

```
body {background-color: color_value;}
```

Here, `color_value` is either an RGB or hex value, a color name, or `transparent`. See Appendix A for a list of color hex values.

Example

Paste the following into the About Me section of your MySpace profile:

```
<style>
a, body, input, table, td, textarea{background-color: transparent;
border: none; border-width: 0;}
body {background-color: 87CEEB;}
</style>
```

How It Will Look

You'll notice that there is now only one background color — Sky Blue — for the whole profile.

Wrapping Up

Simply adding a background image to your profile can make a big visual impact. It is one of the easier ways to make a splash on MySpace. Just bear in mind that not all images are suitable for use as backgrounds.

Background Music

MySpace is well known for promoting the music industry and introducing new bands. For these reasons, and just because it's cool, many MySpace profiles have music playing.

Although the technique for playing audio is similar to that for playing video, I'll cover audio in this chapter and video in Chapter 15.

The Easy Option

Adding music can get a little complicated if you want to write the code yourself — fortunately, there are a couple of easy options, which you take a look at first before you get into the real hack later in this chapter. The first easy option is to simply use the MySpace method of adding audio to your profile. MySpace has its own audio player (see Figure 14-1), which many bands use to play audio. If you come across a band profile in MySpace where there's a song playing using the MySpace player, you'll see that there is an Add link to the right of each track listing).

If you click this link while you're logged in to your account, the player is automatically added to your profile (just below the box that shows your MySpace URL). If you're not logged in, you'll be asked to log in. When you view your profile, the song automatically starts playing. To delete this player, simply log in to your account and select View Profile; you'll see that there is a +delete+ link in the player. Or you can select Home ⇨ Edit Profile ⇨ Profile Songs and click Delete to delete the player.

This is the option recommended by MySpace. It helps to ensure that pirated material is not being played on MySpace (i.e., the artists have given permission for the music to be played).

If you're in a band, you can sign up for a band profile with MySpace, which will allow you to post your band's music.

FIGURE **14-1:** The MySpace audio player — take note of the Add link to the right of each track listing.

The Second Easy Option

The other option is simply to type "MySpace music code" into Google. What you'll see is a list of web sites that provide codes that you can copy and paste into your profile (as described in Chapter 2). Basically what these codes do is call up a music player — usually Windows Media Player — and play an audio track that has been uploaded to a server somewhere on the Internet. It is assumed that sites offering music codes have obtained permission to disseminate these tracks.

Usually these codes contain some kind of advertising, but these are usually quite easy to strip away. Simply identify the <embed> tag and cut away everything except for the <embed> tag and its attributes.

Napster recently launched a free music service that can be used with sites such as MySpace — you can try it out at www.napster.com/napsterlinks/.

The Real Hack

You need to do three things to play your own audio file:

- Source an audio file that you want to play
- Upload it to a file hosting web site or your own web site
- Play the file back using the `embed` tag

Sourcing an Audio File

As you undoubtedly already know, commercially produced music is subject to copyright, which means you can't just rip your favorite band's music and upload it to the Internet — unless you have permission from the band.

Bands that make their music available on MySpace have given permission for their music to be played on MySpace, perhaps in the hope of finding new fans and being discovered. Similarly, the web sites that provide audio codes are often actually providing access to promotional material, and so permission has been given for that material to be made available to you.

If you decide to play audio material from your profile, you need to ensure that you're not infringing on anybody's copyright. Basically, the options available include:

- **Obtaining permission to use somebody else's audio track:** If you happen to know the artist, simply ask him or her for permission to play the track online.

- **Using a public domain track:** Some audio tracks have been placed in the public domain (perhaps by a band trying to develop a profile or because a certain amount of time has passed since the artist died). In the United States, anything before 1923 is in the public domain, while for anything created after that year, the term depends on a number of factors but can be up to 70 years after the last surviving author's death, or up to 120 years after the work's creation. It's actually quite difficult to find public domain audio online, but an alternative is to look at audio released under the Creative Commons system, where certain artists give permission for their work to be used in certain ways — have a look at `creativecommons.org/audio/` to find out more.

- **Recording your own audio:** Using a microphone you can record your own voice or effects directly into your computer. There's a great open source program called Audacity (for both Mac and Windows), available for download from the web site for this book, `www.myspaceismyplace.com`, and also at `audacity.sourceforge.net`, that allows you to record sounds via a microphone connected to the microphone jack on the back of your computer or its sound card. This is useful if you want to record a voice-over, or even to do a basic recording of your own music. While you're downloading that, you may also want the LAME MP3 Encoder (`http://lame.sourceforge.net/`), which will allow you to export MP3 files from Audacity.

Types of Audio Files

You'll come across a number of different types of audio files. Here are the three most popular:

- MP3 is a very popular audio format because it offers high levels of compression while still offering good sound quality. MP3 files have an .mp3 extension.

- WAV is Microsoft's audio format, and offers good sound quality, although the file sizes can be quite large. WAV files have a .wav extension.

- MIDI files are usually quite small and sound like someone playing a synthesizer, which is essentially what is happening. The MIDI file describes how a set of instruments plays a certain song and the sound card reproduces the instruments playing the music. For this reason MIDI files can be quite small. MIDI files have a .mid extension.

Uploading the File to a Web Server

In order to be able to play a music file, you need to upload it to a web server (i.e., it needs to be somewhere that your profile can load it from). You can use the same process I covered in Chapters 8 and 9 to obtain a URL. If you've got your own web site, you can simply upload the music file there to obtain the URL. Unfortunately most image hosting web sites will not allow you to upload music files so you will need to find a more general file hosting web site that accepts different file types. You can find free file hosting services by typing "free file hosting" or "free audio hosting" into Google. You can use any file hosting service as long as it accepts audio files and allows you to hot link to that file. Once you've uploaded the audio file, make sure you take note of its URL.

If you want to try uploading an audio file to a web host, I've made a short MP3 file called Escape (copyright 2006 Daniela Aguilera) available on my web site at www.myspaceismyplace.com.

Playing an Audio File

The <embed> tag allows you to play audio by embedding an audio console in your profile. What happens is that a helper program called a *plug-in* is loaded when the browser encounters the <embed> tag, and it is this player that actually plays the audio file.

Format

```
<embed src="url" autostart="autostart_value" loop="loop_value"
hidden="hidden_value" height="y" width="x" controls="control_type"
align="alignment">
```

Here, autostart_value allows you to specify whether the audio will start automatically. The possible values are true and false.

Also, in this code, *y* is the height of the audio console in pixels or as a percentage, and *x* is the width of the audio console in pixels or as a percentage.

If *hidden_value* is true, the music player is hidden. *url* is the URL (Internet address) of the audio file.

If *loop_value* is set to true, the audio will be repeated; if it is set to a number, the audio will be repeated that number of times. If it is set to false, the audio will be played just once.

control_type can be set to the following:

- console: A full console with stop, play, volume, and pause buttons is displayed
- smallconsole: Only a play button, stop button, and volume slider are displayed
- stopbutton: Only a stop button is displayed
- volumelevel: Only a volume control is displayed

Finally, *alignment* determines where the player will appear and can be set to top, bottom, baseline (bottom edge of text), left, right, or absmiddle.

Example

```
<embed src=" http://www.pospisil.com.au/audio/lost.mp3"
autostart="true" loop="true" width="280" height="45"></embed>
```

Place the preceding code into the About Me section of your MySpace profile. Make sure that you replace http://www.pospisil.com.au/audio/lost.mp3 with the URL of your audio file.

When you go back to edit your code, you may notice that MySpace has automatically added allowScriptAccess="never". Don't worry about this as it's simply MySpace managing a security issue.

How It Will Look

As you can see in Figure 14-2, the audio console simply looks like a little player with pause, play, volume, and so on.

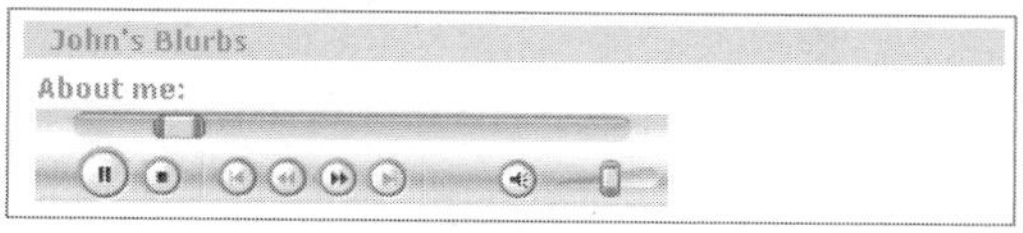

FIGURE 14-2: The audio console gives the visitor some control over how the audio track is played.

Advanced Audio Playback

It's possible to specify that Windows Media Player is loaded as the plug-in that plays your audio. Check out the section "Advanced Video Playback" in the next chapter to see how to do this.

Wrapping Up

Although there are easier ways to add music to your MySpace profile, after reading this chapter you can now embed your own player in your MySpace profile and play music back that you have uploaded to a web server. Take care not to use copyrighted audio.

Playing Videos

While playing videos on your MySpace profile might sound like one of the coolest things you can do, it does pose some special challenges, mainly because video files tend to be quite large.

This means that visitors to your profile need a fast connection to view your video, and the web server hosting your video also needs to have a fast connection to the Internet. Also, if your video files are too large, you may soon find that you are exceeding the bandwidth limits of your hosting service.

Having said that, I should also say that Internet video is in vogue at the moment, and if you use one of the video web sites such as YouTube (see Figure 15-1) or LuLu TV, or MySpace's video function, the whole process of hosting and playing video is quite straightforward, although you still need to prepare your video as described in this chapter.

If you actually want to do the hack yourself, the process is more or less the same as playing audio (see Chapter 14).

The Easy Way Out

The easiest way to add video to your web site is to click the Video tab on the MySpace home page where you can browse a number of videos hosted by MySpace. Codes are provided so all you have to do is to copy and paste them into your profile (as described in Chapter 2).

You can also upload your own video to MySpace, simply by clicking the MyVideos tab when you're in the Videos screen. You then click the Upload button and are taken through a series of windows where you type in a title and a description, specify whether it is public or private, and specify the actual location of the file on your computer's hard disk. The video file can be up to 100MB in size. After your video has finished uploading, it will take a little while to be "processed" before it can be viewed in "My videos."

If you search Google for "MySpace Video" you'll come across a number of web sites offering codes for various videos — mostly music videos — that you can paste into your profile.

There are now quite a few web sites that allow you to upload and share your video, and they even provide you with embed codes that you can paste back into your profile. These web sites, such as YouTube (`youtube.com`), Google Video (`video.google.com`), and LuLu TV (`lulu.tv`) — also give you an audience for your videos. You can also use these web sites to find videos to add to your profile (codes are provided).

FIGURE 15-1: Web sites such as YouTube make the process of working with videos online much easier.

The Real Hack

If you don't want to take the easy path, the first thing you need to do is to obtain some video. As with audio, you need to consider the copyright ownership of any video material you display on your profile (see Chapter 14 for more information on copyright). Also keep in mind that if you play anything obscene on your profile, it will be deleted.

While you might come across a funny video on the Internet, or have access to public domain video, more than likely the video that you'll want to play on your profile is video that you've captured yourself on your video camera or web cam.

The idea of course is to come up with something that is worth watching, or something that gives visitors an insight into who you are. I'm not sure of the value of putting somebody else's video on your profile — unless perhaps you're a fan of a particular band.

Preparing Your Video

The real trick to successfully playing home video on your profile is to get the video as small as possible, while still maintaining reasonable quality. You can do this in two steps:

1. Edit the video so that only the salient parts are shown so that the video doesn't take more than a few minutes to play.

2. Compress the video into a format that is relatively compact and won't take up too much space on your server and won't take long to load when someone visits your profile.

If you're using Windows XP, you'll find that you've already got a movie editing package installed on your computer called Windows Movie Maker (just go to Start ➪ All Programs ➪ Accessories). If you don't have Windows Movie Maker installed on your computer, you can install it from www.microsoft.com/windowsxp/downloads/updates/moviemaker2.mspx.

While Windows Movie Maker is not very sophisticated compared to standalone commercial video editing packages, it's more than powerful enough to do what you need to do.

The first step is to load the video files into Windows Movie Maker. You can do this by selecting File ➪ Import into collections and loading a file from your hard disk, or by downloading video from your video camera by selecting File ➪ Capture Video.

If you don't have a clip, but want to try this technique, I've made available a short section of unedited video footage on the supporting web site at www.myspaceismyplace.com for you to play with.

You'll see that your video will appear in the main window in the center of the screen. If a "storyboard" rather than a timeline is displayed at the bottom of the screen, click the "Show Timeline" button at the top of the bottom section of the screen. As you can see in Figure 15-2, three timelines appear — one for Video, one for Audio/Music, and one for Title Overlay. Drag your video clip (the one that you've just loaded) down onto the timeline. You'll see that the video clip appears as a block on the timeline. The length of the block represents the length of the video clip.

To edit the length of the clip, simply move the mouse pointer to the edge of the clip so that a red double arrow appears. Then, hold the left mouse button and drag the end of a clip to a new starting or finishing point. In this way, you can delete extraneous video. Remember, the shorter you can keep the clip, the better.

Once you're happy with the length of the video clip, it's time to save it into a suitable format for the Internet. Select File ➪ Save Movie File. The Save Movie Wizard appears and you are given the choice of where to save your movie file. Highlight My Computer by left-clicking it, and left-click Next. Now enter a name for your Movie file and left-click the Browse button to locate a directory on your hard disk to save it to. (Use your MySpace working directory to keep all your MySpace files together.) Left-click the Next button. Now it's time to specify the quality and size of the file that you want to create. There's a lot of room for experimentation here, but for the sake of this example, select "Video for dial-up access (38 Kbps)," which brings up a drop-down list from which you should select Other Settings. This creates a very small file (in video terms) of less than 1MB. Left-click the Next button. It may take a few minutes for the video to be resized and compressed, but basically what you'll have is your compressed video ready to be uploaded. The last screen of the Save Movie Wizard gives you the option to play the video. Do so, and you'll see that the video, while compressed and quite small, is still quite viewable — and what's more, it will take up much less space on your server.

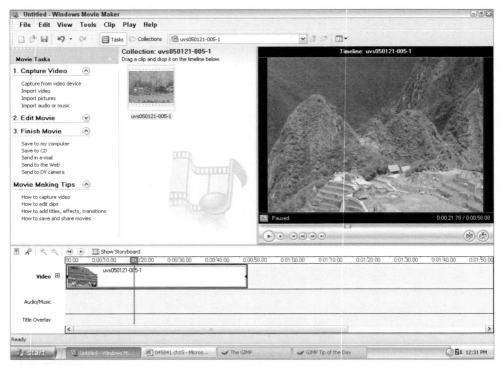

FIGURE 15-2: This screenshot shows the layout of the Windows Movie Maker screen. Note the timelines at the bottom of the screen.

Of course, you can do a lot more with Windows Movie Maker than what I have discussed here. For example, you can add a number of clips to your video, and add transitions and titling. Feel free to experiment to your heart's content.

If you're a Macintosh owner, you'll find that you've got a similar program on your computer called iMovie. While it may look different from Windows Movie Maker, you'll find that the process of importing, trimming (clipping), and saving files is more or less the same.

Hosting Your Video

Now that you have video, you need to find somewhere on the Internet to host or store it. If you have your own web site you can use that, using the same technique I discussed in Chapter 9. Just be aware that depending on how large your video clip is and how many people download it, if you're not careful you might fill up all your storage capacity and exceed your bandwidth limits, and potentially face surcharges from your hosting provider. Check with your hosting provider to see whether this might be a problem for you.

Alternatively you can try a specialized video or file hosting service, which you can find online by typing "video hosting" into Google. Some sites that offer free services include:

- **YouTube** (`youtube.com`): Upload as many videos as you want, but there is a 100MB limit on each video uploaded.
- **Google Video** (`video.google.com`): Upload and share videos of any size.
- **Zippy Videos** (`zippyvideos.com`): This site offers 20MB of free storage for users who register an account, and 10MB of free storage to anonymous users.

The process for uploading video files is similar to that of uploading photos to an image hosting web site, which I covered in Chapter 8.

Playing Your Video

As with audio, the `<embed>` tag allows you to embed video in your profile. When your browser encounters the `<embed>` tag, it loads a helper program, called a plug-in, to actually play the media. If you'd like to try the following technique but haven't created your own web-friendly video clip yet, I've included a short snippet of video footage (mentioned earlier) on the supporting web site at `www.myspaceismyplace.com` for you to practice with. It's a short, 41-second, 320 × 240–pixel video that is about 1.8MB. I've also included a very small 250KB version for you to compare it with.

Format

```
<embed src="url" width="x" height="y" align="alignment">
```

Here, `url` is the web address of the video file you want to play, x is the width of the player window (bear in mind that this includes the player itself), and y is the height of the player window (again, bear in mind that this includes the player itself).

Finally, `alignment` determines where the player will appear; it can be set to `top`, `bottom`, `baseline` (bottom edge of text), `left`, `right`, or `absmiddle`.

Example

```
<embed src="http://www.pospisil.com.au/video/peru.wmv" width="320"
height="286">
```

Place this code into the About Me section of your profile.

Don't forget to put the URL of your video file in place of *http://www.pospisil.com.au/video/peru.wmv*.

Take note that I have added 46 pixels to the height of the player to accommodate the controls (i.e., 286 = 240 + 36).

How It Will Look

You can see from Figure 15-3 that a player has been embedded in the profile. When you go back to edit your code, you may notice that MySpace has automatically added the code `allowScriptAccess="never"`. Don't worry about this as it's simply MySpace managing a security issue.

FIGURE 15-3: A video clip being played from within a profile

Advanced Video Playback

The technique described in the previous section is a simplistic approach. Often when you come across <embed> tags you'll see many different properties, which are used to set particular features of the plug-in that they're using to play the media.

One of the most common plug-ins is Windows Media Player, which is found on most PCs and can play most media files (both video and music), including Microsoft Media formats (.avi, .asf, .asx, .rmi, .wav, .wma, .wax); MPEG (.mpg, .mpeg, .m1v, .mp2, .mp3, .mpa, .mpe); QuickTime (.qt, .aif, .aifc, .aiff, .mov); and MIDI (.mid, .rmi).

In order to ensure that the Windows Media Player is used to play back the media, you'll need to add this code to the `<embed>` tag:

```
type="application/x-mplayer2"
pluginspage="http://www.microsoft.com/windows/windowsmedia/"
```

The first line tells the browser what plug-in to use, while the second line tells the browser where it can obtain the plug-in if it doesn't already have it installed.

Windows Media Player has a number of properties that allow you to have more control over how media is played. Here are some of them:

- `Autostart`: If set to `true`, the media starts playing automatically; if `false`, the Play button needs to be clicked for the media to start playing.

- `ShowControls`: If set to `true`, the controls are shown; if set to `false` the controls are not shown. The controls include play, stop, rewind, and pause. This option increases the height of the video player by 46 pixels.

- `ShowStatusBar`: If set to `true`, the status bar is displayed; if set to `false`, the status bar is not shown. The status bar shows how much of the media has been played and how much has been buffered. It's good to include this as it gives the viewer an idea of how long he or she will have to wait. This option increases the height of the video player by 26 pixels.

- `ShowDisplay`: If set to `true` the file name is shown. This option increases the height of the video player by 74 pixels.

- `AutoRewind`: If set to `true`, the media repeats from the beginning when it finishes.

To see how this would work in practice, let's take the code you used earlier and adjust it to work with Windows Media Player.

Here's the original code:

```
<embed src="http://www.pospisil.com.au/video/perumag.wmv"
width="320" height="286">
```

Let's add the code that specifies Windows Media Player as the plug in:

```
<embed src="http://www.pospisil.com.au/video/perumag.wmv"
type="application/x-mplayer2"
pluginspage="http://www.microsoft.com/windows/windowsmedia/"
width="320" height="286">
```

Now let's add the attributes we covered above:

```
<embed src="http://www.pospisil.com.au/video/perumag.wmv"
type="application/x-mplayer2"
pluginspage="http://www.microsoft.com/windows/windowsmedia/"
width="320" height="386" Autostart="true" ShowControl="true"
ShowStatusBar="true" ShowDisplay="true" AutoRewind="true">
```

Note how I have increased the height to 386 to accommodate the status bar and display. Place this code into the About Me section of your MySpace profile. When you review your profile you'll notice that the media player now has a status bar and display (as in Figure 15-4). In the same way that these attributes can be used to display more controls, they can also be used to hide controls and make the video display more compact. For example, you can hide the controls simply by setting ShowControl to false (i.e., ShowControl="false").

FIGURE 15-4: Calling the Windows Media Player plug-in gives you more control over how your video player appears.

Wrapping Up

Only a few years ago the idea of playing video from the Internet would have been preposterous, and now, as you've seen in this chapter, anyone can do it. As with other content, make sure you don't put up anything that is copyrighted or obscene.

Fun with Links

This chapter covers a couple of lightweight but amusing hacks dealing with links. The first hack changes the cursor when it is passed over a link (or a certain area) on your profile. In the second hack, the link itself is changed when the cursor passes over it.

Changing the Cursor

This hack uses the CSS `cursor` property, which allows you to change the cursor as it passes over a link.

Format

`Selector {cursor: cursor_type}`

Here, `cursor_type` can be one of the following:

- `Auto`: Which simply depends on the browser's settings
- `crosshair`: A small cross
- `default`: No change
- `move`: A small cross with arrows on each tip
- `hand`: A hand
- `help`: A question mark
- `text`: The normal text cursor
- `wait`: Hour glass
- `n-resize`: North arrow
- `s-resize`: South arrow
- `e-resize`: East arrow
- `w-resize`: West arrow

- `ne-resize`: Northeast arrow

- `nw-resize`: Northwest arrow

- `se-resize`: Southeast arrow

- `sw-resize`: Southwest arrow

Example

```
<style>
a {cursor: help;}
</style>
```

To change the cursor when it is moved over a link, simply add the `cursor` property to the link tag. For example, place the preceding code into your style sheet in the About Me section of your MySpace profile.

How It Will Look

It's a little hard to show the changing cursor in a screenshot, but you should find that once you place the preceding code in your style sheet, the pointer turns into a question mark when you move the pointer over a link.

Changing Link Styles

CSS has a number of pseudo classes that allow you to apply a style to a link when certain conditions are met, such as when a link is visited, when it is active, or when you move your mouse pointer over it.

Format

```
a:visited  {property: value;}
a:link     {property: value;}
a:active   {property: value;}
a:hover    {property: value;}
```

The `{property: value;}` style is applied if a link is visited or unvisited, if it has been clicked, or if the mouse is hovered over it. You can use one or all of these pseudo-classes in your profile.

Example

```
<style>
a:hover {color: green; text-decoration: underline; font-size:
large;}
</style>
```

Place this code into your style sheet in the About Me section of your MySpace profile.

How It Will Look

In the preceding example, the link text is made green, large, and underlined when the cursor runs over it.

FIGURE 16-1: You can see that the View More Pics link is large and underlined because the cursor is sitting over the top (not shown).

Advanced Tips

You can use this technique to create some really interesting effects. Try placing the following code in the About Me section of your profile and see what happens (assuming you're using Internet Explorer):

```
<style>
a:hover {cursor: help; color: green; text-decoration: underline;
font-size: large;}
</style>
```

Or you can use this technique to change what existing links look like. Try this:

```
<style>
a:link {font-size: large;}
</style>
```

You'll see in Figure 16-2 that all the links in the profile have been enlarged.

FIGURE 16-2: All existing links have been made large.

Wrapping Up

While neither of the hacks in this chapter is earth shattering, each offers a bit of fun and can add a little unexpected twist to your profile. You should now be able to change the type of cursor that appears when visitors roll their pointer across your profile, parts of your profile, or over links.

Custom Cursors

This hack allows you to design and place your own cursor design in your MySpace profile. It replaces the standard cursor that visitors see when they come to your profile and roll their cursor across your profile.

The Easy Way Out

If you want to take the easy way out, simply type "myspace cursor" into Google and you will be presented with a number of web sites that offer different kinds of cursors and the corresponding code. Copy the code and paste it into the About Me section of your MySpace profile. Invariably, there is advertising in the code, but if you read the rest of this chapter you should able to tell what part of the code actually calls the custom cursor, and which part of the code is advertising.

The Real Hack

If you want to do the hack yourself, a number of steps are involved:

1. Either design your own cursor or find one on the Internet that you like.

2. This cursor needs to be uploaded to a hosting service.

3. A code needs to be inserted into your MySpace profile to load and display the cursor.

Designing a Cursor

Cursors have their own file formats, which you'll be able to identify by the file extensions .cur and .ani. The .cur extension is for static cursors, whereas the .ani extension is for animated cursors.

The easiest and best way to design your own cursor is to use a specialized cursor editor, such as IconArt, which can be downloaded from www.conware-pro.com/products/ia/ (and can also be downloaded via a link at www.myspaceismyplace.com).

Don't be alarmed by the name; IconArt can handle both icons and cursors, including static and animated cursors.

Here's a quick overview of how to design your own cursor:

1. Launch IconArt. You'll see a purple canvas that is 32 pixels wide and 32 pixels high (see Figure 17-1). Don't worry — the purple won't actually show up in your profile. It represents the transparent background that you can't see. On the left side you'll see a series of drawing tools and on the right side you'll see a color palette.

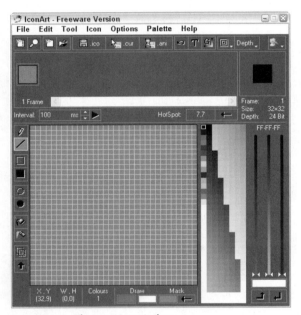

FIGURE 17-1: The IconArt window

2. From the top menu bar, select Palette ➪ Set Palette 256 colors (websafe). Select a darker color from the palette by left-clicking the color of your choice, and then select the pen icon by left-clicking it. Now you can draw your own design. You'll see that there are a number of other tools — such as Line tool and Fill — that you can also experiment with. You can see in Figure 17-2 what my humble attempts amounted to.

3. Once you've created something you're happy with, select File ➪ Save Frame as Cursor. Navigate to your MySpace directory (or the directory where you're keeping your MySpace files) and save your cursor with the name "cursor". The .cur extension will be added automatically.

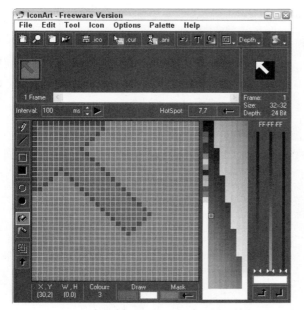

FIGURE 17-2: My humble attempt at drawing a cursor

Finding a Cursor on the Internet

If you find the idea of designing your own cursor too challenging, plenty of cursors are available on the Internet free of charge — just type "free cursor" into Google. Look for cursors with .cur and .ani extensions. These formats are standard, and quite a lot of these cursors are on the Internet, so you shouldn't have too much of a problem finding something you like. Download the cursor to your MySpace directory.

Many cursor sites seem to require you to download toolbars or advertising spyware programs before they provide access to cursors — try to avoid such sites as you really don't need toolbars and spyware clogging up your computer.

Uploading Your Cursor to a Hosting Site

In order to be able to call your cursor from your profile, you need to upload it to an Internet web site — your own or a hosting service (as described in Chapters 8 and 9).

Many image hosting services won't allow you to upload files with .ani or .cur extensions, so you'll probably need to use your own hosting site to store the cursor, unless you can find a reliable web host that allows .ani and .cur files and direct linking.

Obviously, in order to place the cursor code in your profile, you need the URL of the cursor you've uploaded to the Internet.

The Code

Your cursor design is loaded and displayed in your profile using the cursor property, which you encountered in the previous chapter. It allows you to load cursors in either a .cur or .ani file. By defining the cursor property in relation to a particular tag, you can, for example, specify that when the cursor is over the body area of your profile (i.e., the main body of your web page) the cursor becomes the cursor at a specified URL.

Format

```
.selector {cursor: URL("http://URLaddress"), URL("http://
URLaddress2"), cursor_name;}
```

Here, *URLaddress* is the URL of the .cur or .ani file.

URLaddress2 is the URL of the backup cursor (should the first one fail).

Finally, *cursor_name* is the name of one of the pre-defined cursors (a list is provided in the previous chapter). It's good practice to specify a *cursor_name* as a backup in case the first and second cursors fail to load.

Example

```
<style>
body { cursor: URL("http://www.pospisil.com.au/myspace/
cursor.cur"), pointer; }
</style>
```

In this example, you are specifying that when the cursor (or mouse pointer) is over the body area, the cursor design from the specified URL will appear. Don't forget to replace the URL *http://www.pospisil.com.au/myspace/cursor.cur* with the URL where you uploaded the link.

You can also specify cursors for specific areas of the web page or profile. For example, if you want the specified cursor to appear only over parts of the profile that are made up of tables, you can try this code:

```
<style>
table { cursor: URL("http://www.pospisil.com.au/myspace/
cursor.cur"), pointer; }
</style>
```

Notice that the standard cursor appears in the borders of your profile, but as soon as you move over the profile, which is made up of tables, your cursor appears.

Wrapping Up

If you're going to go to the trouble of customizing your profile, why not also customize your cursor? As this chapter shows, with the right tools, your cursor design is limited only by your imagination.

Changing Profile Text

Many of the hacks that you've seen so far have been about adding things to your profile. In this chapter, you look at how to change the text that makes up the existing headings and links in the standard profile. It's really the first step in radically transforming your profile.

How It Works

I've already covered styling the text that you place inside your profile (see Chapters 6 and 7) so this chapter looks at how to style the existing profile text. I'm referring here to the text that has already been placed by the MySpace people.

Now if you haven't been reading the book carefully your first question might be "How can you change something that has already been set?"

The MySpace profile is made up of a number of tables sitting within other tables. This allows the profile to be laid out in the default layout that you see. Text within these tables has generally been styled using CSS classes.

In Chapter 6, you learned that style definitions that appear later in a web page overrule styles that have been set earlier, so that the classes you define in the editable sections of your MySpace profile override those that are set up in the default MySpace profile. It follows, then, that if you know the names of the classes used by the MySpace people to style the text in the profile, you can restyle them as you wish.

CSS also allows you to apply new styles to existing tags or even to a sequence of tags. This means, for example, that by styling the tag sequence `table table table table div`, whenever that combination of tags exists in a profile, a certain style can be set. This allows you to restyle text that hasn't been styled using a class.

Using these two techniques, you can redefine any text that appears in the main profile.

You're going to do all of this very carefully so you can see exactly what's going on — and for this reason I've used a lot of figures.

To really be able to design your own text styles and understand what's going on, you need to have read and understood Chapters 3 and 4, as well as Chapters 6 and 7. All of the text-related properties covered in Chapters 6 and 7 can be used to create the effects you desire.

Well, to get started, take a look at Figure 18-1, which is a very plain version of my profile.

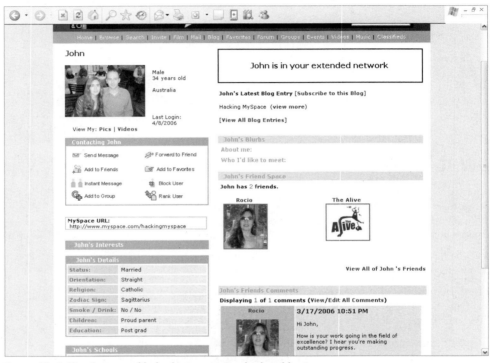

FIGURE **18-1:** Here's my profile looking very standard and boring.

The Codes

In this section, you look at the code required to restyle the text in a standard MySpace profile.

General Profile Text

Changing the general profile text is simply a matter of creating a style for the `table table table td` sequence of tags — these tags correspond to anything that appears in the cells within the main profile that doesn't have its own class to define how it looks.

Place the following code in the About Me section of your MySpace profile:

```
<style>
table table table td {font-family: trebuchet MS, arial, impact;
font-size: medium;}
</style>
```

You can also use this sequence of tags to define how the inner tables appear, so, for example, you can change the background color:

```
<style>
table table table td {background-color: black;}
</style>
```

Be aware that you can use most of the CSS properties you learned about in Chapters 6 and 7. The preceding code is simply an example so that you can see how it works. You can, for example, change the colors and apply different font styles. In Figure 18-2 you'll see that some of the text in the comments, schools, and friend's comments boxes has been changed.

FIGURE 18-2: I've started by restyling the existing text styles in the friend's comments, schools, and comments boxes.

All of the style definitions in this chapter need to be within `<style>` tags, but you can, and you should, put all of the style definitions you use inside one set of `<style>` tags. In the examples in this chapter, I've put the style tags in so that it's clear how they're to be applied — but that's really only for readers flipping through the book who don't read this paragraph.

Links

Links make up a surprisingly big part of your MySpace profile. Changing them is also very easy. As you may recall from Chapter 16, you can change the style of links that have not been visited (unclicked) or that have been visited (clicked) through the use of pseudo classes. Place the following code in the About Me section of your MySpace profile to see how you can change the styling of the links:

```
<style>
a:link {font-family: trebuchet MS, arial, impact; font-size:
medium;}
a:visited {font-family: trebuchet MS, arial, impact; font-size:
medium; color: green;}
</style>
```

You can see in Figure 18-3 how the links will now appear in your profile.

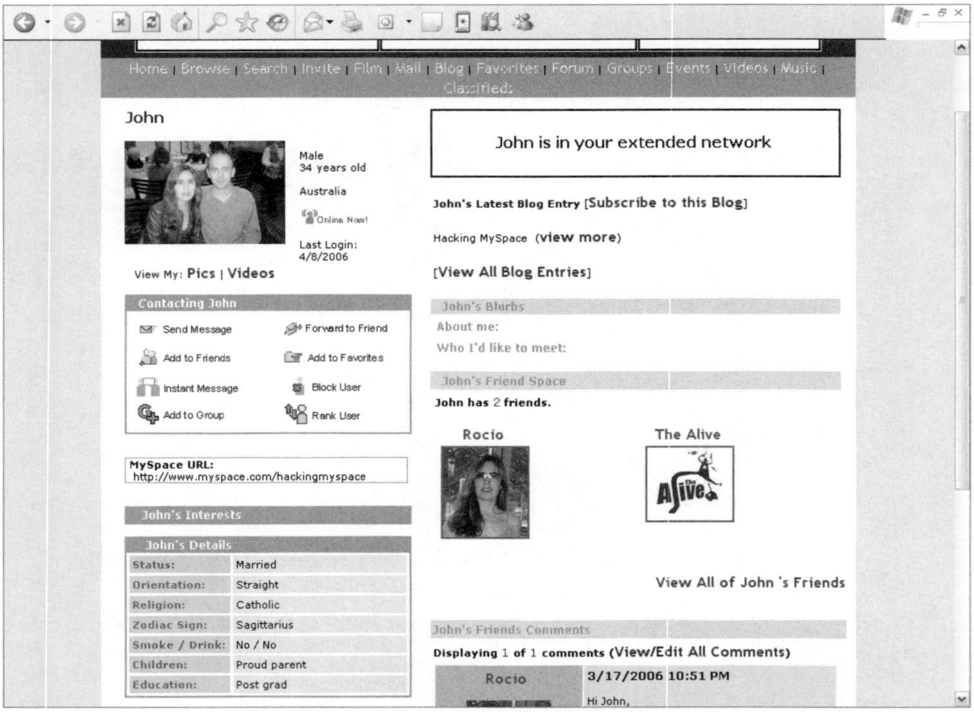

FIGURE 18-3: You can see in this screenshot that everything that is a link has been restyled.

Your Name

Do you want to see your name up in lights? Well you can by redefining the `.nametext` class that defines how your name appears. Place the following code in the About Me section of your MySpace profile:

```
<style>
.nametext {font-family: trebuchet MS, impact, arial; font-size:
xx-large; background-color: yellow;}
</style>
```

Figure 18-4 shows John (or your name in your profile) in xx-large type with a yellow background.

FIGURE 18-4: While you won't see the yellow background in this black-and-white screenshot, you can certainly see that "John" is now dominant.

Left Side Headers

The `.whitetext12` class defines the style of the headings on the left side of your profile. Place the following code in the About Me section of your MySpace profile:

```
<style>
.whitetext12 {font-family: trebuchet MS, arial, impact; font-size: medium;}
</style>
```

You can see in Figure 18-5 that all the headings on the left side of your profile have been restyled.

FIGURE 18-5: The headings on the left side have been restyled.

Right Side Headers

The `.orangetext15` class defines the style of the headings on the right side of your profile. Place the following code in the About Me section of your MySpace profile:

```
<style>
.orangetext15 {font-family: trebuchet MS, arial, impact; font-
size: medium;}
</style>
```

You can see in Figure 18-6 that all the headings on the right side of your profile have been restyled.

FIGURE 18-6: The headings on the right side have been restyled.

Details Box Labels

The `.lightbluetext8` class defines the style of the labels in the details box (where your status, orientation, religion, and so on are shown). Place the following code in the About Me section of your MySpace profile:

```
<style>
.lightbluetext8 {font-family: trebuchet MS, arial, impact; font-
size: medium;}
</style>
```

Figure 18-7 shows the restyled details box labels.

FIGURE 18-7: The details box's labels have been changed.

Extended Network Box

The `.blacktext12` class defines the text in the extended network box. Place the following code in the About Me section of your MySpace profile:

```
<style>
.blacktext12 {font-family: trebuchet MS, arial, impact; font-size:
large;}
</style>
```

I have yet to find a profile that isn't in my extended network, but if you wanted to change the text style, Figure 18-8 shows you what it would look like.

FIGURE 18-8: A startling change to the extended network box

Comment Box Dates

The `.blacktext10` class styles the dates in the comments box. Place the following code in the About Me section of your MySpace profile:

```
<style>
.blacktext10 {font-family: trebuchet MS, arial, impact; font-size:
medium;}
</style>
```

Figure 18-9 confirms my commitment to detail by allowing you to style the dates in the comments box.

FIGURE 18-9: Look carefully and you'll see that the date in the comment toward the bottom of the page has been restyled.

Latest Blog Entry

If you've ever had the urge to restyle the Latest Blog Entry text, just redefine the .btext class. This also happens to restyle the text that tells everyone how many friends you have. Place the following code in the About Me section of your MySpace profile:

```
<style>
.btext {font-family: trebuchet MS, arial, impact; font-size:
medium;}
</style>
```

You, too, can have the satisfaction of restyling "Latest Blog Entry," as you can see in Figure 18-10.

FIGURE 18-10: It's all true — "Latest Blog Entry" has been restyled.

Your Details

The `.text` class changes the text that describes your sex, age, and country next to your photos. Place the following code in the About Me section of your MySpace profile:

```
<style>
.text {font-family: trebuchet MS, arial, impact; font-size:
medium;}
</style>
```

As you can see in Figure 18-11, the critical text that provides salient details about yourself has been changed.

FIGURE 18-11: Your important details have been restyled.

Tip   Don't forget that in addition to being able to change the way text appears in the standard profile, you can also use the `visibility` and `display` properties covered in Chapter 7 to hide text. This might be useful, for example, if you wanted to keep your details private.

URL Box

And finally, this combination of tags allows you to adjust the URL box. Place the following code in the About Me section of your MySpace profile:

```
<style>
table table table table div {font-family: trebuchet MS, arial,
impact; font-size: medium;}
</style>
```

Make sure that visitors to your profile know your URL — see Figure 18-12.

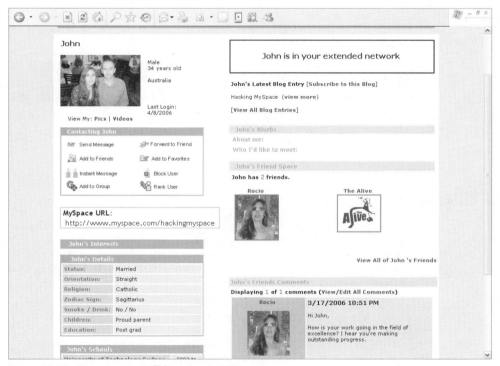

FIGURE 18-12: Now no one will forget your URL.

Working Out Class Names

It's not impossible that at some time in the future the MySpace folks will change the layout of the default profile and perhaps change or add new classes. If this happens, you may find that the codes in this chapter don't work, or that there may be some text that you can't change. Don't panic — it's fairly easy to work out the names of different classes being used to style different elements of your web page.

Let's say, for example, you wanted to know the name of the class that styles the heading "Latest Blog Entry." First select View My Profile from your home page, and then select View ⇨ Source from the Internet Explorer menu bar.

Your default text editor should appear. Do a text search for "Latest Blog Entry" and you should find that you'll be presented with the something similar to this line:

```
<td width="435" style="word-wrap:break-word"><span
class="btext">John's Latest Blog Entry </span>
```

You can see here that the `<span>` tag is being used to apply the `btext` class to the heading, so `btext` is the class you need to change in order to change the Latest Blog Entry heading.

Putting It Together

For the benefit of clarity each class mentioned has been defined within its own `<style>` tags, but if you want to use several (or all) of the styles discussed in this chapter, you can put all the style descriptions together, as in the code that follows. Place this code in the About Me section of your MySpace profile. If you have other style definitions, feel free to include them all within the one set of `<style>` tags.

```
<style>
table table table td {font-family: trebuchet MS, arial, impact;
font-size: medium;}
a:link {font-family: trebuchet MS, arial, impact; font-size:
medium;}
a:visited {font-family: trebuchet MS, arial, impact; font-size:
medium; color: green;}
.nametext {font-family: trebuchet MS, arial, impact; font-size:
xx-large; background-color: yellow;}
.whitetext12 {font-family: trebuchet MS, arial, impact; font-size:
medium;}
.lightbluetext8 {font-family: trebuchet MS, arial, impact; font-
size: medium;}
.orangetext15 {font-family: trebuchet MS, arial, impact; font-
size: medium;}
```

```
.blacktext12 {font-family: trebuchet MS, arial, impact; font-size:
large;}
.blacktext10 {font-family: trebuchet MS, arial, impact; font-size:
medium;}
.btext {font-family: trebuchet MS, arial, impact; font-size:
medium;}
.text {font-family: trebuchet MS, arial, impact; font-size:
medium;}
table table table table div {font-family: trebuchet MS, arial,
impact; font-size: medium;}
</style>
```

You'll see in Figure 18-13 that you can make your profile look quite different just by changing the look of the existing text. I haven't tried to make it particularly beautiful; I just really wanted you to be able to see what I was changing. You can of course use any of the text-styling properties covered in Chapter 6 to really make your profile stand out. Don't forget that in addition to changing fonts, font styling, and font sizes, you can also change color.

FIGURE 18-13: Here's what the profile looks like if you apply all the styles.

Wrapping Up

After working through this chapter you should be able to make some quite profound changes to the way your profile looks. By changing the classes created by the MySpace folks, you can, in effect, override the original classes and create a whole new look.

Customizing Other Parts of Your Profile

So far you've looked at customizing only the main part of your profile, but it is also possible to customize any groups you create, the View More Pictures section, messages you post to forums, as well as your blog — and this is what you will look at in this chapter.

The basic principle of customizing groups, View More Pictures, or your forum posts is the same as customizing your main profile. Basically, you use HTML or CSS to specify how you want it to appear. The problem is that it may not be immediately obvious where you post your code, or if you do manage to place the code, it may not work at first. Luckily, there are ways around these problems.

Customizing Groups

For those who haven't come across the Groups feature of MySpace, it's basically a way to hook up with other members of MySpace and participate in discussions (via forums) on various topics. The range of topics is quite broad — everything from people who want to dance in their underwear to serious political forums.

Let's assume you have a created a group on a topic close to your heart. To edit a group you've created, follow these steps:

1. Log in to your MySpace profile and click the Groups tab at the top of the page, and then select My Groups.

2. Select the group you would like to edit from the list of your groups that appears in the center screen.

   You'll now be presented with an overview of that particular group. You should notice a set of buttons on the top right side (see Figure 19-1).

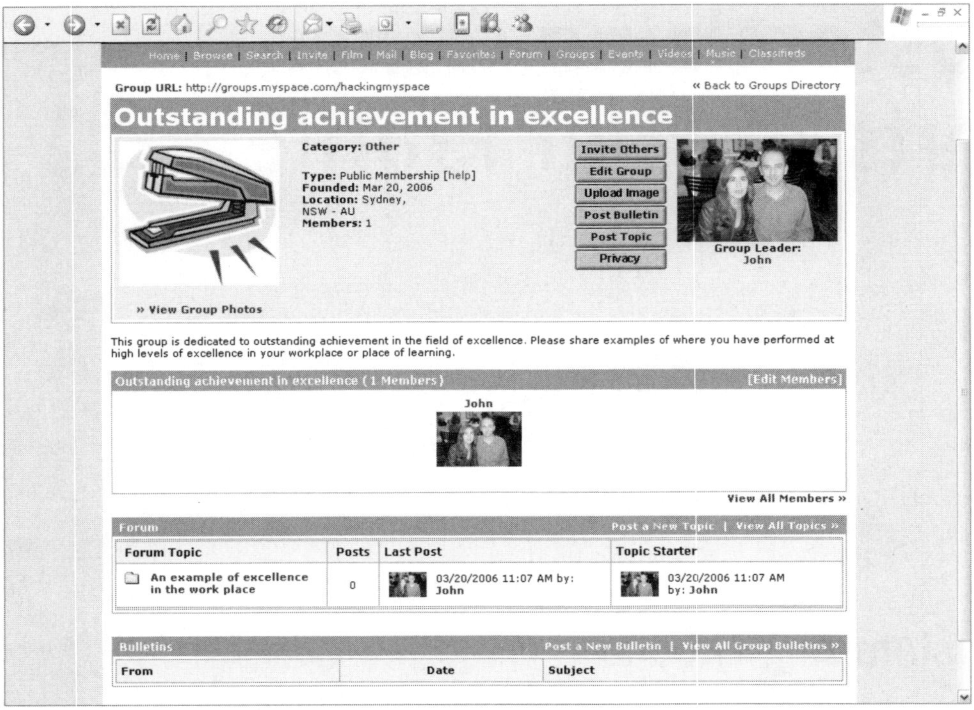

FIGURE 19-1: The screen from which you can edit your group

3. Click the Edit Group button, and you'll be brought to another screen (see Figure 19-2) where you can change the group name, its location, and various parameters such as whether the group is closed or private, whether photos can be posted, and so on. There is also a text box labeled Short Description (and marked no html) and another box that is simply labeled Description (as you'll see in the lower section of Figure 19-2).

To enter HTML or CSS, you need to place it into the Description box — but there is a catch. For example, if you try placing the following code from Chapter 13, it won't work:

```
<style>
a, body, input, table, td, textarea{background-color: transparent;
border: none; border-width: 0;}
body {background-color: 87CEEB;}
</style>
```

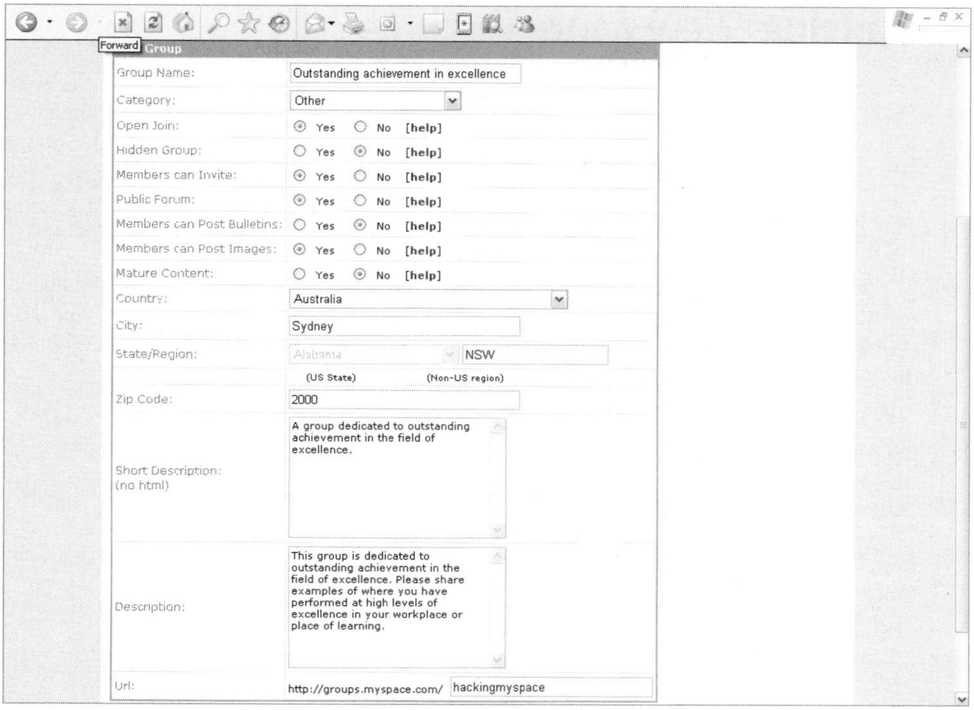

FIGURE 19-2: Code can be entered into the Description text box.

As you may recall this code turns the background of your profile Sky Blue, although the code in its current form won't do anything to your Group page, because you have a Return/Enter at the end of each line. MySpace thinks that the code is finished when it encounters a Return/Enter at the end of each line. The way around this is to run the lines together by removing the Return/Enter. The code will be more difficult to read, but it will still work. Try placing the following code into the Description text box in your MySpace profile:

```
<style> a, body, input, table, td, textarea{background-color:
transparent; border: none; border-width: 0;}body {background-
color: 87CEEB;}</style>
```

Now when you view your Groups page you will notice that the background color has changed. Most HTML or CSS code will work on your Group page if it is placed in the Description text box in this way.

Customizing View More Pictures

The trick to customizing your View More Pictures page is to insert the HTML code into the captions below each picture. To do this, log in to your MySpace profile and select the Upload/Change Photos link, which is located in the Hello box in the top-left corner of your home page.

If you have uploaded some photos, you'll see a thumbnail of each of them along with an Add Caption button below the thumbnail. Click this button and you'll be taken to another page where you can add a caption.

There are a couple of limitations when entering code into the caption box. As with entering code into your Group page, you cannot enter code that has a Return/Enter character. The other bigger limitation is that you can enter only a maximum of 70 characters of code, so you either have to keep your code very short, or split it up.

Try placing this code into a caption:

```
<style> a, body, input, table, td, div{background-color:
transparent; border: none; border-width: 0;}body {background-
color: 87CEEB;}</style>
```

You'll find that it's cut short, so what you need to do is to cut it in two — but keep both <style> tags in each line:

```
<style> a, body, input, table, td, div{background-color:
transparent; border: none; border-width: 0;}</style>
<style> body {background-color: 87CEEB;}</style>
```

The second line is now fine, but you still have a problem with the first line, which is more than 70 characters — and as you may recall the first line is important because it makes the profile transparent so that you can see the background color that is applied in the second line. In order to cut back the length of the first line, you need to think a little more about what you're trying to do. Because the View More Pictures page is a much simpler layout than your main profile, you can get away with making fewer elements transparent. You can also remove the border attributes as there are no borders in the View More Pictures page that you need to worry about. Take a look at the following code:

```
<style> table, td, div {background-color: transparent;}</style>
<style> body {background-color: 87CEEB;}</style>
```

Each line of this code now fits as one caption. To squeeze it down even more, you can remove all spaces, so that the code looks like this:

```
<style>table,td,div{background-color:transparent;}</style>
<style>body{background-color:87CEEB;}</style>
```

To try this code, place the first line of code as a caption for the first picture in your View More Pictures page (as shown in Figure 19-3), and the second line of code as a caption for the second picture in your View More Pictures page.

Your current photos:

Use 'Add Caption' to add/edit photo captions;
'Default' photo is the first photo people see on your profile.

`<style>table,td,div{background-color:transparent;}</style>`

-Update Caption-

FIGURE 19-3: Break the code so it fits in each caption.

You should find that when you click the View More Pictures page, the background color is now Skyblue (see Figure 19-4). You are limited when splitting up code across a number of captions because when someone clicks a picture to view it in detail, only the caption for that picture is shown, which means that only the code in the caption is executed. This is not much of a problem for the preceding example, but it could be a problem if you were trying to do something more complicated.

FIGURE 19-4: The background color has been changed.

It's worth noting you can use this method to apply filters to the photos — which as you know from Chapter 13 work with Internet Explorer only. Nevertheless, if you do want to apply a filter, you do it by styling the `<img>` tag in the following way:

```
<style>img{filter:blur(add=0,direction=225,strength=10);}</style>
```

If you add this to a caption in your View More Pictures page, you'll see that all of the images have become blurred (see Figure 19-5).

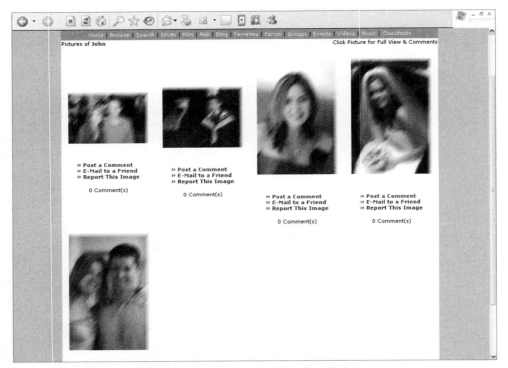

FIGURE 19-5: You can apply filters to images in your View More Pictures page.

To delete code that you've entered into captions, do the following:

1. Select Upload/Change Photos from the main screen.

2. Click Add caption.

3. Leave the text field blank and click the Update Caption button.

4. Click Post Caption to confirm.

Posting Code in Forums

If you've ever tried to post code into forums, you may have noticed that it doesn't seem to accept all tags. Some common tags such as <b> and <h1> work fine, but if you try to link to a picture, for example, MySpace just won't process the code.

There is a way around this — simply use the HTML character code < for the opening brackets.

So, to link a picture to your forum, instead of entering:

```
<img src="http://i45.photobucket.com/albums/f93/pospisil/ch08-image-r.jpg" width="200" height="300" alt="Rocio">
```

you will need to enter the following:

```
&lt;img src="http://i45.photobucket.com/albums/f93/pospisil/ch08-image-r.jpg" width="200" height="300" alt="Rocio">
```

If you are trying the preceding code, please remember to use the URL of your own picture — see Chapters 8, 9, and 10 for more information. Figure 19-6 shows an image displayed in a forum posting.

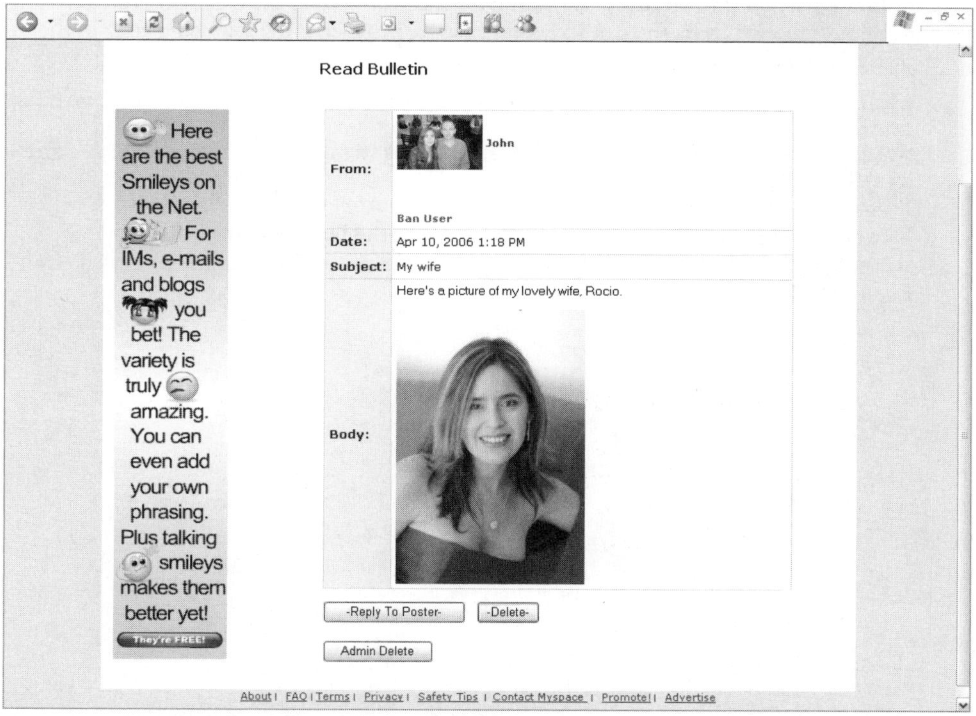

FIGURE 19-6: It is possible to post code in forums.

You don't need to worry about using the character code with the closing bracket. MySpace seems to work fine with the regular > symbol.

Oh, and by the way, even if you use the character code, the forums still won't accept the `<style>` tag, which means that you cannot post CSS code.

Customizing Your Blog

Interestingly, the blog section is the only area that actually has a ready-made provision for a style sheet. You can find it by clicking the Manage Blog link in the Hello box on your home page. You'll be taken to the Blog Control Center, where you can manage your subscriptions to other people's blogs, as well as make adjustments to your own blog. In the My Controls box, click Customize Blog. The Customize My Blog screen appears, and this allows you to make various adjustments to how your blog appears, including adjustment of fonts, colors, background images and music, and so on. In fact, there's such a high level of customization available that most users never need to actually use CSS code. However, right at the bottom of the screen you'll find the section "Your own addition style sheet," and this is where you can place your own class and tag definitions.

Here's a quick example of how you might use it. When your blog is displayed, the subject heading is styled through the `p.blogSubject` class, whereas the blog text is styled using the `p.blogContent` class. You can style these classes by placing the following code in the "Your own additional style sheet" section:

```
p.blogSubject {font-family: comic sans ms, trebuchet ms, verdana;
font-size: x-large;}
p.blogContent {font-family: trebuchet ms, verdana, arial; font-
size: medium;}
```

Don't include `<style>` tags — just the code. Click the Update button, and when the screen is refreshed, click View My Blog. You'll see that your blog has been restyled, as in Figure 19-7.

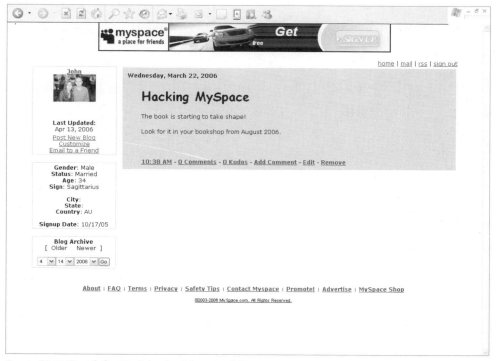

FIGURE 19-7: You define a style sheet for your blog.

Wrapping Up

While most of this book focuses on the main standard profile, this chapter shows that it's also possible to change other parts of your MySpace experience, including Groups, View More Pictures, Forums, and Blog.

Adding a Comments Box

Adding comments to your friends' profiles, and having comments added to yours, is one of the primary means of displaying friendship on MySpace.

Sure, visitors can scroll down to the bottom of your profile if they want to add a comment, but just think of how convenient it would be if you had your own comments box in the middle of your profile. This hack allows you to place a prominent comments box in the middle of your profile, and with a little knowledge of CSS you'll also be able to customize it to your heart's content.

The Basic Comments Box

This comments box will allow your visitors to add their comments about you directly into your profile. Here's the code for adding a basic comments box:

```
<center><form method="post" action="http://
comments.myspace.com/index.cfm?fuseaction=user
.ConfirmComment">
<input type="hidden" name="friendID"
value="XXXXXXXX" >
<b> Enter your comments here </b><br>
<textarea name="f_comments" cols="60"
rows="5"></textarea><br>
<input type="submit" value="Post Comment">
</form></center>
```

I suggest you paste this code into the bottom of your "I'd like to meet" section. You'll need to replace the *XXXXXXXX* with your eight-digit friend ID number. This number is the last eight digits of the URL that appears in your browser when you click View My Profile from your home page. Figure 20-1 shows how the basic comments box would appear in your profile.

FIGURE 20-1: The basic comments box in a profile

You can do a number of other tweaks to this code. If you want to change the size of the text box where the comments are typed, simply change the `cols` and `rows` values in the following line:

```
<textarea name="f_comments" cols="60" rows="5"></textarea><br>
```

The `cols` value determines the width of the text box (in characters), whereas the `rows` value determines the height of the text box (in characters). To create a smaller text box, your line of code might look something like this:

```
<textarea name="f_comments" cols="50" rows="4"></textarea><br>
```

This code creates a text box 50 characters wide and 4 characters high.

Underneath the comments box you'll notice a Post Comment button. You'll see that this label is defined in this line of code:

```
<input type="submit" value="Post Comment">
```

By changing the words "Post Comment" you can relabel the submit button. Here's how it might look:

```
<input type="submit" value="Send Comment">
```

To change the introductory words, which are located in this line of code:

```
<b> Enter your comments here </b><br>
```

simply change them to whatever you want. You can embellish this line using classes or standard HTML tags:

```
<u> Please leave me some comments! </u><br>
```

If you were to apply the example tweaks just described, your code might look something like this:

```
<center><form method="post"
action="http://comments.myspace.com/index.cfm?fuseaction=user
.ConfirmComment">
<input type="hidden" name="friendID" value="XXXXXXXX" >
<u>Please leave me some comments!</u><br>
<textarea name="f_comments" cols="50" rows="4"></textarea><br>
<input type="submit" value="Send Comment">
</form></center>
```

Figure 20-2 shows how this revised code might appear in your profile.

FIGURE 20-2: A slightly revised comments box

Take note that you cannot leave comments about yourself, so you will need to get a friend to try the comments box, or perhaps you can use a second account (if you have one).

Blending Your Comments Box into Your Profile

Now you know how to create a basic comments box, but wouldn't it look neat if you blended your comments box with the style of the existing MySpace profile? As you know from Chapter 18, the class that styles the headings on the right side of your profile is `.orangetext15`. You can style this class to create an extra heading for your comments box.

Here's the code to create a section heading that will blend into a standard MySpace profile:

```
<br><table width="440" height="20" cellspacing="0"
cellpadding="0" bgcolor="ffcc99"> <tr> <td width="440"><span
class="orangetext15">My Comments Box</span></td></tr></table>
```

If you would like a different background color for the section bar, simply change the `bgcolor` value of `ffcc99` to the hex color value of choice (see Appendix A).

Now just add the comments box code (from the "Basic Comments Box" section). I suggest you add this code to the bottom of the "I'd like to meet" section of your MySpace profile:

```
<center><form method="post" action="http://comments.myspace.com/
index.cfm?fuseaction=user.ConfirmComment">
<input type="hidden" name="friendID" value="XXXXXXXX" >
<u>Please leave me some comments!</u><br>
<textarea name="f_comments" cols="50" rows="4"></textarea><br>
<input type="submit" value="Send Comment">
</form></center>
```

As you can see in Figure 20-3, the comments box now blends in with the rest of your profile quite comfortably.

FIGURE 20-3: Your comments box now blends in quite nicely.

Spicing Up Your Comments Box

You can make your comments box much more interesting in a number of ways. One approach is to put the comments box in a table that you can then embellish. Here's an example of how you might do it. Place this text in the About Me section of your MySpace profile. Don't forget to replace the *XXXXXXXX* with your eight-digit friend ID number.

```
<table width="400" height="100" border="2" cell spacing="0"
cellpadding="0" bgcolor="yellow"> <tr> <td width="400">
<center><form method="post"
action="http://comments.myspace.com/index.cfm?fuseaction=user
.ConfirmComment">
<input type="hidden" name="friendID" value="XXXXXXXX" >
<h1> Enter your comments here </h1><br>
<textarea name="f_comments" cols="60" rows="5"></textarea><br>
<input type="submit" value="Post Comment">
</form></center>
</td></tr></table>
```

Figure 20-4 gives you an idea of how you can embellish your contact table.

FIGURE 20-4: You can make your contact table as weird as you like.

If you really want to go all the way, you can create a `.class` in your style definitions and apply the `.class` to your table. (I covered how to create and style classes in Chapter 6.)

Place the following code in the About Me section of your MySpace profile:

```
<style>
.commentbox {font-size: large; font-family: trebuchet MS, arial,
impact; border: medium dashed blue; background-color: yellow;}
.formstyle {font-size: large; font-family: trebuchet MS, arial,
impact;}
</style>
```

Place the following code in the Who I'd like to meet section. Don't forget to replace the *XXXXXXXX* with your eight-digit friend ID number.

```
<table class="comment box" width="400" height="100" cell
spacing="0" cellpadding="0"<tr> <td width="400">
<center><form class="formstyle" method="post" action="http://
comments.myspace.com/index.cfm?fuseaction=user.ConfirmComment">
<input type="hidden" name="friendID" value="XXXXXXXX" >
Enter your comments here <br>
<textarea name="f_comments" cols="60" rows="5"></textarea><br>
<input type="submit" value="Post Comment">
</form></center>
</td></tr></table>
```

In the first section, you defined two classes:

- `.commentbox`: Defines how the table is going to appear
- `.formstyle`: Defines how the actual form is going to appear

To style the table in which the form appears, simply modify or adjust properties in the `.commentbox` class. To style the form itself, simply modify or adjust properties in the `.formstyle` class.

Wrapping Up

You're bound to receive more comments now that you have a comments box in the middle of your profile. And don't forget that the better your understanding of CSS, the more you can adjust the look of the comments box.

Using Marquees and Slideshows

So far you've learned how to insert static images into your profile, and while such images can make a big difference in how your profile looks, you may find that a slideshow makes a much bigger impact.

A slideshow consists of a series of photos that slide across your screen — with one following another. Slideshows are good for creating movement in your profile and for displaying a number of pictures in a confined space. They're also very easy to create through the use of the `<marquee>` tag.

Image Preparation

The first step is to upload a series of pictures to a hosting site that your profile can call them from. For more information on this, check out Chapters 8, 9, and 10. You can either use a photo hosting web site or your own web site. For the purpose of this exercise, upload three pictures to your server so that you have three URLs (the locations of the pictures you've just uploaded). If you're using a photo hosting service such as Photobucket, your URLs might look something like this:

```
http://i45.photobucket.com/albums/f93/pospisil/
rocio.jpg
http://i45.photobucket.com/albums/f93/pospisil/
trishsteve.jpg
http://i45.photobucket.com/albums/f93/pospisil/
wedding.jpg
```

Keep in mind that these URLs probably won't work by the time you read this — I'm showing them so you can see what to expect.

Make your images quite small; otherwise they won't fit very well in the confined space of your MySpace profile. The test images (which you can find on www.myspaceismyplace.com) are 200 pixels wide and 301 pixels high.

A Basic Slideshow

Putting together a basic slideshow is remarkably simple — simply place a number of <image> tags between a pair of <marquee> tags. The code for a basic slideshow looks like this:

```
<marquee>
<img src="url_image1">
<img src="url_image2">
<img src="url_image3">
</marquee>
```

Here, url_image1, url_image2, and url_image3 are the URLs of the images you want in your slideshow.

Example

```
<marquee>
<img src="http://i45.photobucket.com/albums/f93/pospisil/
rocio.jpg">
<img src="http://i45.photobucket.com/albums/f93/pospisil/
trishsteve.jpg">
<img src="http://i45.photobucket.com/albums/f93/pospisil/
wedding.jpg">
</marquee>
```

This is how the code would look with the sample URLs inserted. Of course, when you enter this code into your web site you'll need to use your own URLs. The best place for a slideshow is in the About Me or Who I'd like to meet sections of your MySpace profile.

How It Will Look

While you can't see it in Figure 21-1, onscreen the photos should be scrolling from right to left.

By the way, the <marquee> tag also works with text — just try this:

```
<marquee>It's easy to scroll text</marquee>
```

Controlling Direction

The direction attribute allows you to control the direction of the scrolling images. It has four possible values: left, right, up, and down. The default value is right. Here's how the direction attribute would be placed within the slideshow code:

```
<marquee direction="direction_value">
<img src="url_image1">
<img src="url_image2">
<img src="url_image3">
</marquee>
```

FIGURE 21-1: The basic slideshow is a good way of getting attention.

Here, *direction_value* specifies the direction of the scroll and can be up, down, left, or right.

Example

```
<marquee direction="down">
<img src="http://i45.photobucket.com/albums/f93/pospisil/
rocio.jpg">
<img src="http://i45.photobucket.com/albums/f93/pospisil/
trishsteve.jpg">
<img src="http://i45.photobucket.com/albums/f93/pospisil/
wedding.jpg">
</marquee>
```

When you enter this code into your web site, you'll need to use your own URLs. The best place for a slideshow is in the About Me or Who I'd like to meet sections of your MySpace profile.

How It Will Look

The photos will scroll from top to bottom, as shown in Figure 21-2.

FIGURE 21-2: You can control the direction of the slideshow via the direction attribute.

Misbehavior

The `behavior` attribute allows you to control how the slideshow should scroll. Here's how the code would look:

```
<marquee behavior="behavior_value">
<img src="url_image1">
<img src="url_image2">
<img src="url_image3">
</marquee>
```

Here, `behavior_value` specifies the type of scroll effect, and can be `scroll`, `alternate`, or `slide`. The default value is `scroll`. With `scroll`, the images scroll past and than start again in a continuing loop. With `alternate`, the images appear to scroll back and forward. When the `slide` value is specified, the slideshow is supposed to pause when it reaches the opposite edge, although I haven't been able to see this effect in action in the browsers I tried.

Example

```
<marquee behavior="alternate">
<img src="http://i45.photobucket.com/albums/f93/pospisil/
rocio.jpg">
<img src="http://i45.photobucket.com/albums/f93/pospisil/
trishsteve.jpg">
<img src="http://i45.photobucket.com/albums/f93/pospisil/
wedding.jpg">
</marquee>
```

When you enter the preceding code into your web site, you'll need to use your own URLs. The best place for a slideshow is in the About Me or Who I'd like to meet sections of your MySpace profile.

How It Will Look

Figure 21-3 looks remarkably like Figure 21-1, although if you look at the slideshow onscreen, you'll find that images scroll backward and forward.

FIGURE 21-3: Create some action with the alternate attribute.

Other Useful Attributes

The <marquee> tag has a number of other neat attributes, including: width, height, and loop. Here's how they would be used in code:

```
<marquee width="width_value" height="height_value"
loop="loop_value">
<img src="url_image1">
<img src="url_image2">
<img src="url_image3">
</marquee>
```

Here, width_value is the width of the marquee in pixels or as a percentage.

Also in the code, height_value is the height of the marquee in pixels or as a percentage. The height attribute is especially useful in MySpace profiles if you're using the up or down direction, or you are trying to create a zigzag effect (see the "Zigzag" section, following) and you need to allow some room for the actual up-and-down motion of the images or text.

Finally, loop_value specifies how many times the slideshow is repeated.

Example

```
<marquee width="200" height="301" loop="5">
<img src="http://i45.photobucket.com/albums/f93/pospisil/
rocio.jpg">
<img src="http://i45.photobucket.com/albums/f93/pospisil/
trishsteve.jpg">
<img src="http://i45.photobucket.com/albums/f93/pospisil/
wedding.jpg">
</marquee>
```

When you enter this code into your web site, you'll need to use your own URLs. The best place for a slideshow is in the About Me or Who I'd like to meet sections of your MySpace profile.

How It Will Look

As you can see in Figure 21-4, the slideshow is now constrained to a width of 200 pixels.

FIGURE 21-4: Using the width attribute to contain the slideshow.

Zigzag

By using a `<marquee>` tag within another tag, and then of course closing both tags, you can create a very cool zigzag effect. When you enter the following code into your web site, you'll need to use your own URLs. The best place for a slideshow is in the About Me or Who I'd like to meet sections of your MySpace profile.

```
<marquee behavior="alternate" direction="up" height="400px">
<marquee direction="right">
<img src="http://i45.photobucket.com/albums/f93/pospisil/
rocio.jpg">
<img src="http://i45.photobucket.com/albums/f93/pospisil/
trishsteve.jpg">
<img src="http://i45.photobucket.com/albums/f93/pospisil/
wedding.jpg">
</marquee>
</marquee>
```

Here's another zigzag effect:

```
<marquee behavior="alternate" direction="up"
height="400px"><marquee direction="right" behavior="alternate">
<img src="http://i45.photobucket.com/albums/f93/pospisil/
rocio.jpg">
<img src="http://i45.photobucket.com/albums/f93/pospisil/
trishsteve.jpg">
<img src="http://i45.photobucket.com/albums/f93/pospisil/
wedding.jpg">
</marquee>
</marquee>
```

Don't forget to insert the URLs of your own images.

What's Your Position?

This following hack is more for fun than for anything else at this stage, although its relevance will become more obvious when you get to Chapter 25.

First let's set up a style called box. Place this code in the About Me section of your profile:

```
<style>
.box {background-color: white; position: absolute; left: 50%;
margin-left: -250px;  top:  25%; width: 500px; height: 301px;
z-index: 1; visibility: visible; border: 2px solid black}
</style>
```

Then place this code in the Who I'd like to meet section:

```
<div class="box">
<marquee behavior="alternate" direction="up" height="400px">
<marquee direction="right">
<img src="http://i45.photobucket.com/albums/f93/pospisil/
rocio.jpg">
<img src="http://i45.photobucket.com/albums/f93/pospisil/
trishsteve.jpg">
<img src="http://i45.photobucket.com/albums/f93/pospisil/
wedding.jpg">
</marquee>
</marquee>
</div>
```

What I've done is set up a style for a Div box and then applied that to a Div, inside of which I've placed the code for the marquee. I've used some of the positioning code you looked at in Chapter 7 to reposition the Div box to roughly the center of the screen. You can see in Figure 21-5 that this can work to great effect. Although it's not of great practical use to you right now, you'll see why this concept is important in Chapter 25 when I cover Div overlays.

FIGURE 21-5: Very interesting, but you'll have to wait until Chapter 25 to see how positioning Divs can be used for real hacks.

Wrapping Up

Slideshows offer an easy way to increase visual impact, as well as show a number of images in a confined space. As you can see, in addition to changing the direction of the movement, you can also create zigzag effects, and even place your slideshow anywhere in your MySpace profile.

Changing Your Contact Table

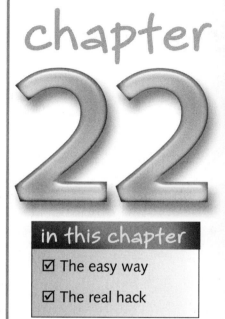
T he contact table is the box in your profile that allows visitors to your profile to send you a message, add you as a friend, send you an instant message, add you to a group, forward your details to a friend, add you to their to favorites, block you, or rank you. As you can see in Figure 22-1, the standard design is quite dull. Fortunately, you can use CSS and the imaging editing program GIMP to make the contact table a lot more interesting.

The Easy Way

The easy way to change your contact table is to type "myspace contact table" into Google. You'll be presented with a large number of web sites offering different styles of contact tables. In most cases, all you have to do is copy the code and paste it into your profile. However, if you're creative, you might want to try your hand at creating a contact table from scratch.

The Real Hack

The existing MySpace contact table consists of a table with eight separate GIF images for each button. Instead of trying to remake each button, you're going to make each existing button transparent and then embed a background image in the table so that when you view the contact table onscreen, what you're actually going to see is the background image.

Creating a Background Image

The first step to developing a unique contact table is to design a background image. You're going to get your hands dirty and create your very own background image from scratch using GIMP.

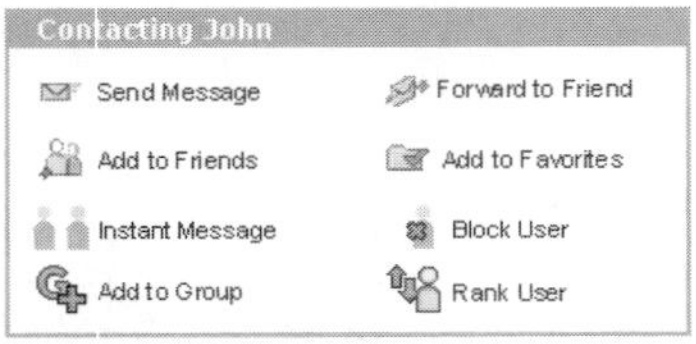

FIGURE 22-1: The standard contact table is quite dull.

The background image needs to be 300 pixels wide and 150 pixels high.

As part of its design, the background image will have the label for each button drawn into it and aligned in such a way that it corresponds to where the standard buttons usually sit.

To make this process easier, I've created a contact table template that you can load directly into GIMP. You can download the template from this book's supporting web site at www.myspaceismyplace.com. The template consists of several layers — an empty background layer and a layer for each button — that contain the text of the buttons laid out in the right positions.

For those who are new to graphics programs, here's a quick explanation of what layers are. In the old days, graphics programs were very much like a traditional oil painting — it was very hard to make a correction if you made a mistake. If you drew a big X across your image, that big X actually became part of your image. Layers were developed to get around this problem. Think of a layer as a transparent canvas placed over the top of the original canvas. You can make as many changes as you like to the layer and the underlying canvas stays the same.

The first step is to embed a background image in the template. You can use any image you like, but for the purpose of this exercise I'm going to use the background image created in Chapter 13. (You can use my background image if you haven't yet worked through that chapter; just download background.jpg from the web site for this book at www.myspaceismyplace.com). Load this background image into GIMP: File ⇨ Open.

Resize this image by following these steps:

1. Select Image ⇨ Scale Image and type **300** into the width box and **150** into the height box. You'll need to click the little chain icon so that it is broken (i.e., so the dimensions of the image are not constrained by its proportions). Then click the Scale button.

2. Save your image (File ⇨ Save As) as backgroundsmall.jpg in your working MySpace directory. When prompted for the quality level, make sure it is at least 85.

3. Leaving the background image onscreen, open the contacttabletemplate.xcf file that you'll find on the web site for this book at www.myspaceismyplace.com. This is the template for the contact table.

4. Open the Layers dialog box (select Dialogs ⇨ Layers). Try to arrange the windows so that you can see everything onscreen (as in Figure 22-2).

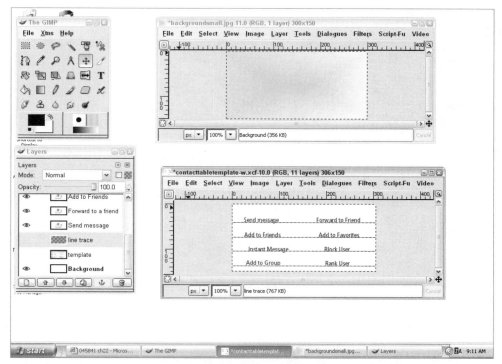

FIGURE 22-2: Arrange the various GIMP windows so that everything is easy to work with.

5. Select your background image window and then select Select ⇨ All. You'll see that the boundary of the image is selected.

6. Copy this into your clipboard by selecting Edit ⇨ Copy, or by pressing Ctrl+C.

7. Select the contact table template window so that it is active. In the Layers window, you should see a number of layers. There's a background layer, and then a layer for each button that contains the text. Select the background layer and then select Edit ⇨ Paste from the template image window. If all is going well, you'll see that the new background has been slotted in behind the button texts, as in Figure 22-3.

   If you want to move the background image around, simply move the cursor over the image and hold down the left mouse button. You'll now be able to move the background image around. You'll notice that when you pass the cursor just outside of the image area there's an anchor next to the arrow.

8. When you're finished, left-click on an area just outside of the image area to anchor the new background.

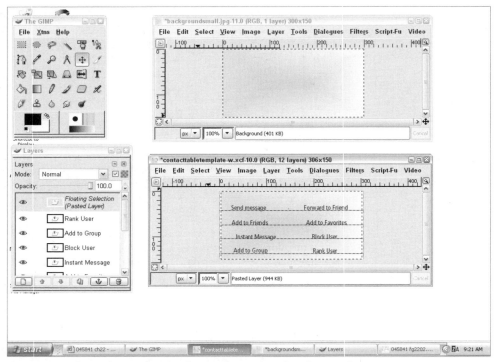

FIGURE 22-3: The background image has been introduced to the template.

9. Close the background image by selecting File ➪ Close from its image window. This should now leave the contact table template open.

Now you need to go through and edit the text for each link, but in order to do that, you need to have the Tool Options window open.

10. From the image window's drop-down menu bar, select Dialogs ➪ Tool Options. A Tool Options window should appear.

11. Click the Text tool in the main tool palette. The Tool Options window will now allow you to adjust the font size and font. (If the Tool Options window shows something else, make sure you have the Text tool selected.) You can also access this window by pressing Shift+Ctrl+T.

12. Click one of the button layers — they are labeled by function so you should not have any problems identifying which layer is for which button. For example, select the layer labeled Send Message by left-clicking it. You'll notice that the corresponding button in the template is highlighted.

Now go to the Tool Options window. Clicking the Aa button allows you to change the font, while changing the font size in the Size text box allows you to directly adjust the size of the font (see Figure 22-4). The selection of fonts available will depend on what fonts you have installed on your system. Because you will be saving the background as a JPEG file, you don't need to worry about using Web-friendly fonts — just use whatever you think looks good. Make a note of the font, font size, and color so that you can make sure all the other buttons look the same. If you want to change the actual text of the button, click the highlighted text with the Text tool. A window appears that enables you to change the text (also shown in Figure 22-4). You may also want to move the text around — simply select the Move layers and selections button in the main tool palette (it looks like a cross with arrows on each tip), and then hold down the left mouse button while moving the text with your pointer. Sometimes it can be difficult to actually pick up the layer you want to move because of the guides and background. To switch off the guides, select View ⇨ Show Guides. (This switches off the guides if they are showing, and switches them on if they're not showing.) To hide the background, simply click the eye icon next to the background layer in the Layers window.

You can also change the color by clicking the Color box, which will bring up a color palette window. After you've mixed your color, click the arrow icon next to the swatches. Your color will be transferred to a swatch, which will make it to use the same color for subsequent buttons.

When you're finished with a button, simply select another button layer and repeat the whole process.

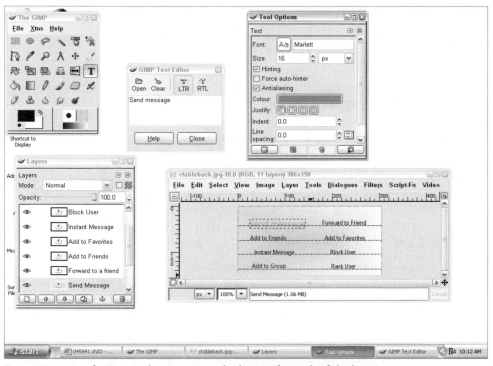

FIGURE 22-4: Use the Text tool options to style the text for each of the buttons.

Feel free to experiment with different fonts to create different effects. When you're finished, make sure you save the file in XCF format (File ➪ Save). This will allow you to come back later and make changes to the text without having to start from scratch.

To actually save the background image, you'll need to select File ➪ Save As. A Save Image dialog box will appear. Type **ctableback.jpg** in the Name text box and save it in your working MySpace directory. (You can navigate to this directory by clicking Browse for other folders.) Click the Save button. When the next window appears, click Export, and then in the next window make sure that Quality is set to at least 85 before clicking OK.

Once you've adjusted all the buttons, your background table should look something like Figure 22-5.

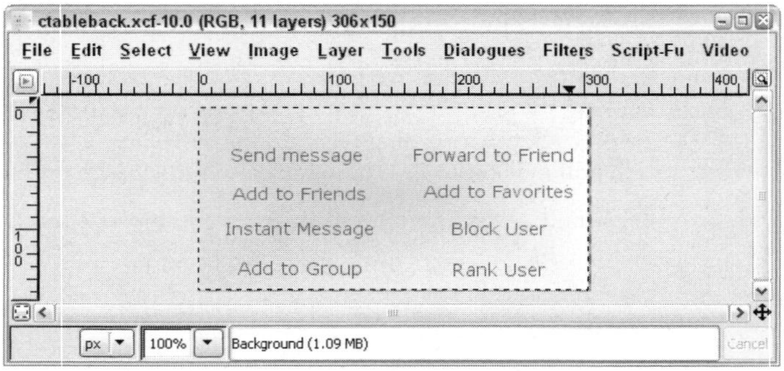

FIGURE 22-5: While this example is very basic, only your imagination limits how you design your own contact table.

You've created a very simple example here, but I'm sure you can see that with some extra time and some creative flair, you could easily create a very interesting contact table.

Uploading the Background Image

In order to be able to display the background image, you'll need to upload it to an image hosting web site or to your own web site. Chapters 8 and 9 provide more information on how to do this. At the end of the process you should have a URL. In the case of this example, the URL looks like this: *http://i45.photobucket.com/albums/f93/pospisil/ctableback.jpg*.

The Code

The code to display the new background image is courtesy of bbz.space (http://bbz-space.com). The code would normally be placed in the About Me section of the MySpace profile.

```
<style>
.contactTable {width: 300px; height: 150px; padding: 0px;
background-image:url("image_url"); background-attachment: scroll;
```

```
background-position: center center; background-repeat :no-repeat;
background-color: transparent; border:0px;}
.contactTable table, table.contactTable td { padding: 0px;
border:0px; background-color: transparent; background-image: none;}
.contactTable a img {visibility: hidden; border: 0px;}
.contactTable a {display: block; height: 28px; width: 115px;}
.contactTable .text {font-size: 1px;}
.contactTable .text, .contactTable a, .contactTable img {filter:
none;}
.contactTable .whitetext12 {visibility: hidden;}
</style>
```

Here, *image_url* is the URL of your contact table background.

The first line of code after the `<style>` tag loads the background image into the contact table — the various background properties specify how the background image will be displayed (many of these were covered in Chapter 13). The rest of the code is basically devoted to hiding the table, images, links, and text that make up the existing table, while still allowing the existing links to work.

Example

```
<style>
.contactTable {width:300px; height: 150px; padding: 0px; background-
image: url("http://i45.photobucket.com/albums/f93/pospisil/
ctableback.jpg "); background-attachment: scroll; background-
position: center center; background-repeat :no-repeat; background-
color: transparent; border:0px;}
.contactTable table, table.contactTable td { padding: 0px;
border:0px; background-color: transparent; background-image: none;}
.contactTable a img {visibility:hidden; border: 0px;}
.contactTable a {display: block; height: 28px; width: 115px;}
.contactTable .text {font-size: 1px;}
.contactTable .text, .contactTable a, .contactTable img {filter:
none;}
.contactTable .whitetext12 {visibility: hidden;}
</style>
If you wanted to keep the little Contacting heading, simply change
the last line from:
.contactTable .whitetext12 {visibility: hidden;}
To
.contactTable .whitetext12 {color: black;}
```

Place this code in the About Me section of your MySpace profile. Don't forget to replace *http://i45.photobucket.com/albums/f93/pospisil/ctableback.jpg* with the URL of your own contact background image.

How It Will Look

Figure 22-6 shows how the new contact table would appear in your profile.

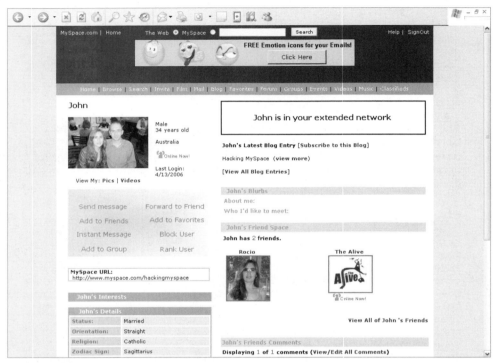

FIGURE 22-6: The new contact table in place in the profile.

Wrapping Up

The contact table is the main communications interface between you and visitors to your profile. You should now be able to create your own contact table from scratch, which can reflect your interests, personality, or the theme of your profile.

Creating Your Own Navigation Bar

This hack allows you to restyle and rearrange the navigation bar at the top of your profile. This hack is based on code written by Willian (www.myspace.com/Willian) and is courtesy of the BBZ MySpace group (http://groups.myspace.com/bbz). Basically, the navigation bar consists of a table with text links to other pages. This hack creates another navigation bar that sits over the top of the existing bar. You can change the look of the links, add or remove individual links, and change the color scheme. The code for this hack is in two parts.

The Hack

The following code will need to be placed in the About Me section of your MySpace profile. The `.navigationbar` class enables you to define the size of the table, a background color, and its position. If you're familiar with CSS, you can just add the `.navigationbar` class to your existing style definitions. Otherwise just add the code as is.

```
<style>
.navigationbar {background-color: color_value;
position: absolute; left: 50%; top: 127px; margin-
left: -400px; width: 800px; height: 26px}
</style>
```

Here, *color_value* is the background color of the navigation bar.

The following code can be placed in the "Who I'd like to meet" section of your MySpace profile:

```
<div class="navigationbar">
<table width="800" height="26" border="0"
cellspacing="0" cellpadding="0">
<tr valign="middle">
<td align="center">
<a href="link_url1">link_name1</a>   |  
<a href="link_url2">link_name2</a>   |  
</tr>
</td>
</table>
</div>
```

Here, `link_url` is the URL that the link goes to, and `link_name` is the link label — what people see onscreen.

The idea is that you will have more than one link in your navigation bar — but you'll see how this works in the text that follows. To make this navigation bar useful, you're going to need to replicate the existing links — or the ones that you deem necessary. You can also add your own links. Incidentally ` ` is an entity that represents a non-breaking space.

Example

```
<style>
.navigationbar {background-color: yellow; position: absolute;
left: 50%; top: 127px; margin-left: -400px; width: 800px; height:
26px}
</style>
```

If you're confident working with CSS, you can place the `.navigationbar` class definition in with the rest of your style sheet. If you don't know what I'm talking about, just place the preceding code as is in the About Me section of your MySpace profile.

Place this code in the "Who I'd like to meet" section of your profile:

```
<div class="navigationbar">
<table width="800" height="26" border="0" cellspacing="0"
cellpadding="0">
<tr valign="middle">
<td align="center">
<a href="http://home.myspace.com/index.cfm?fuseaction=user">
Home</a>
 | 
<a href="http://mail.myspace.com/index.cfm?fuseaction=mail.inbox">
Mail</a>
 | 
<a href="http://blog.myspace.com/index.cfm?fuseaction=blog
.controlcenter">Blog</a>
 | 
<a
href="http://forum.myspace.com/index.cfm?fuseaction=messageboard
.categories">Forum</a>
 | 
<a href="http://groups.myspace.com/index.cfm?fuseaction=groups
.categories">Groups</a>
</tr>
</td>
</table>
</div>
```

How It Will Look

You'll see that the navigation bar in Figure 23-1 has five of the existing links: Home, Mail, Blog, Forum, and Groups.

FIGURE 23-1: Notice the revised navigation bar at the top of the page.

Adding More Links

It's fairly straightforward to add another link; just add the following lines of code after the last link, but before the `</tr>` tag:

```
 | 
<a href="link_url">link_name</a>
```

Replace *link_url* with the URL of the web page you want to link to, and replace *link_name* with the name of the web page. If you want to add more of the existing links — for example, the Videos link — simply click the Movie link, and you will be taken to the MySpace Video, which should look something like this:

```
http://vids.myspace.com/index.cfm?fuseaction=vids.home
```

Your new link will look like this:

```
 | 
<a href=" http://vids.myspace.com/index.cfm?fuseaction=vids.home">
Videos</a>
```

With some links, such as Video links, you'll get a weird looking link that contains your token:

```
http://collect.myspace.com/index.cfm?fuseaction=film&Mytoken=
12BAFA2F-774A-12E6-7AA1120A555DF12832402894
```

Simply delete everything after and including the ampersand (&) symbol, so that it looks like this:

```
http://collect.myspace.com/index.cfm?fuseaction=film
```

Changing the Separator

As you'll see, each link is separated by a | symbol, but you can change this simply by inserting your preferred character in between each link. If you want to use a question mark as the separator, you can use this code:

```
 | 
```

which would become

```
 ? 
```

Changing the Link Style

You can change the style and size of the fonts of the links by creating a style definition for the text in the navigation bar. For example, you could create a new class called .navigationtext, which you would place in the style sheet in the About Me section of MySpace.

```
<style>
.navigationbar {background-color: yellow; position: absolute;
left: 50%; top:127px; margin-left: -400px; width: 800px; height:
26px;}
.navigationtext {font-family: Trebuchet MS, verdana, arial;}
</style>
```

And then you would apply the new style to the links themselves. This code would be placed in the "I'd like to meet" section of your MySpace profile.

```
<div class="navigationbar">
<table width="800" height="26" border="0" cellspacing="0"
cellpadding="0">
<tr valign="middle">
<td align="center">
<a class="navigationtext"
href="http://home.myspace.com/index.cfm?fuseaction=user">Home</a>
 | 
<a class="navigationtext"
href="http://mail.myspace.com/index.cfm?fuseaction=mail.inbox">
Mail</a>
 | 
<a class="navigationtext"
href="http://blog.myspace.com/index.cfm?fuseaction=blog
.controlcenter">Blog</a>
 | 
<a class="navigationtext"
href="http://forum.myspace.com/index.cfm?fuseaction=messageboard
.categories">Forum</a>
 | 
<a class="navigationtext"
href="http://groups.myspace.com/index.cfm?fuseaction=groups
.categories">Groups</a>
</tr>
</td>
</table>
</div>
```

If you look carefully in Figure 23-2 you'll see that the link font has been changed to Trebuchet MS.

Fixing Positioning Problems

If for some reason the navigation bar doesn't quite cover up the existing bar (for example if MySpace has made some changes to the basic profile since this book was written) you can move the navigation bar up and down by adjusting the "top" property, which in the preceding code has a value of 127px.

It's also worth bearing in mind that different browsers do render CSS in different ways. At the time of this writing, the Navbar code works perfectly with Internet Explorer and Firefox, but it doesn't quite work on the Macintosh Safari browser.

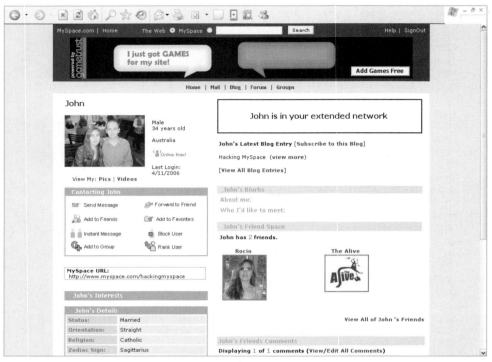

FIGURE 23-2: It's also possible to change the link text font.

Wrapping Up

Changing the navigation bar is a hack that allows you to make a significant change to your profile in terms of influencing where visitors to your profile go next. Don't forget that you can also make adjustments to the design of the navigation bar to suit your taste, and even add links that aren't in the original navigation bar.

Miscellaneous Hacks

This chapter is a collection of interesting hacks that you might want to try out in your profile. The hacks aren't so involved that they deserve an entire chapter, but they create some cool effects that are worthy of a mention.

You'll learn everything from how to create your own custom online now icon to how to move your contact table to how to complete a very simple hack that flips your profile.

The most exciting thing of all is that this is just a taste of all the amazing hacks you'll find out there on the Internet.

Creating a Custom Online Now Icon

If someone visits your profile while you're logged into your MySpace account an online now icon is shown next to your picture. This nifty hack allows you to change that icon to your own design.

If you don't want to go through the hassle of creating your own icon, you can simply type "online now icon myspace" into Google and you come across a number of web sites that offer free online now icons. However, if you want to create your very own online now icon, here's how to do it.

First, you need to create an 80-pixel-wide by 20-pixel-high GIF image, which can be either static or animated. You can use GIMP to do this.

1. Start GIMP and select File ➪ New.

2. In the Create a New Image dialog box, type **80** in the Width text box and **20** in the Height text box. You now have a blank canvas on which to develop your new icon.

You've already used GIMP a number of times, so I won't go step-by-step in this instance. To make up an animated GIF icon, follow a similar process to that outlined in Chapter 12. If you want to use my example GIF, you'll find it on the companion web site for this book at www.myspaceismyplace.com — the file name is onlinenow.gif. Figure 24-1 shows how the icon looks in GIMP.

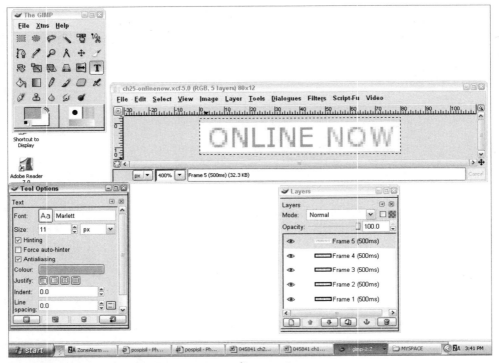

FIGURE 24-1: You can use GIMP to create an online now icon.

Once you've created the GIF file, you'll need to upload it to an image hosting web site (refer to Chapters 8 and 9). At the end of the process you should have a URL that links to your image. For the sample that follows, I'll be using this URL: *http://i45.photobucket.com/ albums/f93/pospisil/onlinenow.gif*.

This link probably won't work by the time the book appears so you'll need to use your own image and URL. Here's the code to place the online now icon into your MySpace profile:

```
<style>
table table table td.text div img {visibility: hidden;}
table table table td.text div{background-
image:url("http://image_url"); background-repeat:no-repeat;}
table table table td.text table table div img {visibility: visible;}
table table table td.text table table div { background-image: none;}
</style>
```

Here, *image_url* is the URL that links to your new icon.

The first line of code hides the original online now icon. The second line of code places your new icon as a background in the place of the old icon. The last two lines stop your new icon from appearing under the photos of your friends in the Friends Space of your profile.

Example

```
<style>
table table table td.text div img {visibility: hidden;}
table table table td.text div{background-
image:url("http://i45.photobucket.com/albums/f93/pospisil/onlinenow.
gif"); background-repeat: no-repeat;}
table table table td.text table table div img {visibility: visible;}
table table table td.text table table div { background-image: none;}
</style>
```

Place the preceding code into the About Me section of your profile. Don't forget to replace *http://i45.photobucket.com/albums/f93/pospisil/onlinenow.gif* with your own URL.

Figure 24-2 shows how the icon will look in the actual profile.

FIGURE 24-2: The new online now icon is in place.

Changing the Color of the Browser Scrollbar

The following code allows you to change the color of the browser window's scrollbar. As you'll see, the code makes use of a number of scrollbar properties to effect the color change. These properties work with Internet Explorer only.

```
<STYLE>
body {scrollbar-face-color: color;
scrollbar-highlight-color: color;
scrollbar-darkshadow-color: color;
scrollbar-arrow-color: color;
scrollbar-track-color: color;
scrollbar-3dlight-color: color;
scrollbar-shadow-color: color;}
</STYLE>
```

Here, *color* is the color of that particular scrollbar feature. Use the color table in Appendix A to pick out appropriate colors.

Example

```
<style>
body {scrollbar-face-color: Salmon;
scrollbar-highlight-color: Silver;
scrollbar-darkshadow-color: SlateBlue ;
scrollbar-arrow-color: MediumBlue ;
scrollbar-track-color: SeaShell;
scrollbar-3dlight-color: Snow;
scrollbar-shadow-color: MediumSlateBlue;}
</style>
```

Place this code in the About Me section of your MySpace profile.

Adding a Scrollbar to Your Blurb

This little hack puts all the sections following About Me — including Who I'd like to meet, Friend Space, and Friends Comments — into a section with its own scroll window.

```
<style>
.blurbscroll {width: width_value; height: height_value; overflow:
scroll;}
</style>
<div class="blurbscroll"><table><tr><td><table><tr><td></div>
```

Here, *width_value* is the width of the scroll box area you want to create and *height_value* is the height of the scroll box. The width of the About Me area is 435 pixels, so it's best to make the width this size or less.

The real key to this hack is the `overflow` property. It specifies what happens if there's too much content for a particular element. The `scroll` value specifies that if there is too much content the browser displays scrollbars so that the content can be viewed.

Example

```
<style>
.blurbscroll {width: 435px; height: 400px; overflow: scroll;}
</style>
<div class="blurbscroll"><table><tr><td><table><tr><td></div>
```

Add this code at the end of your About Me section. Everything below this code will be in a scrollbar. If you're confident working with CSS you can place the `.blurbscroll` class definition in with the rest of your style sheet. If you don't know what I'm talking about, just place the code as is:

As you can see in Figure 24-3, this little hack can make your profile look a little more interesting. You'll need some text in your blurb section in order to be able to see this hack.

You'll need to use a manual submit button to enter this code — Chapter 25 describes how to do this.

FIGURE 24-3: You can have some scrollbars in your blurb section, too.

Flipping Your Profile

This simple hack flips your profile so that the left side is on the right, and vice versa. This hack uses the `direction` property, which is primarily used to switch text from left-to-right to right-to-left, but can also be applied to the tables that make up your MySpace profile. This code should be placed in the About Me section of your profile.

```
<style>
table {direction: rtl;}
table table table {direction: ltr;}
</style>
```

As you'll see in Figure 24-4, the table looks quite different, despite the relatively simple code.

FIGURE 24-4: Flipping your profile is a very easy makeover.

The World of MySpace Codes

After reading this chapter, you should have a good idea of how to use different codes in your profile. While I've tried to give a good overview of some of the different codes available, I've really only scratched the surface. There are plenty of sites — on both MySpace groups and the wider Internet — where you will find amazing codes. Some examples:

- **bbz** (groups.myspace.com/bbz): A great site that contains both tutorial and codes for virtually everything you can imagine. Highly recommended.

- **Free Code Source** (www.freecodesource.com): A general code site that contains quite a lot of useful MySpace code, some of which is drawn from bbz.

- **DivSpace The Remix** (groups.myspace.com/divspace2): An "HTML Militia" offering various codes.

You can also check the companion web site to this book at www.myspaceismyplace.com, which has links to these web sites and more.

Moving Your Contact Table

The contact table can be very easily repositioned by adjusting the .contactTable class, which can be used to specify a position.

```
<style>
.contactTable { position: absolute; top: top_value;  left: 50%;
margin-left: horizontal_value; z-index: 1; }
</style>
```

Here, `top_value` is used to control the vertical position of the table, and can be expressed as a percentage of the HTML page or as a number of pixels from the top of the browser window.

`horizontal_value` is used to control the horizontal position of the table, and working this out is a little more complex. Whereas the top of a web page is always fixed, the edge of the left and right sides of a web page can vary depending on the size of the browser window. To get around this problem, this code uses the `left` property to place the section in the center of the page, and then the `margin-left` property to position the section relative to the center of the page. This is quite a nifty work around, and once you understand this principle, it's actually quite simple.

Example

```
<style>
.contactTable { position: absolute; top: 300;  left: 50%; margin-
left: 100px; z-index: 1;}
</style>
```

Place this in the About Me section of your profile — you can also place the class definition directly into your style guide if you feel confident doing this.

You'll notice in Figure 24-5 that this code places the contact box so that it lines up with the right side of the profile. How does this work?

FIGURE 24-5: The contact box has been moved to the right side of the profile.

Because the standard MySpace profile is about 800 pixels wide, if you place something in the middle (using `left: 50%;`) and then move it 400 pixels to the left of that centered position (using `margin-left: -400px;`), you'll be able to roughly line up the element to the left side of the profile. To align the box to the right side, you need to know that the contact box is

300 pixels wide (easily found out by searching the profile source code for `.contactTable` style). For the contact box to be aligned with the right edge, it needs to be placed 300 pixels from the right side of the profile, or 100 pixels from the middle. That's why I set `margin-left` to 100px.

Try this code:

```
<style>
.contactTable { position: absolute; top: 510px;  left: 50%;
margin-left: -375px; z-index: auto;}
</style>
```

Figure 24-6 shows how I've now placed the contact table in a new position at the bottom of the profile. Note that in order to get it to align with the left edge of where the profile actually starts I've had to allow a margin of 25 pixels (−400 + 25 = −375).

FIGURE 24-6: Here the contact table is tucked into the bottom left of the screen.

Wrapping Up

While none of the hacks in this chapter are earth shattering by any means, they are fun, and give you a small taste of the hacks you'll come across if you start looking online. You'll find some pointers on where to find more hacks in the World of MySpace Codes sidebar.

Div Overlays

Div overlays are the Holy Grail of MySpace customization. Most of the hacks you've looked at so far simply allow you to modify the standard MySpace profile. Div overlays, on the other hand, allow you to build a completely new profile from the ground up.

This chapter brings together a number of different concepts that I have covered in other chapters of the book. If you really want to understand how to create your own Div layouts, you're going to need to understand HTML (Chapters 3 and 4) and CSS (Chapters 6 and 7).

As you may recall from Chapter 4, the `<div>` tag allows you to mark out logical divisions in your HTML code. You can think of the opening and closing tags (`<div>` and `</div>`) as containers for your content. Using CSS, you can style and position whatever lies within `<div>` tags in almost any way you see fit.

The Div overlay technique entails hiding the existing standard profile and then using Divs to build a new profile over the top of the old one — literally.

This involves adding back whatever MySpace functionality you require, as well as your own features. Your new-found freedom comes with limits — whatever you do, don't cover up the advertising banner. And you always need to include a "Block me" link in your new profile.

To help you understand how Div overlays work, you'll be working through an example Div overlay by Nick Edwards (www.myspace.com/twisted_spikes), who has very kindly allowed me to use his Div overlay code here. You should also check out Nick's MySpace group where there are a number of Div templates available (groups.myspace.com/freedivs).

The steps involved in creating a Div overlay include:

1. Erasing or hiding the existing profile

2. Restyling the parts you want to keep

3. Styling new profile sections

4. Placing new Div sections in the profile

5. Within these Divs, placing the new content and linking to the standard MySpace functions

By the time you've completed this chapter you should be able to easily customize Div templates you come across, if not create your very own Div layouts.

Tip   In some of the code in this chapter you'll come across properties containing `!important`. Typically, the latest rule (lowest in the stylesheet) takes precedence over earlier rules. When a property contains `!important`, that property takes precedence no matter what comes after.

Hiding the Existing Profile

The next few sections of this chapter basically explain what the Div code does and how it works. I'll present the code that you actually put into your profile a little later in the chapter.

In order to place your Div overlay, you need to hide the existing MySpace profile. You can do this by making the color of the elements transparent, by hiding them using the `visibility` property, or by stopping them from being displayed using the `display` property. The `visibility` property has two relevant attributes — `hidden` and `visible`. When an element is hidden, it simply means it isn't shown. When an element is visible, it is shown.

The following code hides much of the old profile, but leaves a few sections — such as the navigation bar — visible. As you'll see, it styles tags and sequences of tags to hide and unhide different parts of the profile.

```
<style>
table {visibility: hidden;}
div table tbody tr td a.navbar,
table tr td script {visibility: visible;}
table tbody tr td a.navbar,
table tbody tr td input,
{visibility: visible;}
body table td {background-color: transparent;}
table tr td div div {display: none;}
div table tbody tr td form input,
div table tbody tr td a img,
div table tbody tr td div a,
div table tbody tr td
{visibility: visible; color: red;}
</style>
```

If you place the preceding code into your existing MySpace profile, you'll see that it blanks out most of your profile.

Restyling the Existing Text

Now that you've hidden most of the existing profile, it's time to style the parts that you want to keep. Before each section of code I've noted what that line actually does — don't include this comment in your code. By changing the properties in this code, you can customize these elements in the way that you see fit.

This code would normally sit in the About Me section of your profile:

```
<style>
```

The following styles the way that links appear in the profile (i.e., red italic):

```
a, a.man, a:link, a:visited{color: CC0033; font-size: 10pt; font-weight: bold; text-decoration: underline; font-style: italic;}
```
The following styles the way links appear when they are active and changes the color of the links to green when you hover the pointer over them.

```
a:active, a:hover {color: 00ff00; font-size: 10pt; font-weight: bold; text-decoration: underline; font-style: italic;}
```

This line makes a lot of commonly used tags white, while making their backgrounds transparent:

```
td, table, tr, span, li, p, div, textarea, div {color: ffffff; font-weight: bold; font-decoration:none; font-style: normal; background-color: transparent;} td, li, p, div, textarea {border-color: ffffff;} table {border-color: ffffff;}
```

This section styles the navigation bar links — the first makes all the links in the navigation bar 12pt and bold, the second line makes the links red, the third line makes active links green, the fourth line makes visited links green, and the fifth line makes the links red when the cursor hovers over the top:

```
a.navbar{font-size: 12pt; font-weight: bold;}
a.navbar:link{color: CC0033;}
a.navbar:active{color: 00ff00;}
a.navbar:visited{color: 00ff00;}<<This is the code for green
a.navbar:hover{color: CC0033;}<<This is the code for red
```

These classes are used to define the way that text appears in the profile:

```
.nametext{font-size: 12pt; color: ffffff; font-weight: bold;}
.blacktext10{font-size: 12pt; color: CC0033; font-weight: bold;}
.blacktext12{font-size: 12pt; color: ffffff; font-weight: bold;}
.btext, .itext, .text{font-size: 12pt; color: ffffff; font-weight: bold;}
.orangetext15{font-size: 12pt; color: ffffff; font-weight: bold;}
.lightbluetext8{font-size: 12pt; color: ffffff; font-weight: bold;}
.tmz_imp{font-family: arial; color: ff0000; font-weight: bold;}
a img{border-color: ffffff; border-width: 2px; border-style: solid;}
a:hover img{border-color: 00ff00; border-width: 2px; border style: solid;}
```

This section specifies the color of the scroll bar:

```
body{scrollbar-arrow-color: ffffff; scrollbar-track-color:000000;
scrollbar-highlight-color: ffffff; scrollbar-base-color: ffffff;
scrollbar-face-color: 000000; scrollbar-shadow-color: ffffff;
scrollbar-darkshadow-color: ffffff;}
```

This makes the background color of the body black:

```
body {background-color: 000000;}
</style>
```

Styling the New Sections

Now that you've created a blank canvas, it's time to start setting up the new profile. In this section of code you're going to create a number of new classes that you'll use to style elements that will make up the new overlay.

This code would also sit in the About Me section of your MySpace profile:

```
<style>
```

The .background class positions and styles the background:

```
.background {background-color: transparent; position: absolute;
left: 50%; top: 190px;
margin-left:-460px; width: 960px; height: 600px; z-index: 0;
visibility: visible !important; overflow: none; color: white;}
```

The .row class styles the row block that appears in the upper section of the Div overlay:

```
.row {background-color: 000000; position: absolute; left: 50%;
top: 190px; margin-left: -400px; width: 750px; height: 75px;
visibility: visible !important; overflow: none; color: white;
border:2px solid white;}
```

The .column1 class styles the left column of the Div overlay. It specifies that the background color is black, and it specifies its position, width and height, and border:

```
.column1 {background-color: 000000; position: absolute; left: 50%;
top: 300px; margin-left: -400px; width: 350px; height: 500px;
visibility: visible !important; overflow: auto; color :white;
border: 2px solid white;}
```

The .column2 class styles the row block that appears in the upper section of the Div overlay:

```
.column2 {background-color:000000; position: absolute; left: 50%;
top: 300px; margin-left: 0px; width: 350px; height: 500px;
visibility: visible !important; overflow: auto; color: white;
border: 2px solid white;}
</style>
```

If you want to change how the row and columns appear in your profile, make the changes by adjusting the .row, .column1, and .column2 classes.

If you wanted to add more sections (or boxes) you would need to create some additional classes in this section, specifying where the section would appear, along with its color, size, width, height and so on. Most of the properties here are pretty obvious, and I've covered them in previous chapters — the really tricky part is the positioning of the sections (I covered positioning in Chapter 7).

You can see in the preceding code that the Y or vertical coordinate is specified using the top property and is simply the number of pixels that the section is from the top of the profile, For example the .column2 class contains the property top: 300px, which simply means that column 2 will be 300 pixels from the top of the page. That's easy. But the Y or horizontal coordinate is not so straightforward. Because the top of a web page is always fixed, the edge of the left and right sides of a web page can vary depending on the size of the browser window. To get around this problem, this code uses the left property to place the section in the center of the page, and then the margin-left property to position the section relative to the center of the page. This is quite a nifty workaround, and once you understand this principle, it's actually quite simple.

Because the standard MySpace profile is about 800 pixels wide, if you place something in the middle (using left: 50%;) and then move it 400 pixels to the left of that centered position (using margin-left: -400px), you'll be able to roughly line up the element to the left side of the profile.

When you're working out the positions of different elements, you need to be conscious of their dimensions and how they will relate to other elements. Take a look at the two column classes in the preceding code (.column1 and .column2) — they're each 350 pixels wide, and column 1 is placed 400 pixels to the left of the center (using the margin-left property), which leaves a nice 50-pixel gutter between the two columns. If you have a look at the .row class, you'll notice it's 750 pixels wide, which is the same width as the two columns and gutter (350 pixels + 350 pixels + 50 pixels).

As an example, pretend you want to add a bottom row to this layout. You need to specify a class called .row2 (which you can very easily base on the existing .row class) and adjust it so that it appeared at the bottom of the page. Now you know that the columns are placed 300 pixels from the top of the page, and that each column is 500 pixels in height.

However, if you placed the bottom row 800 pixels from the top of the page, it would be right up against the columns. It would be nice to have the bottom column the same distance from the bottom of the columns as the top row is from the top of the columns. You can work out this distance because you know that the top of the columns is 300 pixels from the top of the page. You also know that the top row (from looking at the .row class) is 190 pixels from the top of the page and that it is 75 pixels high, which means that its bottom edge is 35 pixels from the top of the columns (300 pixels – 190 pixels – 75 pixels = 35 pixels). So this means that if you placed the second row 835 pixels from the top of the page, it would appear to be the same distance from the columns as the top row.

Here's what the class definition would look like:

```
.row2 {background-color: 000000; position: absolute; left: 50%;
top: 835px; margin-left: -400px; width: 750px; height: 75px;
visibility: visible !important; overflow: none; color: white;
border:2px solid white;}
```

> **Tip**
> While putting together this layout I thought I had stumbled onto some kind of incompatibility issue when the second row, discussed previously, did not display correctly in Firefox. Having a careful look at the code I realized I had typed "top: 835 px;" rather than "top: 835px;" — the difference was a single space. Explorer seems to tolerate these kinds of bad habits, but Firefox does not.

Hiding Comments

This next part really is a hack. It's a small section of code that hides any comments that may be in your profile. Place the code into the "Who I'd like to meet" section of your profile. Use the standard Edit Profile function to do this. Safe Mode won't work because the submit button is hidden when the code is previewed. In the "old days" you would have had to use something called manual submit to make the changes, but this is not necessary now.

```
<style> .comt {display: none; visibility: hidden;} </style>
<div class="comt"> <table> <tbody> <tr> <td> <table> <tbody> <tr>
<td>
```

This code opens a Div that hides comments.

Placing New Content

Now this is when the fun starts — it's here where you recreate your profile. What you're doing in this code is applying the classes you defined earlier to a series of `<div>` tags. This is why this technique is often referred to as Divs or Div overlays. The code that follows is actually just the shell of your new profile. To actually remake your profile you'll have to add content and links between the `<div>` tags. I'll get back to that shortly.

This code would be placed into the Interests section of your profile.

```
<div class="background">
</div>
<div class="column1">
Content for column 1
</div>
<div class="column2">
Content for column 2
</div>
```

```
<div class="row">
Content for row - you might want to insert contact table links
here
</div>
```

If you've done everything as described, your profile should now look like Figure 25-1.

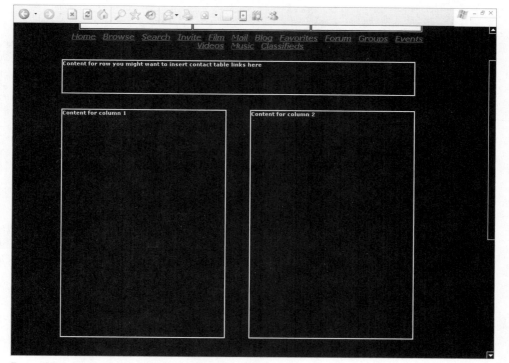

FIGURE 25-1: You've just created your first div layout.

If you want to add more Divs you need to set up additional classes (as discussed in "Styling the New Sections") and you also need to add some Divs here. For example, if you want to add another row, you need to set an additional class — as we did for .row2 in "Styling the New Sections" — and apply it to a Div:

```
<div class="row2">
Content for row 2
</div>
```

You can see in Figure 25-2 that there is now an extra row at the bottom of the profile. With a little careful planning it's not hard to build up a very interesting layout.

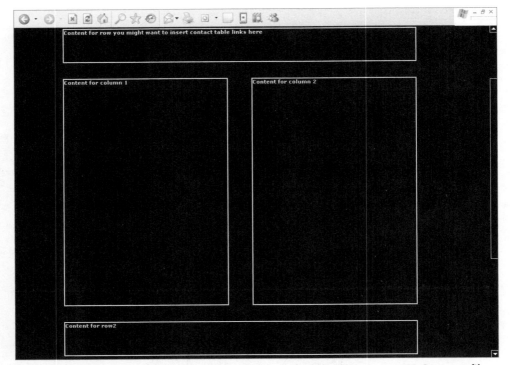

FIGURE 25-2: With some planning, it's easy to change and add sections to your MySpace profile.

Restoring the Contact Table Functions

Now that you've got the shell of our Div template up and running it's time to restore some of the functionality of the original MySpace profile. What this involves is creating links back to the standard MySpace functions such as Send Message and Add to Friends.

In case it's not obvious, when you click the Send Message icon in the standard profile, you're actually clicking a link to:

```
http://mail.myspace.com/index.cfm?fuseaction=mail.message&
friendID=xxxxxxxx
```

Here, *xxxxxxxx* is your eight-digit friend ID number, which is the last eight digits of the URL that appears in your browser when you click View My: Profile from your home page.

Here are the link addresses to the functions found in the contact box:

- **Send Message:**

```
mail.myspace.com/index.cfm?fuseaction=mail.message&friendID=xxxxxxxx
```

- **Forward To Friend:**

```
mail.myspace.com/index.cfm?fuseaction=mail.forward&friendID=xxxxxxxx&f
=forwardprofile
```

- **Add To Friends:**

```
collect.myspace.com/index.cfm?fuseaction=invite.addfriend_verify&
friendID=xxxxxxxx
```

- **Add to favorites:**

```
collect.myspace.com/index.cfm?fuseaction=user.addToFavorite&friendID=
xxxxxxxx&public=0
```

- **Instant Message:**

```
chat.myspace.com/index.cfm?fuseaction=messenger&strDestinationUserID=
33492166&sendType=0
```

- **Block User:**

```
collect.myspace.com/index.cfm?fuseaction=block.blockUser&userID=
xxxxxxxx
```

- **Add To Group:**

```
groups.myspace.com/index.cfm?fuseaction=groups.addtogroup&friendID=
xxxxxxxx
```

- **Rank User:**

```
collect.myspace.com/index.cfm?fuseaction=RateImage.UserRating&UserID=
xxxxxxxx
```

To make this into something useful, you would add some links to the row Div, which might look like this:

```
<div class="row">
<p class="contactbarmain">WELCOME TO JOHN'S MYSPACE PROFILE</P>
<p class="contactbarmain">
<a class="contactbar"
href=http://mail.myspace.com/index.cfm?fuseaction=mail.forward&
friendID=33492166&f=forwardprofile>Send message</a> | 
<a class="contactbar"
href=http://mail.myspace.com/index.cfm?fuseaction=mail.message&
friendID=33492166>Forward to friend</a> | 
<a class="contactbar" href=http://collect.myspace.com/
index.cfm?fuseaction=invite.addfriend_verify&friendID=33492166>Add
to friends</a> | 
```

```
<a class="contactbar" href=http://collect.myspace.com/
index.cfm?fuseaction=user.addToFavorite&friendID=33492166&public=
0>Add to favorites</a> | 
<a class="contactbar" href=
http://chat.myspace.com/index.cfm?fuseaction=messenger&
strDestinationUserID=33492166&sendType=0>Instant
message</a> | 
<a class="contactbar" href= http://collect.myspace.com/
index.cfm?fuseaction=block.blockUser&userID=33492166&public=0>
Block user</a> | 
<a class="contactbar"
href=http://groups.myspace.com/index.cfm?fuseaction=groups
.addtogroup&friendID=33492166>Add to group</a> | 
<a class="contactbar" href=
http://collect.myspace.com/index.cfm?fuseaction=RateImage
.UserRating&UserID=33492166>Rank</a>
</p>
</div>
```

This would, of course, sit in the Interests section of your MySpace profile, and would replace the skeleton code that was there, which looked like this:

```
<div class="row">
Content for row - you might want to insert contact table links
here
</div>
```

Don't forget that you'll need to replace *33492166* with your own friend ID number — that ID number works with my profile only. Notice that I have used a couple of classes — .contactbarmain and .contactbar. The first class, .contactbarmain, is basically used to center the heading and the links, whereas .contactbar is used to style the actual links (and you'll see I created a style for each possible link condition).

I created a specific class for the contact links because I wanted them to look different from the other links on the page. Here are the classes that I created. They would need to be added to the style sheets in the About Me section.

```
a.contactbar {font-size:8pt; font-weight: normal; color: ffffff;
font-style: normal;}
a.contactbar:link {font-size:8pt; font-weight: normal; color:
ffffff; font-style: normal;}
a.contactbar:active {font-size:8pt; font-weight: normal; color:
ffffff; font-style: normal;}
a.contactbar:visited {font-size:8pt; font-weight: normal; color:
ffffff; font-style: normal;}
a.contactbar:hover {font-size:8pt; font-weight: normal; color:
00ff00; font-style: normal;}
.contactbarmain {text-align: center;}
```

With the Div code and classes correctly placed, the profile now has contact functions back in place — as you can see in Figure 25-3. I used a very simple approach to add the links back to MySpace, but you can create buttons using GIF images to make your profile more interesting.

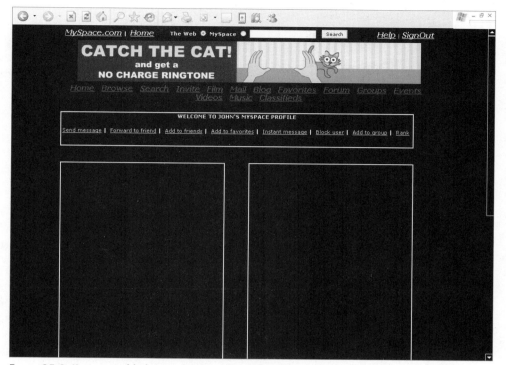

FIGURE 25-3: I've now added some functionality back into the MySpace profile.

If you want to be clever, you can design your own icons for your contact table that you could then link back to the contact table functions.

Tip If in the future some of these URLs change, it's quite easy to work out the new ones. Just click the function you're trying to work out and the new URL is displayed in your browser when you're taken to that function.

Placing Your Profile Picture

Now that you have complete control of your profile, you can place your profile picture wherever you want and make it whatever size you want. The simplest way to place a new profile picture is to upload a new profile image to a hosting site (see Chapters 8 and 9) and to link back to it (see Chapter 10).

You're going to place your new profile image, along with your personal information, in column 1, which means it will be placed between the `<div>` tags you placed in the Interests section:

```
<div class="column1">
Content for column 1
</div>
```

Here's what it looks like when I place my profile picture in column 1:

```
<div class="column1">
<p class= "profilecaption">
<img src="http://i45.photobucket.com/albums/f93/pospisil/
Mainprofile.jpg" border="0" alt="Pospisil Family"></p>
<p class= "profilecaption ">The Pospisil family - Baby Grace, John
and Rocio</p>
</div>
```

You can see that I have created a new class, `.profilecaption`, that basically allows me to center both the image and the caption. The class looks like this, and needs to be added to the style sheet in the About Me section:

```
.profilecaption {text-align: center;}
```

Placing the image inside the `<p class= "profilecaption">` tags might seem like a round-about way of centering the image, but because of the vagaries of CSS you can't center the `<img>` tag directly, unless you do something like use the clunky and obsolete `<center>` tag.

Adding Personal Information and Profile Functions

To add your personal information, you basically write it directly into the profile. In this example, you're going to write it into column 1 under the profile picture. You're going to add back these functions (the corresponding links are shown):

- **View Pics:**

  ```
  http://viewmorepics.myspace.com/index.cfm?fuseaction=user
  .viewPicture&friendID=xxxxxxxx
  ```

- **View Videos:**

  ```
  http://vids.myspace.com/index.cfm?fuseaction=vids.uservids&
  friendID=xxxxxxxx
  ```

- **View All Friends:**

  ```
  http://home.myspace.com/index.cfm?fuseaction=user.viewfriends&
  friendID=xxxxxxxx
  ```

- **Add Comment:**

  ```
  http://comments.myspace.com/index.cfm?fuseaction=user&
  circuitaction=viewProfile_commentForm&friendID=xxxxxxxx
  ```

- **View All Comments:**

  ```
  http://comments.myspace.com/index.cfm?fuseaction=user
  .viewComments&friendID=xxxxxxxx
  ```

- **View All Blogs:**

```
http://blog.myspace.com/index.cfm?fuseaction=blog.ListAll&
friendID=xxxxxxxx
```

- **Subscribe To Blog:**

```
http://blog.myspace.com/index.cfm?fuseaction=blog
.ConfirmSubscribe&friendID=xxxxxxxx
```

- **View All Groups:**

```
http://groups.myspace.com/index.cfm?fuseaction=groups
.myGroups&UserId=xxxxxxxx
```

Your friends ID number will need to replace the *xxxxxxxx*.

Here's how I integrated these functions into my profile. You'll note that I have added the code to the end of the existing code in the column 1 <div> code. I've also added some personal details.

```
<div class="column1">
<p class=profilecaption>
<img src="http://i45.photobucket.com/albums/f93/pospisil/
Mainprofile.jpg" border="0" alt="Pospisil Family"></p>
<p class="profilecaption">The Pospisil family  Baby Grace, John
and Rocio</p>
<p class="profiletext"> I'm a married 34-year-old-male living in
Australia</p>
<p class="profiletext"> View my <a class="profilelink"
href=http://viewmorepics.myspace.com/index.cfm?fuseaction=
user.viewPicture&friendID=33492166>photos</a> or view my <a
class="profilelink" href=
http://vids.myspace.com/index.cfm?fuseaction=vids.uservids&
friendID=33492166>videos</a>, alternatively you can <a
class="profilelink" href=
http://comments.myspace.com/index.cfm?fuseaction=user&
circuitaction=viewProfile_commentForm&friendID=33492166>add a
comment</a>, or you can <a class="profilelink" href=
http://comments.myspace.com/index.cfm?fuseaction=user.viewComments
&friendID=33492166>view my comments</a>.</P>
<p class="profiletext">Read my <a class="profilelink" href=
http://blog.myspace.com/index.cfm?fuseaction=blog.ListAll&friendID
=33492166>blog</a>, and if you like it, <a class="profilelink"
href= http://blog.myspace.com/index.cfm?fuseaction=
blog.ConfirmSubscribe&friendID=33492166>subscribe</a>. View my <a
class="profilelink"
href=http://home.myspace.com/index.cfm?fuseaction=user.viewfriends
&friendID=33492166>friends</a>. View my <a class="profilelink"
href=http://groups.myspace.com/index.cfm?fuseaction=groups
.myGroups&UserId=33492166>groups</a>.
```

```
</p>
</div>
```

Notice the `.profiletext` and `.profilelink` classes in this code. Basically these classes are designed to ensure that the links and the text in the profile are consistent. This is what the classes look like (obviously they would be sitting in the style sheet in the About Me section of the profile):

```
.profiletext {text-align: left; margin-left: 10px; font-weight:
normal;}
a.profilelink {font-size:8pt; font-weight: normal; color: ffffff;
font-style: normal;}
a.profilelink:link {font-size:8pt; font-weight: normal; color:
ffffff; font-style: normal;}
a.profilelink:active {font-size:8pt; font-weight: normal; color:
ffffff; font-style: normal;}
a.profilelink:visited {font-size:8pt; font-weight: normal; color:
ffffff; font-style: normal;}
a.profilelink:hover {font-size:8pt; font-weight: normal; color:
00ff00; font-style: normal;}
```

When you view your profile (see Figure 25-4), you'll notice that it is beginning to take shape.

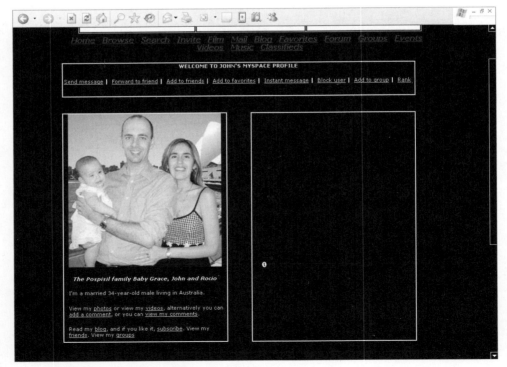

FIGURE 25-4: The profile is now starting to take shape.

Adding Content

You're going to use the second column to add content — basically the same stuff that usually appears in the About Me, Who I'd like to meet, and Interests sections of MySpace. This content needs to be placed in-between these <div> tags (which are located in the Interests section of the profile:

```
<div class="column2">
Content for column 2
</div>
```

I also created an additional class, .profileheading, which looks like this (and of course sits in the style sheet):

```
.profileheading {align: center; font-weight: bold;}
```

Here's the code for the column 2 Div — you'll notice it's mostly information about me.

```
<div class="column2">
<p class="profileheading">About Me</p>
<p class="profiletext">I'm a writer based in Sydney Australia. I
was happily going about my life until late in 2005 when my agent
in New York gave me the opportunity to pitch a book about MySpace
to John Wiley and Sons - yes the same Wiley that publishes the
Dummies guides.</p>
<p class="profiletext">Obviously, this was an opportunity of a
lifetime, so I promptly put together a proposal, and before I knew
it, I had a contract to write Hacking MySpace: Mods and
customizations to make MySpace your space</p>
<p class="profiletext">The book is designed to give novices an
understanding of HTML and CSS, and some step-by-step guides on how
to use these to completely customize their profile.</p>
<p class="profiletext">So right now I'm trying to meet an
impossible deadline! Feel free to drop me a note, or to add me as
your friend.</p>
<p class="profileheading">Interests</p>
<p class="profiletext">What, with this book, a six-month-old baby,
and a real job, you think I have time for interests? At the moment
I'm very busy, but when this book is finished I'm looking forward
to spending more time with my adorable daughter, Grace, and my
equally adorable wife, Rocio.</p>
<p class="profileheading">You may know me from</p>
<p class="profiletext">Well, OK, you probably don't know me. I've
written a number of books here in Australia, including How to buy
a computer (that went through four editions), How to get more from
your computer, and How to start a small business in the real
world. All of these were published by CHOICE Books. I am also
the founding publisher of <a class="profilelink" href=
http://www.freeaccess.com.au >FREE ACCESS</a> and <a
class="profilelink" href= http://www.total-image.com.au >TOTAL
IMAGE</a> magazines. Also check out my <a class="profilelink"
```

```
href= http://www.cogentinsights.com >blog</a> about the
blogosphere.</p>
</div>
```

Well, as you can see from Figure 25-5, you're finished — or are you?

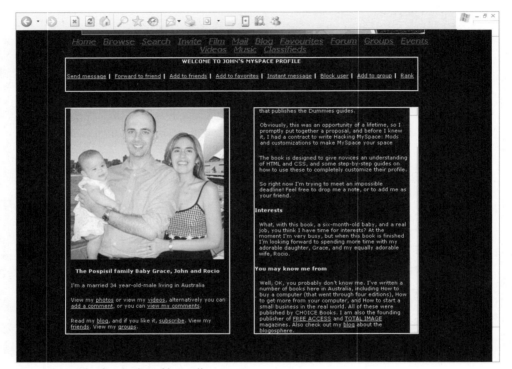

FIGURE 25-5: The finished profile, well not quite

Customizing the Template

Well, Nick's Div template has served me very well, but now that I've put in the content, there are a few opportunities to make it work a little better for this particular situation.

Adjusting the Divs

You'll notice that a scrollbar has appeared on the second column because I've put in too much content. I think that looks a bit messy, so the solution is to make the columns a little longer.

The other change I'd like to make is to get rid of the white borders. Both of these problems can be easily solved by restyling the `.column1`, `.column2`, and `.row` classes, which are printed here and, as you'll recall, are located in the About Me section:

```
.row {background-color: 000000; position: absolute; left: 50%
;top: 190px; margin-left:-400px; width: 750px; height: 75px;
visibility: visible !important; overflow: none; color: white;
border: 2x solid white}
.column1 {background-color: 000000; position: absolute; left: 50%
; top: 300px; margin-left: -400px; width: 350px; height: 500px;
visibility: visible !important; overflow: auto; color: white;
border: 2px solid white;}
.column2 {background-color: 000000; position: absolute; left: 50%;
top: 300px; margin-left: 0px; width: 350px; height: 500px;
visibility: visible !important; overflow: auto; color: white;
border: 2px solid white;}
```

To make the columns longer, you simply need to change `height: 500px;` to `height: 600px;` in the `.column1` and `.column2` classes.

To hide the borders, simply change `border: 2px solid white;` to `border: 0px none;` in all three classes.

I'd also like to make the navigation bar links a little smaller. Simply find this class in the About Me section:

`a.navbar{font-size: 12pt; font-weight: bold;}` and change `font-size: 12pt;` to `font-size: 8pt;`

Also add the `font-size: 8pt;` property to the following navbar styles:

```
a.navbar:link{color: cc0033;}
a.navbar:active{color: 00ff00;}
a.navbar:visited{color: cc0033;}
a.navbar:hover{color: 00ff00;}
```

Changing Colors

Now that you've adjusted the Divs and the navigation bar, you might also take the opportunity to change the colors. I developed a color scheme using Color Scheme Generator 2 (`wellstyled.com/tools/colorscheme2/index-en.html` — see Chapter 27 for more information) and decided to use the following color scheme:

- **Background color:** BFE5FF (a light blue color)
- **Text:** 00497B (a dark blue color)
- **Links:** 171BB5 (a purple blue color)
- **Headlines and captions:** 0069B0 (a medium blue)

Now that I know what colors I want, I need to go through the style sheet to identify which classes need to be adjusted.

Background Color

If you look halfway through the style sheet, you come across this line:

```
body {background-color: 000000;}
```

This styles the body tag so that its background is black. To change it to the light blue color, you need to change it to:

```
body {background-color: bfe55ff;}
```

If you preview the profile, you find that the profile background has changed, but not backgrounds of the Div boxes. As you'll recall, the Div boxes are styled by these classes:

```
.row {background-color: 000000; position: absolute; left: 50%
;top: 190px; margin-left: -400px; width: 750px; height: 75px;
visibility: visible !important; overflow:none; color: white;
border: 0px none}
.column1 {background-color: 000000; position: absolute; left: 50%
; top: 300px; margin-left: -400px; width: 350px; height: 600px;
visibility:visible !important; overflow: auto; color: white;
border: 0px none;}
.column2 {background-color: 000000; position: absolute; left: 50%;
top: 300px; margin-left: 0px; width: 350px; height: 600px;
visibility:visible !important; overflow:auto; color:white; border:
0px none;}
```

Let's change the attribute for the `background-color` property in each of these classes from `000000` to `transparent` — so that it looks like this `background-color: transparent;`.

All you have to do now is to change the body tag color to change the background for the whole profile. It also means you could easily slot in a background image if you wanted to (see Chapter 13).

Text Color

If you view the profile after changing the background color you see that it's now very difficult to read the profile text because the white text is difficult to read on the light blue background. So let's change it.

You might remember that you created a new style for your profile text:

```
.profiletext {text-align: left; margin-left: 10px; font-weight:
normal;}
```

To change the color, let's add the following color property, `color: 00497b;`, so that the `.profiletext` class looks like this:

```
.profiletext {text-align: left; margin-left: 10px; font-weight:
normal; color: 00497b;}
```

Links

If you were to view the profile after changing the `.profiletext` class, you would see that while it's now possible to read the text, the links are still white and difficult to read. So find the following styles and change `color: ffffff;` to `color: 171bb5;`.

```
a.profilelink {font-size:8pt; font-weight: normal; color: ffffff;
font-style: normal;}
a.profilelink:link {font-size:8pt; font-weight: normal; color:
ffffff; font-style: normal;}
a.profilelink:active {font-size:8pt; font-weight: normal; color:
ffffff; font-style: normal;}
a.profilelink:visited {font-size:8pt; font-weight: normal; color:
ffffff; font-style: normal;}
```

Leave the following style as it is:

```
a.profilelink:hover {font-size:8pt; font-weight: normal; color:
00ff00; font-style: normal;}
```

When the mouse is over the link, the link turns green (although you may want to change the color to something more attractive).

You also need to change the color in the navigation bar styles to `171bb5;`.

```
a.navbar:link{color: CC0033; font-size: 8pt;}
a.navbar:active{color: 00ff00; font-size: 8pt;}
a.navbar:visited{color: CC0033;font-size: 8pt;}
```

However, leave the following style the same:

```
a.navbar:hover{color: 00ff00;font-size: 8pt;}
```

The color changes when the mouse passes over the top. And finally, you need to change the color of the contact links by changing the color property to 171bb5 in the following styles.

```
a.contactbar {font-size:8pt; font-weight: normal; color: ffffff;
font-style: normal;}
a.contactbar:link {font-size:8pt; font-weight: normal; color:
ffffff; font-style: normal;}
a.contactbar:active {font-size:8pt; font-weight: normal; color:
ffffff; font-style: normal;}
a.contactbar:visited {font-size:8pt; font-weight: normal; color:
ffffff; font-style: normal;}
```

And again, leave this style as is:

```
a.contactbar:hover {font-size:8pt; font-weight: normal; color:
00ff00; font-style: normal;}
```

We can have saved space for a number of these classes as they share exactly the same properties; for example, you can group three of the contact bar classes as follows:

```
a.contactbar, a.contactbar:link, a.contactbar:active {font-
size:8pt; font-weight: normal; color: ffffff; font-style: normal;}
```

I've left each class separate in this demonstration to make it easier to follow, and also to make it easier for fine-tune each class.

Headlines and Captions

To change the headlines and captions to a medium blue color, simply add this property — color: 0069b0; — to the following classes:

```
.contactbarmain {text-align: center;}
.profilecaption {text-align: center; font-style: italic;}
.profileheading {align: center; font-weight: bold;}
```

Browser Scrollbars

Because you've gone through so much trouble to get the colors right, you may as well change the scrollbar colors. Find this style in the stylesheet:

```
body{scrollbar-arrow-color: ffffff; scrollbar-track-color:000000;
scrollbar-highlight-color: ffffff; scrollbar-base-color: ffffff;
scrollbar-face-color: 000000; scrollbar-shadow-color: ffffff;
scrollbar-darkshadow-color: ffffff;}
```

Let's apply the color scheme to the scrollbars, so the style looks like this:

```
body{scrollbar-arrow-color: 0069b0; scrollbar-track-color: 0069b0;
scrollbar-highlight-color: 0069b0; scrollbar-base-color: bfe5ff;
scrollbar-face-color: bfe5ff; scrollbar-shadow-color: 00497b;
scrollbar-darkshadow-color: 00497b;}
```

The Finished Div Overlay

The whole point of this exercise is to demonstrate how a Div template works, and how to customize a pre-made template. If you understand the CSS that I've been using, you should actually be in a position now to create your own Div overlays. Figure 25-6 shows the finished profile.

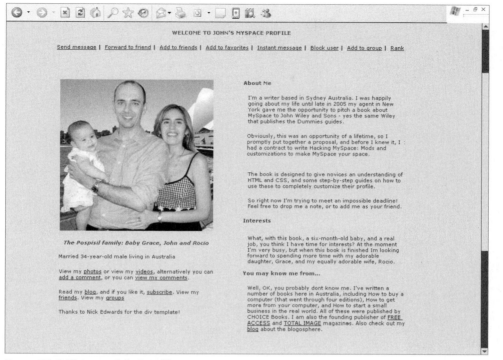

FIGURE 25-6: The completed profile

The Original Code

To help you see how the original code has been modified, here is the original Div template, along with the template that was customized. The idea is that you would start with the original code and customize it in much the same way that you have customized it in these chapters. Thanks again to Nick Edwards for allowing me to use his code for this tutorial. This code is available from www.myspaceismyplace.com so please don't try to type it in yourself.

This code would be placed in the About Me section:

```
<style>

table {visibility: hidden;}
div table tbody tr td a.navbar,
table tr td script {visibility: visible;}
table tbody tr td a.navbar,
table tbody tr td input,
{visibility: visible;}
```

```
body table td {background-color: transparent;}
table tr td div div {display: none;}
div table tbody tr td form input,
div table tbody tr td a img,
div table tbody tr td div a,
div table tbody tr td
{visibility: visible; color: red;}a, a.man, a:link, a:visited
{color: cc0033; font-size: 10pt; font-weight: bold; text-
decoration: underline; font-style: italic;}
a:active, a:hover {color: 00ff00; font-size: 10pt; font-weight:
bold; text-decoration: underline; font-style: italic;}
td, table, tr, span, li, p, div, textarea, div {color: ffffff;
font-weight: bold; font-decoration: none; font-style: normal;
background-color: transparent;} td, li, p, div, textarea {border-
color: ffffff;} table {border-color: ffffff;}
a.navbar {font-size: 12pt; font-weight: bold;}
a.navbar:link {color: cc0033;}
a.navbar:active {color: 00ff00;}
a.navbar:visited {color: cc0033;}
a.navbar:hover {color: 00ff00;}
.nametext {font-size: 12pt; color: ffffff; font-weight: bold;}
.blacktext10 {font-size: 12pt; color: cc0033; font-weight: bold;}
.blacktext12 {font-size: 12pt; color: ffffff; font-weight: bold;}
.btext, .itext, .text {font-size: 12pt; color: ffffff; font-
weight: bold;}
.orangetext15 {font-size: 12pt; color: ffffff; font-weight: bold;}
.lightbluetext8 {font-size: 12pt; color: ffffff; font-
weight:bold;}
.tmz_imp {font-family: arial; color: ff0000; font-weight: bold;}
a img {border-color: ffffff; border-width: 2px; border-style:
solid;}
a:hover img {border-color: 00ff00; border-width: 2px; border
style: solid;}
body {scrollbar-arrow-color: ffffff; scrollbar-track-color:
000000; scrollbar-highlight-color: ffffff; scrollbar-base-color:
ffffff; scrollbar-face-color: 000000; scrollbar-shadow-color:
ffffff; scrollbar-darkshadow-color: ffffff;}
body {background-color: 000000;}
.background {background-color: transparent; position: absolute;
left: 50%; top: 190px;
margin-left:-460px; width: 960px; height: 600px; z-index: 0;
visibility: visible !important; overflow: none; color: white;}
.row {background-color: 000000; position: absolute; left: 50%;
top: 190px; margin-left: -400px; width: 750px; height: 75px;
visibility: visible !important; overflow: none; color: white;
border:2px solid white;}
.column1 {background-color: 000000; position: absolute; left: 50%;
top: 300px; margin-left: -400px; width: 350px; height: 500px;
visibility: visible !important; overflow: auto; color :white;
border: 2px solid white;}
```

```
.column2 {background-color: 000000; position: absolute; left: 50%;
top: 300px; margin-left: 0px; width: 350px; height: 500px;
visibility: visible !important; overflow: auto; color: white;
border: 2px solid white;}
</style>
```

This code would need to be placed in the "Who I'd like to meet" section of your profile:

```
<style> .comt {display: none; visibility: hidden;} </style>
<div class="comt"> <table> <tbody> <tr> <td> <table> <tbody> <tr>
<td>
```

This code would be placed in the Interests section of your profile:

```
<div class="background">
</div>
<div class="column1">
Content for column 1
</div>
<div class="column2">
Content for column 2
</div>
<div class="row">
Content for row - you might want to insert contact table links
here
</div>
```

The Modified Code

Here's the template code with all of the changes I've discussed in this chapter. This code fits in the About Me section of the profile. Please don't try to type in the code yourself — it's available at www.myspaceismyplace.com:

```
<style>
table {visibility: hidden;}
div table tbody tr td a.navbar,
table tr td script {visibility: visible;}
table tbody tr td a.navbar,
table tbody tr td input,
{visibility: visible;}
body table td {background-color: transparent;}
table tr td div div {display: none;}
div table tbody tr td form input,
div table tbody tr td a img,
div table tbody tr td div a,
div table tbody tr td
{visibility: visible; color: red;}
a, a.man, a:link, a:visited{color: cc0033; font-size: 10pt; font-
weight: bold; text-decoration: underline; font-style: italic;}
```

```
a:active, a:hover {color: 00ff00; font-size: 10pt; font-weight:
bold; text-decoration: underline; font-style: italic;}
td, table, tr, span, li, p, div, textarea, div {color: ffffff;
font-weight: bold; font-decoration: none; font-style: normal;
background-color: transparent;} td, li, p, div, textarea {border-
color: ffffff;} table {border-color: ffffff;}
a.navbar {font-size: 8pt; font-weight: bold;}
a.navbar:link {color: 171bb5; font-size: 8pt;}
a.navbar:active {color: 171bb5; font-size: 8pt;}
a.navbar:visited {color: 171bb5; font-size: 8pt;}
a.navbar:hover {color: 00ff00; font-size: 8pt;}
.nametext {font-size: 12pt; color: ffffff; font-weight: bold;}
.blacktext10 {font-size: 12pt; color: cc0033; font-weight: bold;}
.blacktext12 {font-size: 12pt; color: ffffff; font-weight: bold;}
.btext, .itext, .text {font-size: 12pt; color: ffffff; font-
weight: bold;}
.orangetext15 {font-size: 12pt; color: ffffff; font-weight: bold;}
.lightbluetext8 {font-size: 12pt; color: ffffff; font-weight:
bold;}
.tmz_imp {font-family: arial; color: ff0000; font-weight: bold;}
a img {border-color: ffffff; border-width: 2px; border-style:
solid;}
a:hover img {border-color: 00ff00; border-width: 2px; border
style: solid;}body {scrollbar-arrow-color: 0069b0; scrollbar-
track-color: 0069b0; scrollbar-highlight-color: 0069b0; scrollbar-
base-color: bfe5ff; scrollbar-face-color: bfe5ff; scrollbar-
shadow-color: 00497b; scrollbar-darkshadow-color: 00497b;}
body {background-color: bfe5ff;}
.background {background-color: transparent; position: absolute;
left: 50%; top: 190px; margin-left:-460px; width: 960px; height:
600px; z-index:0; visibility: visible !important; overflow: none;
color: white;}
.row {background-color: transparent; position: absolute; left:
50%; top: 190px; margin-left:-400px; width: 750px; height: 75px;
visibility: visible !important; overflow: none; color: white;
border:0px none}
.column1 {background-color: transparent; position: absolute; left:
50% ; top: 300px; margin-left:-400px; width: 350px; height: 600px;
visibility: visible !important; overflow: auto; color: white;
border:0px none;}
.column2 {background-color: transparent; position: absolute; left:
50%; top: 300px; margin-left:0px; width: 350px; height: 600px;
visibility: visible !important; overflow: auto; color: white;
border:0px none;}
a.contactbar {font-size: 8pt; font-weight: normal; color: 171bb5;
font-style: normal;}
a.contactbar:link {font-size: 8pt; font-weight: normal; color:
171bb5; font-style: normal;}
a.contactbar:active {font-size: 8pt; font-weight: normal; color:
171bb5; font-style: normal;}
```

```
a.contactbar:visited {font-size: 8pt; font-weight: normal; color:
171bb5; font-style: normal;}
a.contactbar:hover {font-size: 8pt; font-weight: normal; color:
00ff00; font-style: normal;}
.contactbarmain {text-align: center; color: 0069b0;}
.profilecaption {text-align: center; font-style: italic; color:
0069B0;}
.profiletext {text-align: left; margin-left: 10px; font-weight:
normal; color: 00497b;}
.profileimage {align: center;}
.profileheading {align: center; font-weight: bold; color: 0069b0;}
a.profilelink {font-size: 8pt; font-weight: normal; color: 171bb5;
font-style: normal;}
a.profilelink:link {font-size: 8pt; font-weight: normal; color:
171bb5; font-style: normal;}
a.profilelink:active {font-size: 8pt; font-weight: normal; color:
171bb5; font-style: normal;}
a.profilelink:visited {font-size: 8pt; font-weight: normal; color:
171bb5; font-style: normal;}
a.profilelink:hover {font-size: 8pt; font-weight: normal; color:
00ff00; font-style: normal;}
</style>
```

This code would go into the "Who I'd like to meet" section of your profile:

```
<style> .comt {display: none; visibility: hidden;} </style>
<div class="comt"> <table> <tbody> <tr> <td> <table> <tbody> <tr>
<td>
```

This code would go into the Interests section of your profile:

```
<div class="background">
</div>
<div class="column1">
<p class=profilecaption>
<img
src="http://i45.photobucket.com/albums/f93/pospisil/Mainprofile
.jpg" border="0" alt="Pospisil Family"></p>
<p class="profilecaption">The Pospisil family Baby Grace, John and
Rocio</p>
<p class="profiletext"> Married 34 year-old-male living in
Australia</p>
<p class="profiletext"> View my <a class="profilelink"
href=http://viewmorepics.myspace.com/index.cfm?fuseaction=user
.viewPicture&friendID=33492166>photos</a> or view my <a
class="profilelink" href=
http://vids.myspace.com/index.cfm?fuseaction=vids.uservids&
friendID=33492166>videos</a>, alternatively you can <a
class="profilelink" href=
http://comments.myspace.com/index.cfm?fuseaction=user&
circuitaction=viewProfile_commentForm&friendID=33492166>add a
```

```
comment</a>, or you can <a class="profilelink" href=
http://comments.myspace.com/index.cfm?fuseaction=user.viewComments
&friendID=33492166>view my comments</a>.</P>
<p class="profiletext">Read my <a class="profilelink" href=
http://blog.myspace.com/index.cfm?fuseaction=blog.ListAll&friendID
=33492166>blog</a>, and if you like it, <a class="profilelink"
href=
http://blog.myspace.com/index.cfm?fuseaction=blog.ConfirmSubscribe
&friendID=33492166>subscribe</a>. View my <a class="profilelink"
href=http://home.myspace.com/index.cfm?fuseaction=user.viewfriends
&friendID=33492166>friends</a>. View my <a class="profilelink"
href=http://groups.myspace.com/index.cfm?fuseaction=groups.
myGroups&UserId=33492166>groups</a>
</p>
</div>
<div class="column2">
<p class="profileheading">About Me</p>
<p class="profiletext">I'm a writer based in Sydney Australia. I
was happily going about my life until late in 2005 when my agent
in New York gave me the opportunity to pitch a book about MySpace
to John Wiley and Sons - yes the same Wiley that publishes the
Dummies guides.</p>
<p class="profiletext">Obviously, this was an opportunity of a
lifetime, so I promptly put together a proposal, and before I knew
it, I had a contract to write Hacking MySpace: Mods and
customizations to make MySpace your space</p>
<p class="profiletext">The book is designed to give novices an
understanding of HTML and CSS, and some step-by-step guides on how
to use these to completely customize their profile.</p>
<p class="profiletext">So right now I'm trying to meet an
impossible deadline! Feel free to drop me a note, or to add me as
your friend.</p>
<p class="profileheading">Interests</p>
<p class="profiletext">What, with this book, a six-month-old baby,
and a real job, you think I have time for interests? At the moment
I'm very busy, but when this book is finished I'm looking forward
to spending more time with my adorable daughter, Grace, and my
equally adorable wife, Rocio.</p>
<p class="profileheading">You may know me from</p>
<p class="profiletext">Well, OK, you probably don't know me. I've
written a number of books here in Australia, including How to buy
a computer (that went through four editions), How to get more from
your computer, and How to start a small business in the real
world. All of these were published by CHOICE Books. I am also the
founding publisher of <a class="profilelink" href=
http://www.freeaccess.com.au >FREE ACCESS</a> and <a
class="profilelink" href= http://www.total-image.com.au >TOTAL
IMAGE</a> magazines. Also check out my <a class="profilelink"
href= http://www.cogentinsights.com >blog</a> about the
blogosphere.</p>
</div>
```

```
<div class="row">
<p class="contactbarmain">WELCOME TO JOHN'S MYSPACE PROFILE</P>
<p class="contactbarmain">
<a class="contactbar"
href=http://mail.myspace.com/index.cfm?fuseaction=mail.forward&
friendID=33492166&f=forwardprofile>Send message</a> | 
<a class="contactbar"
href=http://mail.myspace.com/index.cfm?fuseaction=mail.message&
friendID=33492166>Forward to friend</a> | 
<a class="contactbar"
href=http://collect.myspace.com/index.cfm?fuseaction=invite
.addfriend_verify&friendID=33492166>Add to friends</a> | 
<a class="contactbar"
href=http://collect.myspace.com/index.cfm?fuseaction=user.
addToFavorite&friendID=33492166&public=0>Add to
favorites</a> | 
<a class="contactbar" href=
http://chat.myspace.com/index.cfm?fuseaction=messenger&
strDestinationUserID=33492166&sendType=0>Instant
message</a> | 
<a class="contactbar" href=
http://collect.myspace.com/index.cfm?fuseaction=block.blockUser&
userID=33492166&public=0>Block user</a> | 
<a class="contactbar"
href=http://groups.myspace.com/index.cfm?fuseaction=groups.
addtogroup&friendID=33492166>Add to group</a> | 
<a class="contactbar" href=
http://collect.myspace.com/index.cfm?fuseaction=RateImage.
UserRating&UserID=33492166>Rank</a>
</p>
</div>
```

Adding Back Your Comments and Friends

Well now that I actually look at my profile, I realize that I miss not having my friends and comments. Fortunately, it's not too hard to add them back. Thanks to Nick Edwards from Free Divs (groups.myspace.com/freedivs) and Mark McDonald and the team from BBZ (groups.myspace.com/bbz) for their assistance with this code.

The first step is to delete the existing code in the "Who I'd like to meet" section of your MySpace profile, and replace it with the following code:

```
<DIV class="comt"><table><tr><td><table><tr><td>
```

When you view your profile, you'll find that you can see your friends and comments behind your Divs. That's okay because the Div that places the friends and comments is styled using a class called .comt. By adding a class definition called .comt to our style guide, you can position the comments and friends anywhere you like. Add this to your style guide:

```
.comt {visibility: visible; width: 740px; height: 800px;
position: absolute; top: 910 px; left: 50%; margin-left: -375px;
overflow: visible;}
```

You see that your friends and comments are now below your Div profile. You can position your friends and comments anywhere you like by adjusting the top and margin-left properties. If you would like your Friends and Comments to appear in a scrolling box, just change the overflow property to auto, and use the height property to set the height of the scrolling box. Obviously, you can also adjust the width of this section by adjusting the width property.

Now I need to tidy up some of the fonts. I've included a comment above each section of code. Don't include this comment when you enter the code into your profile. The code is printed without comments a little further on.

This code adjusts the text in the Friends and Comments section:

```
.comt td b, .redtext, .comt td td td b, .comt td td td table,
.btext, .comt td td td  {font-size: 11px; color: 00497b; text-
decoration: none; font-style: normal; font-weight: normal;}
```

This code adjusts the links in the Friends and Comments section:

```
.comt td td td a, .comt td a, .comt td b a, .redlink, .comt td td
td a:visited, .comt td a:visited, .comt td b a:visited,
a.redlink:visited {font-size: 11px; color: 171bb5; text-
decoration: none; font-style: normal; font-weight: normal;}
```

This code adjusts the links in the Friends and Comments section when a mouse pointer is over the top:

```
.comt td td td a:hover, comt td a:hover, .comt td b a:hover,
a.redlink:hover {font-size: 11px; color: 0069b0; text-decoration:
none; font-style: normal; font-weight: normal;}
```

This code adjusts the data and time text, and also adjusts the width of the comment area:

```
.blacktext10 {font-size: 11px; color: 00497b; display: block;
width: 500px; text-align: left;}
```

This code adjusts the headings:

```
.orangetext15 {font-size: 11px; font-weight: bold; color: 0069b0;}
.comt td td td table {width: 150px;}
```

This code adjusts the width of the comment text area:

```
.comt td td td b, .comt td td td {width: 400px; border: none;}
```

Here's the code again without the comments:

```
.comt td b, .redtext, .comt td td td b, .comt td td td table,
.btext, .comt td td td  {font-size: 11px; color: 00497b; text-
decoration: none; font-style: normal; font-weight: normal;}
.comt td td td a, .comt td a, .comt td b a, .redlink, .comt td td
td a:visited, .comt td a:visited, .comt td b a:visited,
a.redlink:visited {font-size: 11px; color: 171bb5; text-
decoration: none; font-style: normal; font-weight: normal;}
```

```
.comt td td td a:hover, comt td a:hover, .comt td b a:hover,
a.redlink:hover {font-size: 11px; color: 0069b0; text-decoration:
none; font-style: normal; font-weight: normal;}
.blacktext10 {font-size: 11px; color: 00497b; display: block;
width: 500px; text-align: left;}
.orangetext15 {font-size: 11px; font-weight: bold; color: 0069b0;}
.comt td td td table {width: 150px;}
.comt td td td b, .comt td td td {width: 400px; border: none;}
```

This code would be placed in your style sheet, which should be located in the About Me section of your MySpace profile.

The Easy Way Out

Of course, if you find all of this too difficult, a much easier way is to use an online friends generator, which allows you to specify how you would like the Friends and Comments section to look, and then generates the code for you. A couple generators that you might want to check out are:

- **R4wr** (r4wr.com/friends/): Offers a very complete friends generator that started life as a Top Eight generator

- **HTmate.com** (www.htmate2.com/friendgen/): Another friends generator that is worth checking out

Div Layers

Our example Div is fairly straightforward — three Divs over a background — but what if you wanted to overlap Divs, so that you had layers of Divs, rather than Divs just floating separately. Often this technique is useful if you want to show text or images over an existing image (which might be set in a Div). The question arises: How do you specify which Div layer should be on top, and which one should be below. This is where the z-index property comes to the rescue. Its format is:

```
Selector {z-index: value;}
```

Here, value specifies the order in which an element is displayed. Elements with higher z-index values are shown on top of elements with lower values. Please note that z-index works only with elements that have been positioned.

Div Generators

If you want a quick hit, there are a number of Div generators that take a lot of the hard work out of creating the Div overlay. For example, the BBZ's overlay generator at www.bbzspace.com/overlay/ allows you to select from a number of Div layouts, as well as to set colors and border styles. You will still need to use your CSS skills to add the content to the Div overlay, but it's certainly a much quicker way to get started. And you can always modify the overlay if you want something a bit different.

Working with Other Sites

Now that you've developed your own Div overlay, you can seamlessly link your profile directly to your Photobucket (www.photobucket.com) or Flickr (www.flickr.com) photo album, or to your blog at an external blogging service such Blogger (www.blogger.com). There's no need necessarily to rely on the services offered by MySpace.

Group Divs

You can also create Div layouts for your groups. Thank you to Mark McDonald and the team from BBZ (groups.myspace.com/bbz) for providing the code for this section. The following code places a Div over the existing group profile but leaves the members and the forums intact underneath.

When you create a Group Div based on the code here, you won't be able to access the Edit Group button that normally appears when a moderator views one of his or her groups. For this reason, before you start playing with Group Divs, it's vitally important that you go to your Edit Your Myspace Group page and save it as a favorite in your browser. That way you'll be able to easily edit your profile when your Edit Group button disappears (and it will if you use this code).

Don't forget to save the Edit Your Myspace Group page as a favorite in your browser, otherwise you won't be able to edit your group!

The Descriptions section is the only place in the Groups Editor that accepts HTML code, so all code needs to be placed there. Also, <style> tags don't seem to be recognized so you can't use classes. All styles actually need to be applied inside the Div tags.

```
</td></tr></table></td></tr></table></td></tr></table></div><div
style="position: absolute; left: 50%; top:125px; margin-left:
-400px; height: 800px; width: 800px; background-color:white;
border:transparent 0px white;">

Place content here

</div>
```

You would obviously place your content where it says "Place content here." While you could possibly put all your content into one big Div (like the preceding one), the reality is that you're more likely to place your content into a number of Divs. For more Div layers, add this code into the description after the existing code:

```
<div style="position: absolute; top: 400px; left: 50%; margin-
left: -200px; height: 60px; width: 500px; background-color:
yellow;">

Place more content here

</div>
```

You can add as many Divs as you want. Obviously you can adjust the size and position of each Div, and you can change properties such as background-color. Finally, after you've placed all of your Divs, place this code:

```
<div style="display: none;">
```

Don't forget that you'll also need to add back the Group links; otherwise your group won't have all the functionality it normally has. You'll need to work out your group ID number, a nine-digit number that appears in the URL at the top of your browser if you go to the group from your home page (as opposed to just typing in the group URL). For example, the URL that appears when I visit my group is:

```
http://groups.myspace.com/index.cfm?fuseaction=groups.
groupProfile&groupid=102476972&Mytoken=D75262D3-5F6E-8FEF-
ED3EAEEE8EFE304B60886660
```

The group ID number is the nine-digit number just after groupid=. In this case, the group ID is 102476972.

Here are the URLs of the links that you will need to include in your Div overlay. Place your nine-digit group ID where you see *xxxxxxxx*.

- **Join:**

  ```
  groups.myspace.com/index.cfm?fuseaction=groups.join&groupID=
  xxxxxxxx
  ```

- **Invite Others:**

  ```
  groups.myspace.com/index.cfm?fuseaction=groups.groupInvite&
  groupID=xxxxxxxx
  ```

- **Resign:**

  ```
  groups.myspace.com/index.cfm?fuseaction=groups.resign&groupID=
  xxxxxxxx
  ```

- **Upload Image:**

  ```
  groups.myspace.com/index.cfm?fuseaction=groups.ImageForm&
  groupID=xxxxxxxx
  ```

- **Post Topic:**

  ```
  forum.myspace.com/index.cfm?fuseaction=messageboard.PostThread
  &groupID=xxxxxxxx
  ```

- **Post Bulletin:**

  ```
  bulletin.myspace.com/index.cfm?fuseaction=bulletin.edit&
  groupID=xxxxxxxx
  ```

- **Privacy:**

  ```
  groups.myspace.com/index.cfm?fuseaction=groups.privacy&
  groupID=xxxxxxxx
  ```

- **View Group Photos:**

  ```
  groups.myspace.com/index.cfm?fuseaction=groups.groupImages&
  groupID=xxxxxxxx
  ```

Don't forget that you'll need to turn them into links with an <a> link tag, so that the first link would look something like this:

```
<a href=http:// groups.myspace.com/index.cfm?fuseaction=groups.
join&groupID=102476972>Join</a>
```

Admittedly, this is a very barebones overview of developing a group Div, but if you've managed to develop a Div for your main profile by following this chapter, this should be enough information to get you started.

Using Flash in Your Profile

Sometimes when you come across an amazing profile, you might wonder how the person created it. Well usually a number of factors are at play. First the creator of the profile is very talented and has a lot of time on his or her hands. And second, if it involves amazing images and multimedia effects, it's usually done in Flash.

Macromedia Flash is a multimedia authoring program, which incidentally is now distributed by Adobe. Multimedia files created by Flash have a .swf extension. It's possible to play files directly from your profile, as long as you (and people visiting your site) have a Flash player installed — which 98 percent of people do because Windows XP comes bundled with a Flash

player. If your system doesn't have it installed, the Flash player can be downloaded from
www.adobe.com.

To actually create Flash multimedia, you'll need to purchase a program that allows you to
develop Flash movies. You choose the "real-thing" in either Flash Basic or Flash Professional,
now distributed by Adobe (www.adobe.com); or other commercial programs such as Swish
(www.swishzone.com), Koolmoves (www.koolmoves.com), or SWF Quicker 2.2
(www.sothink.com). Many of these programs are available for a free trial period, so you can
try out the software before you buy. This is also a good way of getting a taste of whether you
will want to go further with Flash.

A finished Flash movie has a .swf extension, whereas a Flash movie under development has an
.fla extension (this just means that you can open it up and edit it). Some Flash software allows
you to open .swf files.

To create a Flash-based web site, you would need to cover the existing profile using the techniques discussed in this chapter, and then launch the Flash animation from within a Div, which
you would need to size and position appropriately.

You could then use this code to load the Flash file:

```
<embed src="http://url.swf" menu="false" quality="high" width=x
height=y type="application/x-shockwave-flash" pluginspage="
http://www.adobe.com/products/flashplayer/">
```

Here, url is the URL of the Flash file, x is the width of your Flash movie, and y is the height
of your Flash movie.

MySpace is home to a number of groups dedicated to helping you learn more about Flash,
including the Copenhagen Flash Tutorials (groups.myspace.com/copenhagentutorials),
which features video and written tutorials on how to create Flash-based MySpace profiles.

You'll also find a lot of resources online simply by searching for "Flash tutorials" on Google.

Wrapping Up

Well, you've just made it through the most difficult chapter in this book. Div overlays open up
a whole new world of possibilities, which is why they're considered the ultimate hack. Be aware
that this chapter is just an introduction to Div overlays. Once you've mastered this technique,
the possibilities are limited only by your imagination.

Design and Photography

J ust because you can do something doesn't mean you have to do it, which is why this part of the book looks at design and what you need to consider when putting together a profile that will work at an aesthetic level as well as at a technical level. Good design, after all, is often quite minimalist — less equals more. Some of the best MySpace profiles are quite simple, but they have the right balance of technical innovation and stylish design.

It's very easy to forget that MySpace is primarily about communicating with other users, and so Chapter 26 looks at content — what messages you're going to publish to the world via your profile. The creators of some of MySpace's most outstanding profiles share their secrets in Chapter 27.

This section also looks at photography. A big part of the impact of any profile is its photographs, which involves taking good photographs in the first place and knowing how to use a photo editing package to correct any problems.

Sending the Right Message

MySpace is all about communicating — whether it's through your profile, your posts to forums and groups, or through your comments about other people's profiles.

The word "communicate" comes from the Latin "communis" or "common" — so when you communicate with someone you are trying to create commonality with that person by sharing information.

Writing 300 years before the birth of Christ, the Greek thinker Aristotle developed a model for oral communication that consisted of three elements: the speaker, the subject, and the person being addressed (the listener or the audience).

This might seem very obvious, but the reality is that many people approach the communications process from the point of view of "What do I have to say?" They seem to forget about the listener, but without a listener, there is no communication. Before planning the design of your profile page, it's a good idea to think about the message or purpose of your profile.

For the purpose of developing a communications model for MySpace, I'm going to build on Aristotle's model and consider four elements that you should look at when creating content for your profile. These elements include the following:

- **Purpose:** What is the purpose of your profile? What are you trying to achieve?

- **You:** That's right, you! You're the "speaker" after all, but don't forget that on MySpace you can choose who you want to be.

- **Audience:** Well, this is actually more like your target market — who is it that you're hoping to communicate with.

- **Content:** If you know what you're trying to achieve, you can work out what you need to say.

in this chapter

☑ Purpose

☑ You

☑ Audience

☑ Content

☑ The next step

Purpose

To some degree, the purpose of your profile shapes your message. If you're not absolutely clear about what the purpose of your profile is, you're going to have some serious problems developing content. If the purpose isn't absolutely clear, grab a piece of paper and a pencil and try writing answers to some of these questions to crystallize your purpose:

- What do you want your profile to achieve? What are your objectives?

- What do you want your profile to look like?

- What kind of comments do you want people to leave?

- What kind of people will your profile be attracting?

- What kind of friends do you want to make?

You

How you present yourself on MySpace is part of the communications process because it influences how your message is received.

How will you translate who you are into your MySpace profile? Or, do you want to create a MySpace persona that differs from your real-life persona? Is it dishonest to create a profile that doesn't match your real-life persona? Certainly there are situations where it is deceitful and clearly wrong. For example, if a 50-year-old male posed as a cool 18-year-old male in order to approach young women for some kind of gratification (whether real-world contact was made or not), that would clearly be wrong. On the other hand, there's nothing wrong with simply making yourself sound a little more interesting (or perhaps a little more cool) as long as you're being fundamentally honest about yourself. And by the way, most people are pretty good at detecting a fake — so even if you choose to create a completely misleading profile, most people will probably pick up that it's not real.

There's also another reason why you should think very carefully about how you present yourself online — you really don't want to attract inappropriate attention. It is a fact that some people do use MySpace in a predatory fashion to lure gullible people into inappropriate situations. Now while you shouldn't let the possibility of danger stop you from living the life that you want to live, that possibility does mean that it is important to be responsible about the kind of information and images you put online. You might think you look cool in your swimsuit, but it could also attract the attention of unsavory characters. Obviously, at the end of the day it's up to you how you present yourself, but you should be aware that not everyone has good intentions.

Audience

Now that you know why you want to create a profile, you can start to think about the kinds of people you would like to have visiting your profile and have as your friends. It's important to think about this before proceeding because having a good idea about your target audience will help you craft the right message.

As mentioned, if no one receives your message, no communication has taken place. Your message needs to take into account the needs and interests of your intended audience. You should also know that there will be some people who will view your profile who are not the intended audience, and because of the anonymity of the Internet, you might never know who they really are.

Keep in mind that you cannot be all things to all people; it's much easier to engage a smaller and well-defined audience with similar interests, than a large broad audience with a wide range of interests.

Content

Now that you know why you're developing a profile, and who you're trying to reach, you can start to think about developing the content — what it will be about and what form it will take. Of course there is an interrelationship between this step and designing your profile, but before you start working out designs, you need to know what content you are going to have to play with.

At this stage you should also start thinking about a theme. A theme is a unifying idea that brings together all the elements of your profile. The theme could be anything from your favorite movie, to a feeling, a color, or a more abstract concept such as "nature." Because your MySpace profile is all about expressing yourself, the theme should also be tied to your personality. Having a theme for your profile will help you to create a sense of consistency throughout.

For the purpose of developing a MySpace profile, there are a number of different types of content you should consider.

Main Profile Text

The main profile is essentially a summary of who you are, and you need to think carefully about what to include and what to exclude. Obviously, you should aim to be as interesting as possible, but at the same time keep in mind that a wide audience will be looking at your profile, and you don't want to divulge information that is inappropriate. That being said, you do need to provide some personal information about yourself; otherwise your profile will be dull and boring.

You'll also need to think carefully about the style of your writing, whether it's witty, serious, aloof, or otherwise. The style should reflect your personality (and the theme of your profile), or at the very least the persona you're trying to project.

If spelling is important to you, write your text in a word processor rather than directly into MySpace so that you can check spelling before placing your text in your profile. Using a word processor to compose the longer sections of your MySpace site first can help not only in keeping a copy of your original thoughts and writings on your PC, but it also helps you avoid retyping information in case the web page you are typing into accidentally gets closed, your computer freezes, or a blackout strikes!

Your Main Profile Image and Your Supporting Images

Often people's very first impressions of you are formed by your main profile image. That's why it's important to make sure this image is as flattering as possible. Please go to Chapter 28 for some ideas on how to take better photos, and Chapter 29 on how to edit your photos in GIMP. People often also browse the images in the View More Pics section of your profile, so it's important to make sure these images are up to par.

You also need to consider carefully what photos you post. They need to be aligned to the theme of your profile, and as already mentioned, you need to consider the wide audience of people who will be viewing your profile.

Blogs

In addition to the content for your main profile, you should also think about the kinds of content you'll need for your blog (if you choose to keep one). A blog is a great way to keep your profile fresh and relevant, but you do need to keep the blog updated regularly, and you need to try to write about something interesting. If you've got a purpose, and if you've developed a theme, you should find that the content of your blog follows naturally.

Once you've got your blog started, let your friends know about it. Read and subscribe to other blogs to help build your relationships with other bloggers, and to generate interest in your own blog.

Writing a Plan for Your Profile

If you've read this chapter and you still don't have much of an idea of what your profile is going to be about, the following planning exercise might help.

Planning can be very useful because it helps you save time by avoiding unnecessary steps. If you have a clear idea about what you want to do, you'll also find it faster to get going. Usually when people put together a profile, their planning process takes place subconsciously or on-the-fly — they just do their profile, and whatever comes out, comes out.

While this obviously works for some, what you're going to do here is to take this subconscious process and actually carry it out step-by-step. This will help you develop a clearer idea of what you're trying to achieve and how to get there, and also help you if you've gotten stuck.

Incidentally, if you're currently taking a business studies course (or if you've done one in the past) you'll notice that some of the concepts here have been lifted from the business world. Nevertheless, they work equally well for your MySpace profile as they do for business ventures. And just remember: This is all simply a tool to help you get to where you want to go.

continued

Take a blank piece of paper and write four headings: Vision, Mission, Objectives, and Strategies. Keep in mind that this is a process to help you understand what it is that you want to achieve with your profile. It might seem a bit pretentious to do all of this just for a profile, but bear with me, and you'll find that even just by writing down a few notes, you'll have a clearer idea of what it is that you're trying to achieve.

Under the Vision heading, write your thoughts on the following questions. How do you imagine your final profile will look after you've initially created it? If you like it, you can then imagine what your profile might be like after being online for 12 months. Write down how you think it will look after 12 months of updates, changes, comments from friends, and more. Write down what kinds of comments you think people might leave. What kind of people will your profile attract? What kind of friends might you make? Try to make your vision ambitious, but not impossible. Some examples might include:

- "To have a profile site with lots of photos of my friends and where friends and I meet and chat online."

- "To help my band become successful!"

Or in my case:

- "To create a profile that uses a Div overlay to tell the world about this book."

Under the Mission heading, write the mission or purpose of your profile. If you can, limit the mission to about one or two sentences. Try to answer the question "What do I want my profile to do on a day-to-day basis?" Your vision and mission may overlap, but the distinction is that the mission is what it has to do, whereas the vision can be a little more aspirational. An example of a mission statement might be:

- "My profile is a place where I can keep in touch with my real-world friends, as well as make new online friends."

Or:

- "My profile has the job of helping to increase the popularity of my band!"

Or in my case:

- "My profile should be a place where people can get in touch with me about this book on a daily basis."

Now by developing a vision and mission for your profile, you should have a pretty clear idea of what it is that your profile is about and what you need to do in order to realize your vision and achieve your purpose. Under the Objectives heading, write down what you want to achieve with your profile. Here are some sample objectives:

- "Create a profile that stands out."

- "Have at least 100 friends in the first three months."

continued

Writing a Plan for Your Profile *continued*

Now that you know what you want to do, it's time to work out how you're going to achieve those objectives. This is where strategy comes in. When developing a profile, there are three main activities you can undertake to achieve your objectives:

- **Profile appearance:** How your profile looks. This includes the design of your profile, as well as the mods and customizations that you apply to it. This is what most of this book is about. The appearance of your profile should be aligned with your vision and mission.

- **Content:** The images and text you place on the profile. Essentially, this is what visitors to your profile read and see.

- **Promotion:** These are the activities you undertake to get more people to your profile, which can mean participating in groups, leaving comments, and adding friends. But before you get to this point, you need to make sure your profile is just right.

Wrapping Up

The primary aim of this chapter is to suggest that you consider factors other than "what you want to say" when working out what you want to place on your MySpace profile. What is your target audience interested in? What will catch your audience's attention? These are the kinds of questions you should be asking yourself. Of course, engaging with your audience is difficult if you don't know what you want to say to them, and that's why it's also important to have a clear idea of what your profile is about — its purpose.

Profile Design for Maximum Impact

What makes good design? The truth is there's no right or wrong design, just design that works or doesn't work. If a certain design allows you to effectively send the right message to the intended audience, then you can call that a good design. When it comes to MySpace profiles, you often know right away whether a design is good or not. It's a number of characteristics that contribute to whether something works or doesn't — everything from the fonts, the composition of the page, the images used, the theme, and so on.

Talent, of course, plays a large part in developing a good design, but there are things that less-talented people like me can do to help ourselves along, and this chapter details a process that anyone can use to help develop a profile design.

The design process has six steps:

- Considering form and function
- Conceptualization
- Developing a color scheme
- Selecting fonts
- Selecting images
- Laying out your profile

In this chapter, you look at several outstanding MySpace profiles that everyone can learn from. Bear in mind that many of these outstanding profiles use Flash, which I discussed in Chapter 25.

Interestingly, several of the creators of the outstanding profiles featured in this chapter speak about how they went through several generations of profile development that started with relatively simple HTML and CSS coding, and then moved to Div overlays, and then to Flash.

Considering Form and Function

Many designers are guided by the idea that "form follows function." In the context of MySpace profile design, form consists of the elements — fonts, images, layout — that give the profile a look and feel. Function is the objective of the profile — for example, to promote a band or to meet friends.

In order for a profile to function, it needs form. And of course, form without function is just a decorative profile that doesn't do anything.

What all of this means is that how a profile looks and feels is driven by what its purpose is. If you're not sure what the purpose of your profile is, take some time to go back to Chapter 26, which has some exercises that will help you establish what you're doing in your profile.

Is the "form follows function" concept really important on MySpace? Absolutely! How many profiles have you come across that don't have a point? Quite a few I bet! What do you think when you see such a profile? Nothing! And that's the problem.

For these reasons, it's important to consider the function of the profile you're about to design before you start designing it. You should also consider the practical limitations of the project. I covered many of the key concepts in the last chapter, "Sending the Right Message." Some of the questions you might ask yourself are:

- Who is my target audience?
- What am I trying to get the target audience to do? Become my friend? Become a fan of my band?
- How much time do I have to spend developing the profile?
- What are the limitations of my skills?

At this early stage you might also start thinking about a theme for your profile. A theme is a single unifying idea that ties all the different elements of your profile together. It helps to give your profile a strong sense of unity and purpose, and you'll see that some of the featured profiles later in the chapter have quite strong themes.

Conceptualization

Conceptualization is basically brainstorming. It's about playing with different ideas and different layouts, and coming up with something that you like and think will work.

Despite the amazing design tools that you might have access to, the best way to conceptualize a MySpace profile (and indeed most design pieces) is to simply take a piece of paper and a pen, and sketch out your ideas.

One approach to brainstorming is simply to come up with as many ideas as you can, which basically means you might come up with as many as ten or twenty rough sketches. Try to get the proportions roughly right, but don't worry about details; the aim is to get the general idea of what it is that you would like to do down on paper.

Because you're sketching a design, you need to draw only representations of various elements — for example shaded boxes with parallel lines for text, or boxes with crosses through them for photos. While there are different conventions around, use whatever you're comfortable with. Figure 27-1 shows an example of what a sketch might look like.

Once you've got a rough idea of what the profile should look like, it's time to start thinking about colors, fonts, and images, and how they will fit into your design.

FIGURE 27-1: An example of a sketch to help you brainstorm your design

Developing a Color Scheme

Color is an important part of any design, and it can also be quite difficult. With color you can convey meaning, as well as emotion. Some combinations of colors work well together, while other combinations are quite uncomfortable. The challenge is to use a palette of colors that work well together, and at the same time support the theme or objective of the profile.

Some people have a natural talent for picking colors, while others (myself included) do not. One approach is to select one or two dominant colors that you use for headings and text, for example, and then some complementary colors that can be used as a background color. Another approach is to pick out key colors from a photograph that you might be planning to feature in the profile.

However, having said all of that, the easiest way to decide on a color scheme is to use one of the online tools to create the color scheme.

One of the best online tools for picking a color scheme is Petr Stanicek's Color Scheme Generator 2, which you can find at `wellstyled.com/tools/colorscheme2/index-en.html` — see Figure 27-2.

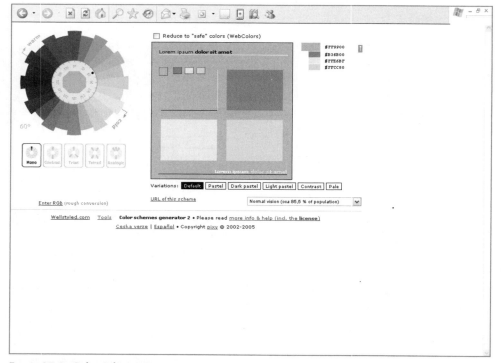

FIGURE 27-2: Color Scheme Generator 2

In Color Scheme Generator 2, you enter a base color, either by clicking on the color wheel or by entering an RGB code as a six-digit hexadecimal code, and the tool automatically develops a color scheme that it shows in real time. The hex values of the color scheme are displayed on the right side, so you can very easily use the codes in your CSS properties. You can also select different color schemes based on the same base color by selecting a variation of the color scheme, or by trying a different color scheme. A Web Safe check box allows you to convert the color scheme to Web-safe colors. There is more information on how this works at the web site.

Other tools you can use to help you develop a color scheme include:

- **Colormixers** (`http://colormixers.com/mixers/cmr/`): An easy-to-use, but very effective, tool for creating nice color schemes. Simply enter the primary color and the software does the rest.

- **Color Palette Creator** (`http://slayeroffice.com/tools/color_palette/`): Computes a ten-color palette from a base color you enter in hex format.

- **Color Schemer** (`http://www.colorschemer.com/online.html`): Creates 16 complementary and contrasting colors from your base color.

Selecting Fonts

It may be a little tempting to go crazy and use lots of different fonts, but too many fonts can make your page look messy and out of control. The general rule is that you don't need to use more than three or four fonts on a page — personally I think you probably don't need more than three.

Try to pick fonts that reflect the theme and purpose of the profile. Select a font for the main text, and perhaps another for headings.

Be consistent — use one font for headlines and one font for body text. It is very distracting when people use a different font for each headline, or if they abruptly change fonts in the middle of a paragraph.

Selecting Images

Images are a very important part of your profile and can make a big contribution to the look-and-feel of your profile, as well as to the story you're trying to tell.

Use images selectively, and make sure that they fit in with the theme and tone of the profile design you're developing.

It's very easy to clutter a profile with lots of inane clipart images. Try to avoid lots of little images. Instead, prioritize the importance of your images and make the important images larger than the less important ones. Place each image with purpose.

Laying Out Your Page

Once you've decided on a color scheme and fonts and images that support your concept, it's time to start making your design a reality. If you've got the skills, you can create a Div overlay profile (see Chapter 25) — taking this approach obviously means you have a lot more freedom to create almost any kind of profile you can imagine.

If you don't have the skills to create a Div overlay profile, there's a lot you can do to modify the existing template, especially if you take onboard some of the ideas on color, fonts, and images that I've discussed in this chapter.

You can change the fonts and colors of your own content quite easily by using CSS (as discussed in Chapters 6 and 7) as well as the standard profile text (see Chapter 18).

The Profile Hall of Fame

As I've been working on this book, I've come across some great profiles. Some of the creators of these profiles have been kind enough to offer some insights into how they put together their profiles. Please keep in mind that this is just a sample of all the great profiles out there — not a complete list. If I missed your profile, it may be that I just didn't see it. I plan to feature more profiles at the book's companion web site at www.myspaceismyplace.com, so if you've got a profile that you think should be featured, please feel free to get in touch with me at john@myspaceismyplace.com.

Bear in mind that when you go to visit some of these profiles, they may have changed substantially, or indeed be completely different. These guys like to innovate.

The interesting theme that comes through as you read these case studies is that almost all of these featured MySpacers started out with no or little programming or design knowledge. They are almost all self-taught, and some of them have even used MySpace as a stepping stone to a career in web design.

Here then, is my MySpace hall of fame, where in their own words, the creators of these amazing profiles describe why and how they put together their creations.

Dan Hill

Profile URL: www.myspace.com/copenhagen

Dan's Story

It all started with pneumonia. I got sick and was home from school for about five days. My friend had told me how to create a simple HTML web page using the `<html>`, `<head>`, and `<body>` tags and I figured that this would be a good time to experiment. I sat down and started throwing stuff together and I got excited when I figured out how to change the background color of the page. But a bunch of words centered on a page can only do so much.

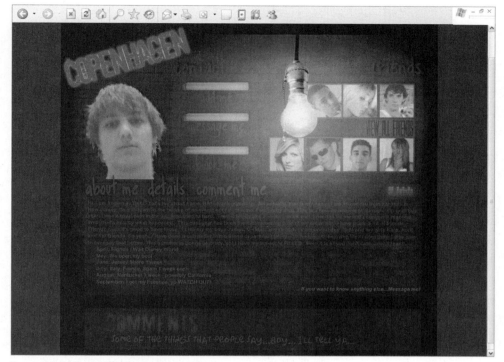

FIGURE 27-3: Dan Hill's MySpace profile

To make a long story short, I ended up learning how to make tables, add images and sounds, and do mouse-over effects. Before I knew it, I was making full blown websites (though I have to admit they were graphically challenged).

Then came MySpace. Lo and behold, I signed up for the program and started adding my friends to my Friends list. But my profile looked just like all the other ones, so I decided I would spice it up a bit. Then I realized that some members used CSS (cascading style sheets) to customize their profiles. I had never even thought about how to design using this language. I started Googling for everything I could find on CSS and I came across all of the things I would need in order to make my profile what I wanted it to be.

Soon I realized that my profile just wasn't going cut it with just CSS. People were starting to catch on to the fact that they could customize their profiles with Thomas's Myspace Editor and now my profile was just one of the bunch. I needed something new, something not many had seen before — I needed a Div (a type of profile created with layers positioned on the screen with attributes, aka an overlay). So I tried this and it worked for a while until I noticed other people were catching on to this new "Div" fad. So I again decided I needed something better. This is when I started adding images and styles to my profile that made it look like a web site, rather than a profile on MySpace. But this still didn't float my boat. I needed Flash.

Flash is a program that allows you to create web sites with extremely high levels of animation, excitement, and user interaction. I had seen some Flash profiles before, but I was extremely intimidated by this program and had no clue where to start. Google came to the rescue, and by reading online tutorials and guides, I finally began my first Flash profile.

It was simple as simple can be, but it made a splash in the MySpace world. Friend requests and e-mails poured into my Inbox as people wanted me to help them with their profiles as well and make profiles for them. Of course I didn't have the time to make profiles for all 45 million (at the time) users on MySpace, but I helped out where I could.

My MySpace profile was beginning to get old yet again when people learned the tricks of the trade and began putting together Flash MySpace profiles of their own. Mine again looked like everyone else's. I needed something new . . . something hip and cool with nice music that the user could turn off and on. In Figure 27-3, you can see what I created. The user came to the page and saw a light bulb. When the bulb was clicked, the flickering and buzzing ended, the bulb illuminated, and the profile kicked into high gear. Music began and links and navigation were then visible. With realistic fluorescent light bulb buttons and a red-and-black color scheme, the profile was deemed by many as my greatest work. My profile at myspace.com/copenhagen had become a profile to remember.

But I wasn't going to stop there. I created a group (groups.myspace.com/copenhagentutorials) that helps people learn Flash and accelerates the process. Before I knew it, two or three Flash profiles started popping up on MySpace daily. The group offers Video Flash Tutorials as well as a place to ask questions about Flash and how to use it. MySpace gave me the edge I needed to start my own Internet-based career as well. I am the current owner and founder of four web sites, all of which are personal portfolios for up and coming projects. But those web sites would not be possible without the help of MySpace and pneumonia.

Dan's Tips

First, let me say that everything I know about web design and HTML, CSS, and Flash, I have learned on my own with no help — so basically anyone can do this sort of thing.

Begin studying things such as tables and basic HTML. Search on Google for tutorials on these topics. You should next begin learning basic CSS (cascading style sheets). This type of coding is crucial to the building and maintaining of a Flash profile.

Master these two things and I'd say you are well on your way to building something impressive. Know how to use Photoshop or a similar graphics program. Plain profiles without a theme or thought to them are boring.

Know what you can and can't do with your MySpace profile. Try to do the things you can't. I know it sounds ludicrous — but if you simply work with what you know and don't venture out into the world of computers and the things that are available to you, you will never get any better at what you do.

The Take Away

- You'll need to learn how to use Flash if you want to create media rich profiles.
- Learn HTML and CSS, before taking on Flash.

- Use Google to find online resources such as tutorials and guides on HTML, CSS, and Flash.

- Don't be afraid to push yourself beyond the limits of what you think is possible.

- It's important to come up with a theme.

Elda Ramirez

Profile URL: www.myspace.com/eldaadriana

Elda's Story

I have always liked graphic design so when I found out that MySpace lets you modify your profile I thought it was the perfect opportunity to learn.

I started by looking at web sites that tell you how to customize your profile. I found a couple of profile generators but I wanted to learn how to do it myself, so I searched for tutorials that talked about HTML and CSS. I didn't have a clue what the code meant so I Googled it and found out what it did.

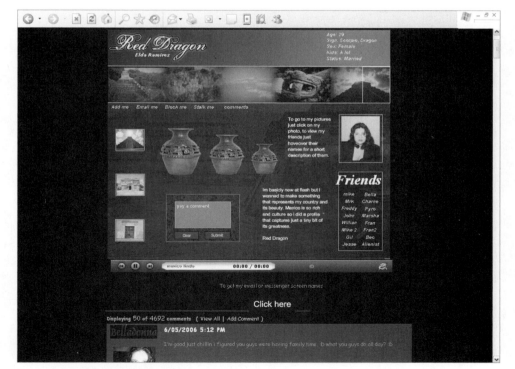

FIGURE 27-4: Elda Ramirez's profile

Little by little, I started understanding HTML and CSS. I started with the basic profile by just changing the background, contact table, extended network banners, and online icons. Then I found a great site that helped me modify my Friends list, which included changing your friends' pictures, selecting the number of friends you want to list on the front page, and so on.

I thought I was doing well, so I decided to do a Div profile. A Div profile covers your main profile and then lets you create and place your own tables anywhere you want. There are a lot of groups and sites that provide help with MySpace customization. BBZ (`groups.myspace .com/bbz`), a group about how to customize your profile, was a big help. The best web sites that I have found are:

- **#bbz.space** (`www.bbzspace.com`): A search engine for tutorials that has lot of generators
- **Skem9.com** (`www.skem9.com`): A great forum for help that has pre-made layouts, generators, and really cool graphics for your page
- **Private Pyro** (`live.privatepyro.com`): A great site if you want a music player on your profile that can play more than one song

From there, I started messing around with Flash, which is a really fun program for designing web pages, making videos, creating music players, and in fact pretty much any type of animation for web design. Soon I was creating full Flash profiles.

I am really surprised by how much I have accomplished on MySpace. It is not only a networking site, but also it is an opportunity to practice web design. Every page is a new challenge for me.

I have never studied HTML or any type of coding, so it's been a very steep learning curve over the past ten months, and I still have a lot to learn.

The Take Away

- You don't need formal study to learn how to code HTML and CSS, or how to use Flash.
- Don't be afraid to use online resources — that's what they're there for.
- A lot can be accomplished in a relatively short period of time.

Valerie Burgess

Profile URL: `www.myspace.com/shadowwraith`

Valerie's Story

I have a 20-year-old daughter who had a profile on MySpace as well as a number of other social networking sites.

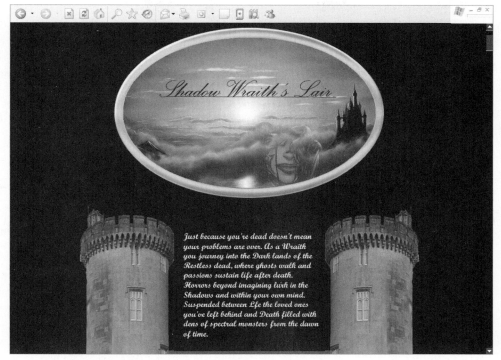

FIGURE 27-5: Valerie Burgess's profile

I quickly noticed one huge difference between these sites and MySpace, and that was the fact that on MySpace.com you could greatly customize your profile to fit your personality. I had just recently retired from the computer field and was looking for opportunities to fill my time, and a place, where even at my age, I could hang out with people with similar interests.

I have never been all work and no play, and you'll notice that my profile has a strong medieval theme. I played Dungeons and Dragons before it was even created for the computer. I have always had a passion for this era. I even have a room in my home dedicated to medieval and renaissance artifacts. So it only made sense that when I came to MySpace that I would build a page that reflected my passion for this era and the games I played. And because you cannot post in the forums in the first seven days after you join, I took this time to explore the site. I recommend that new MySpace users spend this time doing the same, so that they might find their way around the site because it is quite large.

When I first came to MySpace there were very few coders and even fewer codes to work with. At this time we were only beginning to uncover and discover the strengths and abilities to create truly customized profiles within the MySpace environment.

At first, like most, I began with a typical themed HTML/CSS profile. But because of the lack of challenge, I began designing something much more complex. I decided to just completely cover up my entire profile with a CSS overlay, and use Macromedia Flash to create a complete custom complex look and feel, but one that still reflected my interest and passion.

For the first year while I was on MySpace I volunteered my time in the Myspace.com Forum, which is now known as the Customizing Forum, and which you can find from the main MySpace page by going to Forum ⇨ MySpace ⇨ Customizing. I will never forget what my first question was when I arrived on the scene, and I quickly began to realize that this was not an uncommon question: "Where do I place my codes?"

Of course, the answer always was "In the About Me section of your profile." It seemed as though many people who knew how to code web pages outside of MySpace quickly found themselves very confused and overwhelmed.

It's important that people understand that customizing a MySpace page is totally different from coding a page over which you have total control. In reality, customizing a MySpace profile is accomplished by manipulating and changing (messing up) the original MySpace tables in order to create a new look and feel.

Valerie's Tips

If you're new to MySpace.com, your level of knowledge determines where I direct you for help on getting started.

If you're not familiar with HTML and CSS, I usually recommend that you start out quickly by obtaining a free profile layout from one of the many sites offering such services. This is probably the fastest way for any user to get up and running quickly with a custom profile.

The number of themes to choose from out there is huge, so it's still possible to fit one to your personality. In most cases, the complete codes are provided and the graphics are pre-hosted for the user. And usually, you are instructed as to where to place these codes. I explain to newcomers that they can then actually learn a lot just by looking at these codes that are provided to them.

For people more familiar with HTML and CSS I direct them to the large number of MySpace groups that provide codes and help. These codes are readily available and can be easily copied and pasted into any profile for a custom look and feel.

Also by just frequenting these groups, users can begin to grasp the concepts of customizing within the MySpace environment so that they may begin creating their own custom codes and profile.

I direct advanced users, who are well versed in the use of applications such as Macromedia Flash, straight to the groups specializing in Flash.

The Take Away

- Create a profile that reflects your passion; it's also a good way to develop a theme.
- Coding for a MySpace profile is not like coding a regular web site — and you need to be aware of the differences if you already know how to code in HTML and CSS.

- You can learn about customization by using profile generators and looking at the code to try to understand what it does.

- MySpace groups are a great way to find codes and get help.

Michelle Mannor

Profile URL: `www.myspace.com/illvixen`

Michelle's Story

I created the profile in Figure 27-6 because I got tired of looking at the default layout. I wanted something appealing so that users would add me to their Friends list. So many times I have come across profiles that are just horrible and very unappealing.

My first experience with creating a profile wasn't the greatest, I will tell you that.

I knew nothing about HTML or CSS until I got to MySpace and my profile was voted as the worst. But after learning HTML and CSS over a period of a year, I have developed beautiful creations that have been very popular.

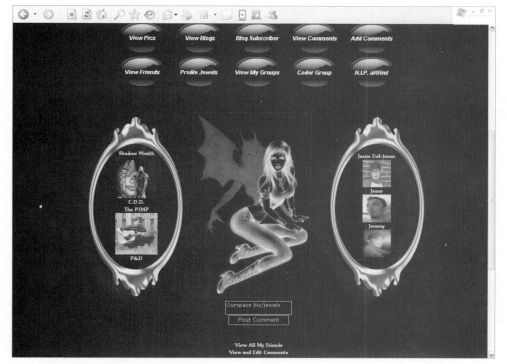

FIGURE 27-6: Michelle Mannor's profile

The types of profiles I enjoy creating have CSS and Div classes coded in them. I have tried Div styles but they just do not work well in all browsers. So if anyone wants to create a complete overlay I recommend using Div classes, instead of Div styles. By way of explanation, in a Div style the properties are placed in the actual Div tag. Here's an example of a Div style:

```
<div style="margin-right:150px; border-style: double">content in
here</div>
```

Now here is an example of a Div class:

```
<div class="Layer1" style="margin-left: -395px; margin-top: 10px;
width:
800px; height: 1500px">Content here</div>
The properties for the Div are defined in a style sheet
<style type="text/css">
.Layer1 {position: absolute; left: 50%; top:155px; z-index:9;
overflow:none; border style:ridge; border-width:0px; border-color:
silver;}
</style>
```

Notice how the CSS `.layer1` matches with the `div class="layer1"`. This is what your content is going to be based on. Not only are you working with your CSS but also with your Div class and you are most likely guaranteed to have a cross-browser–compliant profile.

Now if you want to hide sections such as your Friends space and comments, this would be when Div style is useful. Here is an example of what I used for my profile:

```
<div style="display:none;">
<table><tr><td><table><tr><td><table><tr><td>
```

This was placed to display nothing of the default layout. I placed it in the Interests section, but other users can place it in other sections as well.

I used Flash navigations to create the contact buttons. It's awesome because it brings the effects out and makes it fun for the users to contact me.

I am all about easy navigation and clean looking layouts. I feel that good web design is about making your sites look clean and crisp, as well as being user-friendly.

Simplicity is the key to a successful web site.

The Take Away

- Use .classes rather than styles when creating Div overlays
- Keep your profiles looking clean, and easy to navigate.

Kevin Turner

Profile URL: www.myspace.com/kevturner007

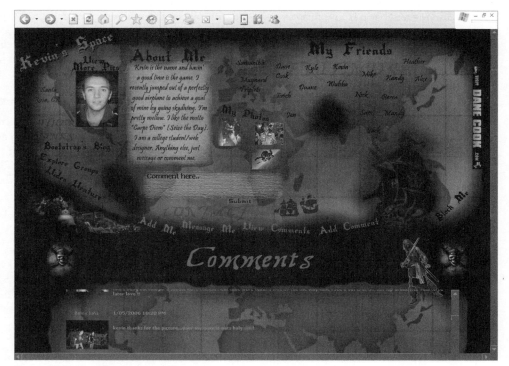

FIGURE 27-7: Kevin Turner's profile

Kevin's Story

MySpace is a place where I can express my thoughts. When I first got started on MySpace, I was just a normal kid who didn't know anything about coding, or customization, or anything along those lines. I was turned on to the new MySpace craze by my brother, Kyle, in April 2005. By the same time the next year, I had one of the most tricked out and outstanding profiles on MySpace.

I am a self-taught coder, but more than that, I was able to learn all of my web design skills through MySpace. I would see something that I liked on another person's profile, and I would apply that same technique to my own. I basically started out with just the simple code generators that are all over the Internet. Once I got started coding I didn't stop.

At first, I used only pre-made codes that are available anywhere, but as I became bored with every new thing, I started to look for another way of doing things. The way, I later found, was through the use of Div overlays.

With a Div overlay I could do almost anything with my profile, and that was the main attraction for me. I didn't understand how to use them at first, but as I messed around, I learned more, I was able to have enough knowledge so that I could at least apply the coding to my profile. Keep in mind that I was learning all of this with the help of MySpace Groups.

There are several help groups that can assist you with any number of things, including profile customization. One example of these groups is HTML Masters (groups.myspace.com/html), which is a great help group that can answer almost any question that you might have about coding, customization, or just MySpace in general. There are also great groups to go to for tutorials on how to do things; one such group is BBZ, which is located at groups.myspace.com/bbz. There are also places to hang out and just chat about customization or whatever you like; I personally like to go to DIV-Space (groups.myspace.com/divspace2) for that. The point is that you can find a lot of help with customization in the MySpace groups, and the best part is that it is free!

Once I had learned the basics of Div overlays, I began designing and customizing my own profile the way I wanted it to look. I also learned about Div classes, which are a cleaner way of using Div overlays — there is more information about that in the groups. I change my profiles regularly and they usually have some sort of theme to them, such as a tropical beach, the Mafia, Indiana Jones, or my current pirate profile.

I try to do two things when I am creating a profile: make it easy to browse through and make it fun to view.

I usually include a matching song to the theme of the profile; for example, a song from *Pirates of the Caribbean* is playing on my current pirate profile. Another element of my profile that makes it especially different is that I use Flash. Basically, by using a program to create a Flash Movie, I am able to upload it onto my profile, and I can do almost anything I want with this movie. I can add moving parts, link buttons, movie clips, music clips, and any graphic designs that I have.

I use Macromedia Flash MX, which is the common Flash Movie–creating program on the market, although there are many other programs that are worthy in their own right. I actually started off by using a program called Koolmoves, which is a very user-friendly way to learn and create Flash Movies.

All of my recent designs for my profile have included a main Flash Movie that has everything I need included in it, such as the basic MySpace links, along with the different contact links. I also include a custom Friend section in my Flash Movie, and I have a photo album section that links to several different albums of photos that I have collected over the years. I created my MySpace profile for my friends to enjoy, but because other people can view my profile, I make sure it showcases me positively.

One thing a person might notice as he or she first views my page is that it has a lot of moving parts and links that lead you to other places. Each moving piece of my profile is its own movie with movements that are activated when a user hovers over each link with the cursor. I am using a special feature on my profile right now: As you hover over each link, a flame engulfs the text in the link. All of these moving parts and hover effects can be applied using a Flash program, which is why I like using Flash. It is so versatile and useful. To make the moving parts in my profile there must be several separate still frames that run in a main timeline together. Each frame has its own set of elements and can either be linked to outside web sites, or inside of MySpace, or the frames can interact with other frames in the Flash Movie, such as a button that triggers a music clip to play or a movie trailer to play. Basically, through the use of Flash, I can create anything I want in terms of graphic design and creativity on my profile.

Another thing that makes my profile unique are the custom-made graphics. I use multiple graphics creation and picture editing programs to give my profile that extra special look. I also use special fonts that can be found for free and all you have to do is download them and poof, there is another way to make a custom profile or even a graphic. I also like to use fonts that have something to do with the current theme of my profile, such as an old English–style font for my pirate page; for my Indiana Jones profile I used a font similar to the one used on the movie cover of that movie. Essentially, the idea is to stick with a theme and add as much cool stuff to it as possible without making the profile seem crowded; simplicity is also a good thing.

I was once just a novice that didn't know anything about coding or customization of a web site, but in just a few months I was able to acquire skills that could rival even the best coders on MySpace, so it is true that even a non-programmer can create some great things on MySpace. There are all sorts of resources on the Internet, in books, and even in public groups on MySpace, and all of them have helped me to create my own custom MySpace, which I call Kevin's Space.

The Take Away

- Try to keep all the images, fonts, and text consistent with your theme.

- Groups are a great source of information.

- Using Flash Movies can create a rich multimedia experience for visitors to your profile.

Michael Sabine

Profile URL: www.myspace.com/gonesyko

When I found MySpace.com, right away I saw the potential for advertising and the ability to reach a large number of people at once. The first thing I did was browse tons of profiles to see how people set them up. The one thing I didn't like right off the bat was the standard MySpace layout. Being a web designer, I wanted to have something that was different from anything that was on MySpace and that would stand out from the crowd.

I started finding a few profiles that were doing something different and right away set out to find out how I could manipulate the MySpace code. If they could do it, I knew, so could I. Designing for MySpace is different from designing a normal web site because you are basically going in and breaking their code to make it work for you. This was a little tricky, but through searching help forums and doing a bit of reading, I learned how I could get my profile the way I wanted. After finding out how I could get my profile to work like a Flash web site, I got busy designing.

The one thing I noticed with people that were using Flash in MySpace profiles was that the Flash was always a completely separate element from the background. I didn't like this. I wanted my Flash and my background to blend seamlessly. So the first thing I did was take a screenshot of the standard MySpace profile design. This would turn out to be my template. I then opened that up into Photoshop. I am also not a fan of scrollbars and I wanted everything to be visible to the eye right away. So using the screenshot, I set about designing my profile around the MySpace banner at the top, and at the same time, keeping everything in a size that wouldn't need a scrollbar.

FIGURE 27-8: Michael Sabine's profile

After I had everything designed to my liking, I put everything into Flash, but used Flash only for the center of my design. I placed the background image directly into my MySpace profile. That way, when it came time to place my Flash onto the background, it was already there, and was just a matter of moving the Flash up or down or left or right to get everything to line up evenly.

This is where I also discovered that it's a good idea to work in Safe Mode on MySpace, and how important Manual Submit is. When you are editing a MySpace profile in Safe Mode with some advanced codes that cover everything up, sometimes these codes also cover your submit button. So there is no way to tell MySpace, yes I like it, submit. So you have to type:

```
javascript:document.forms[1].submit()
```

into your browser address bar and hit Enter. This then works exactly as if you had hit the submit button. Once I had that figured out, everything else was straightforward and simply a matter of tightening up the design. And that is the short and skinny of how I put a MySpace profile together.

Note

From John: Incidentally, the MySpace folks have changed the standard Edit Profile function, so that it's no longer necessary to use Safe Mode and Manual Submit to enter difficult code.

The one tip I would say when designing your profile would be to get creative. With the capability to cover up all the stuff from MySpace, there is no limit to what you can place there.

The Take Away

- Integrate your Flash Movie with your background image, rather than putting everything in the Flash Movie.

- Use a graphics program to create the images for your site, before moving them over to Flash.

Wrapping Up

The concept "form follows function" is as relevant to MySpace as it is to the world of design generally. Once you know function, you can work the form the profile needs to take — and this includes fonts, color schemes, and image selection. The six featured MySpace profiles have been selected to help inspire you. The stories of the profiles' creators are also fascinating, and you should note that most of creators are self-taught; they knew nothing about profile coding or design before joining MySpace. The message is — if they can do it, so can you!

Taking Winning Photos

P hotos are an important part of a good MySpace profile, and yet it seems that many MySpace members don't make much of an effort. Your main photo is what most people see first when they browse or search profiles. The photos in your View My Pics collection give people an insight into who you are as a person. A great photo, like Figure 28-1, can really make your profile shine. Then why is it that so many MySpace photos are so terrible?

FIGURE 28-1: A well-taken photo can make your profile shine.

Even with a very basic digital camera, it's possible to take good photos. With this in mind, the following tips are designed to help you take better photos. And yes, I have to admit to taking many of the following examples of shockingly poor-quality photos.

Choosing Your Subject

Decide what you're really interested in, and work on getting the best photo of this subject, whether it is a person, animal, mood, culture, or anything else. Keep things that will distract attention from the subject out of the picture (see Figure 28-2 for an example of what not to do). Check at the edges of the picture, and recompose if necessary. For example, you might close in on the subject so that it fills up the photo, or you might move so a trash can (or whatever) is kept out of your picture.

Look before you shoot. Train yourself to look around the subject before you push the shutter button, to check if there are things such as poles or trees that may appear to be sticking out of your subject's head. If taking a photo of a group of people, make sure you can see your subjects clearly, and that people's faces aren't being blocked by others. If they can't see you, you can't see them — and your photo won't show them!

FIGURE 28-2: Too much clutter in the background takes focus away from the subjects.

If you're planning to take a photo of yourself for your main profile image, try to make sure that the photo shows you — not your bedroom, living room, or bathroom in the background. And yes, I've seen plenty of photos on MySpace that appear to have been taken in someone's bathroom. Try to avoid taking your own photos by simply holding the camera at arms length. Just ask a friend or family member to do it for you — surely you're not that embarrassed about having your photo taken.

Being Quick

If your subject may stop smiling, run off, fly away, or just get bored of waiting for you to take the picture, take the shot right away. You need to be quick, or you may miss the moment, as in Figure 28-3. The great thing with a digital camera is that you don't need to worry about wasting film. When you've taken the picture, a camera with a built-in screen will let you check that you've got the picture you wanted. With most digital cameras there's a lag between pressing the button, and the picture being taken — because they usually focus after you press the button. A good idea for quicker photos is to aim your camera and half depress the shutter button, this will focus the camera ready for you to fully push it and take your shot.

FIGURE 28-3: Be quick, or you'll miss the moment.

Framing the Picture

Your subject needs to be large in relation to the surroundings; otherwise it can get lost in the picture – just as in Figure 28-4.

This is where a zoom feature offers flexibility. There are two types of zoom fitted to digital cameras: optical and digital. An optical zoom works in the same way as a traditional camera zoom lens: The lens moves so a different image is captured. A digital zoom just enlarges part of the picture, which means the resolution (picture quality) is effectively reduced.

FIGURE 28-4: The subjects are too small in relation to the background.

Taking as Many Photos as Possible

Take more photographs, lots more. If you've ever seen a professional photographer you may have noticed that he or she doesn't take just one photo. Professional photographers take a series of photos, maybe dozens or hundreds, hoping to get a few shots that are perfect. One of the biggest benefits of digital photography is that there are no film and processing costs, so why not try a few different angles? Get down low or up high. Zoom in or zoom out. After all, you can simply keep the best and delete the rest. (See Figure 28-5 for one that I should have deleted.)

By the way, all of this means nothing if your camera is in a drawer at home. Most digital cameras these days are quite compact, so do make it a habit to take your camera with you wherever you are. You can take photos for your MySpace profile that are a bit more exciting than you and your friends sitting on a sofa in your living room.

FIGURE 28-5: To get the perfect shot, you may need to take many shots — many of which won't turn out.

Foreground/Background

Think about how you can get the foreground and background of the picture to work together. Remember that you may need to compromise on the focusing — you can't have both the foreground and background in sharp focus. Cameras with automatic focusing generally focus on what's in the center of the picture. If your primary subject is off-center, point the camera at the subject first and half depress the shutter button, this will set the focus. Then recompose the picture (while keeping your finger on the button) and take the picture.

The Importance of Lighting

Light alters the viewer's idea of an image by evoking warmth, coolness, brightness, and darkness and establishing shape, form, contrast and color. Ensure your subject is illuminated in a manner that agrees with your visual concept. Any disagreement between light and subject can ruin a potentially successful image (see Figure 28-6).

You'll get better results using natural light than taking photos indoors with a flash (unless you have a professional lighting setup and studio, but that's a different story).

FIGURE 28-6: Bad lighting can really ruin a photo opportunity.

Take into account the kind of light you're working with. Where are the shadows falling? It's generally best to shoot with the sun behind you (unless you want a silhouette effect). Look at how the light is affecting your subject. Is he or she squinting? Is the light shining brightly on the whole subject or just on parts of it?

Try shooting earlier or later in the day and avoid the harsh light of midday, which tends to cast shadows that can make it difficult to take good photos. Overcast days offer a flat, even light that is great for portraits. Directional light from just after sunrise and just before sunset can transform your landscapes into something truly spectacular.

Using Fill-in Flash

Use fill-in flash. Often when your subject is in deep shadow or the contrast is high on a bright sunny day, you end with a silhouette you didn't want or deep ugly shadows under the nose, eyes, and chin. Fill-in flash fires a small burst of flash to fill out shadows caused by too much contrast. Use this function to balance the available light and the flash light (see Figure 28-7).

FIGURE 28-7: Fill-in flash saved this photo.

Understanding Your Camera

Learn how to use your camera and software. Today's cameras allow amazing flexibility and control over the image. As you read the manual (yes . . . read the manual) try each function on the camera to see what creative possibilities it allows.

The same goes for the computer software. Creativity does not end when you press the shutter. Even simple computer manipulation can improve an image out of sight. Take the time to experiment and enjoy. In Chapter 29, I look at some ways the software editing package GIMP (available for download via a link on this book's web site at www.myspaceismyplace.com) can be used to improve the appearance of your photos.

Composition

When you take a photograph, it's important to consider how the elements that make up the picture work together. Check out Figure 28-8 to see what a photo looks like when there has been no thought about composition.

Decide which parts of the scene are important, and use the viewfinder to help you position the camera so these elements relate to each other. Make sure you keep the horizon level. Consciously place your subject where you think it will look best. Adjust the perspective so that the lines of the photo show a pattern or lead the eye to the main subject.

FIGURE 28-8: A photo where there has been no thought about composition

Try to look for unusual or non-standard viewpoints from which to begin your composition. Lowering and elevating your camera viewpoint adds interest by revealing even the most everyday subjects from a different perspective.

Avoiding Camera Shake

It's important to keep the camera stable while taking a photo, particularly when there isn't much light because a longer exposure is required. This can cause camera shake, which will make the photos look blurred.

Camera shake is when the camera moves while you're taking a picture (see Figure 28-9). Camera shake is more noticeable when you're zooming in on a subject from far away. It's particularly an issue with powerful zoom; some cameras have optical zooms of up to 10 times. Even cameras with shorter zooms can be affected dramatically by camera shake. The best way to combat camera shake is to use a sturdy support for your camera.

Most cameras can be fitted to a tripod, but you can also try to steady the camera by leaning against something such as a wall or table, or you can try placing the camera on a table or other sturdy surface. As a general rule, the smaller the camera the more difficult it is to hold steady.

FIGURE 28-9: Camera shake can make a photo look blurry.

Tips for Taking a Good Profile Shot

The profile shot is arguably the most important image in your MySpace profile. It's what visitors first see when they're browsing or searching profiles, and therefore it's how they get their first impression of who you are. With that in mind, here are some tips on how to take a profile photo with maximum impact.

- Don't take your own photos — there's nothing worse than a photo taken by someone holding a camera at arm's length. Go on, ask a friend or family member to take it for you.

- Make sure your image fills up the photo — remember the aim is to show you, not the background.

- Keep the background as neutral as possible, and definitely avoid taking photos in places such as your bedroom or the bathroom.

- Try to take your photo in natural light — you'll get a better image, and that's another excuse to avoid taking the photos inside your home.

- It's better to keep the photo just of you, although if you're married or in a relationship, including your loved one in your photo is a good way to keep unwanted attention away (and it also helps to stop your partner from getting jealous).

- And while I don't mean to sound prudish, my suggestion is that women especially should think carefully before posting images that are provocative — even if you're just wearing a swimsuit or looking flirtatious. While you might think your photo is simply fun, it's bound to bring unwanted admirers. But of course, that is completely up to you.

Wrapping Up

None of the tips in this chapter are particularly difficult, but if you follow them, you will notice a profound improvement in the quality of your photos. Because images are such an important part of your profile, spending a little extra time taking the photographs is incredibly worthwhile.

Photo Editing

I n the last chapter, you looked at how to take nice photos, but the reality is often that try as you might, you just can't get the right shot.

Fortunately, in the age of computers it's relatively straightforward to fix many problems. In this chapter, you use GIMP, a free image editing program, to fix a few a common photographic problems. You've used GIMP in a number of chapters in this book, and the installation process is described in Chapter 10.

The Basics

Loading images into GIMP is straightforward. Simply left-click File from the drop-down menu of the main GIMP window, and then left-click Open. Navigate to the image file you want to load and left-click the Open button.

To save an image, simply select File ➪ Save. To save a file with a different file name, or in a different format, select File ➪ Save As. To change the file name, simply change the name of the file in the Name text box. To change the file type, simply click Change File type (By Extension) and select the file type you would like to save the image in. If you're going to be using a photo on the Internet, you would usually select JPG.

Once you've entered a file name and selected the file type, click the Save button. If you're saving your file as a JPG, you'll then have the option of adjusting the Quality. The higher the quality, the larger the file size.

If you're going to work on an image, I suggest that as soon as you load the image, you use Save As to save the image with a different file name. It's important to keep a separate copy of the original image; otherwise, it's very easy to save an edited image over it, meaning that you'll never be able to use the original image for anything.

Cropping

To crop a photo means to cut away the superfluous parts of the image. You'll be surprised at how often well–thought out cropping can improve a poor image.

Take a look at Figure 29-1. You'll see that the subjects of the photo are lost — they're too small compared to the background.

FIGURE **29-1: The subjects of this image are too small compared to the background.**

Cropping allows you to cut away some of the background so that it does not dominate the image.

Let's load this image into GIMP (you'll find it on the companion web site for this book at www.myspaceismyplace.com) — or you can use your own image. Locate the "Select rectangular regions" tool, where you'll find the main GIMP tool palette (it looks like a rectangle with a dashed border). If you're unsure whether you've found the right tool, just hold the mouse pointer over the tool icon for a few moments and the name of the tool is displayed. Now select the point where you want the top-left corner of the image to start, and holding down the left mouse button drag down the selection to the new bottom-right corner of the image. Release the mouse button. You can see in Figure 29-2 that I have selected the part of the image that I want to keep.

If you make a selection, but find that it's not right, simply left-click the image and try again. If you want to keep the same aspect ratio as the original image, simply ensure that you have the Tool Options window visible (Dialogs ⇨ Tool Options) and select Fixed Aspect Ratio from the drop-down options menu (which should be showing Free Select). When you've got the selection right, select Image ⇨ Crop Image. Your image will now be cropped. As you can see in Figure 29-3, the sample photo is now much better.

FIGURE 29-2: The part of the image that I want to keep has been selected.

FIGURE 29-3: At least in this cropped photo, you can now see who the subjects are.

Be aware that you can really crop images successfully if they are quite high resolution to start with — at least 2 megapixels, but preferably 3 or 4 megapixels.

Resizing and Rotation

Resizing and rotation are two common functions that sometimes come in handy. Resizing is handy if you need only a smaller image and you want to minimize file size. Rotation is useful if the original image was taken by turning the camera sideways, and the image appears in the wrong orientation.

To resize an image, select File ⇨ Scale Image. A window appears that allows you to set the width and height (as you can see in Figure 29-4). If you want to keep the same aspect ratio, make sure the chain link icon between the width and height boxes is unbroken. When you put in a new width value, the height value will change automatically to ensure that the image keeps the same proportions. If the chain link icon is broken, then you will be able to put in independent values for width and height, meaning that you will be able to, in effect, stretch the image. When you've finished, click the Scale button.

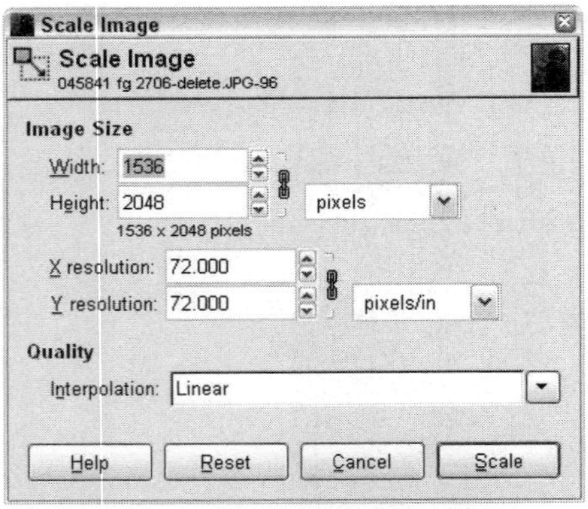

FIGURE 29-4: The Scale Image window

To rotate an image, select Image ⇨ Transform. From the menu you can then select Rotate 90 degrees CW (clockwise), Rotate 90 degrees CCW (counter clockwise), or Rotate 180 degrees.

Adjusting Brightness and Contrast

Sometimes photos can be underexposed, which makes them look too dark, or overexposed, which makes them look too light. Figure 29-5 shows an underexposed photo; there wasn't enough light when this photo was taken and a flash wasn't used to compensate. Fortunately, GIMP has a number of tools that can be used to improve the appearance of such images.

FIGURE 29-5: This image is underexposed and is therefore too dark.

Brightness Contrast

The first thing you can try is to adjust the brightness and contrast of the image (by selecting Tools ➪ Color Tools ➪ Brightness Contrast). As you can see in Figure 29-6, you'll be presented with a window showing two sliders.

FIGURE 29-6: The Brightness Contrast window

The top slider allows you to adjust brightness, while the bottom slider allows you to adjust contrast. Ensure that you have the Preview checkbox selected so that you can preview how your image will look as you experiment with the sliders. When you achieve the effect you want, click OK and the changes will be applied to your image. Sometimes, however, simply adjusting brightness and contrast will not allow you to sufficiently improve the appearance of an image, in which case select the Cancel button so that you can try another approach.

Color Levels

Another way to adjust color and contrast is to adjust the color levels (by selecting Tools ➪ Color Tools ➪ Levels). Figure 29-7 shows what the Adjust Color Levels window looks like. Make sure the Preview checkbox is selected so that you can see how your adjustments will affect your photo.

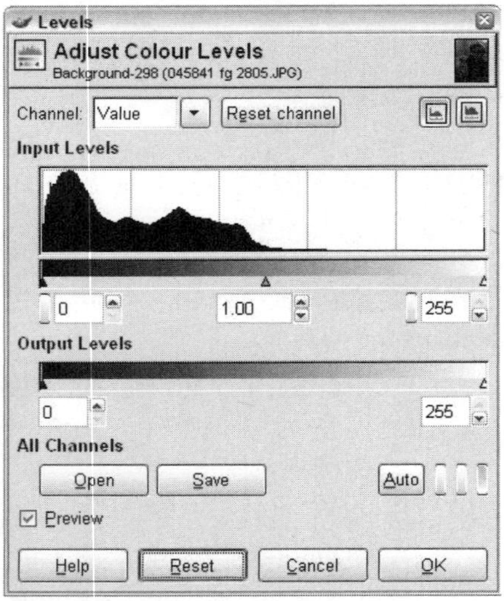

FIGURE 29-7: The Adjust Color Levels window

The first thing to try is to click the Auto button. GIMP attempts to adjust the color levels automatically. Sometimes this works, which is fine. But often you'll find that it's not quite right, in which case just click the Reset button.

To the right of the Auto button are three buttons (they should look like eyedroppers). If you run your mouse pointer over each of them, you'll see the following labels: Pick Black Point, Pick Gray Point, and Pick White Point. Let's say you click the Pick White Point button. You then find a spot on your photo that you know should be white (but it appears gray because the photo is too dark) and click the left mouse button. GIMP then automatically adjusts the colors in the photo so that point does become white. Picking a white point can be a very easy way to correct underexposed images (too dark) while picking a black point can be an easy way to correct overexposed images (too light).

The graph beneath the Input Levels diagram is called a *histogram*. It shows the distribution of pixels according to their brightness — black on the left through to white on the right, and of course all gradations of brightness in between. As you can see in Figure 29-7 there are a lot of very dark pixels in the sample image. Below the graph you'll see three triangles. Moving these triangles allows you to adjust the brightness of the pixels. One approach that usually works well is to move the black triangle (the one on the far left) to the left edge of the graph (its existing position in Figure 29-7) and the white triangle (the one on the far right) to the right edge of the graph. This should provide a good level of contrast (although there are always exceptions to the rule). Adjust the middle gray triangle to adjust the brightness. When you have finished, left-click OK.

Color Curves Window

The third method of adjusting contrast and brightness is to adjust the color curves (select Tools ➪ Color Tools ➪ Curves). Figure 29-8 shows the Adjust Color Curves window, which at first probably won't mean very much. As with the Adjust Color Levels window, there's a histogram that shows the distribution of pixels by their brightness (this is the gray solid graph). Darker pixels are on the left, and lighter pixels are on the right.

Over the top of the histogram is a curve that should be a straight line going from the bottom-left corner to the top-right corner. This curve represents your new brightness values. Changing the shape of this curve allows you to control the brightness of different parts of your image.

Check that you have the smooth curve option selected by left-clicking the Smooth Curve button under the Curve Type heading. Double-click on the curve. A control point appears.

With your mouse pointer over a control point, click and hold down the left mouse button to move the control point and adjust the curve. To delete a badly placed control point, simply position your mouse pointer over it, hold down the mouse button, and move it off the curve until it pulls away. You shouldn't need more than three or four control points.

When you adjust the curve, the brightness of your photo will change. A steep curve improves the contrast, whereas a shallow curve creates a more washed out effect. Confusingly, the curve uses the vertical axis to show which brightness levels are being manipulated. It'll take you a little bit of experimentation to get a feel for it, but for example, I was able to get a good result using the curve in Figure 29-9. The advantage of using color curves over color levels is that it allows you a finer level of control.

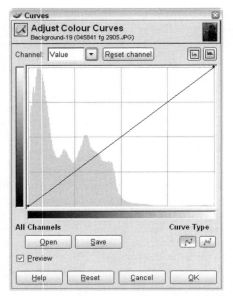

FIGURE 29-8: The Adjust Color Curves window

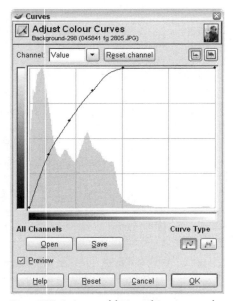

FIGURE 29-9: I was able to achieve a good
result using this color curve.

In most cases you should be able to get the results you want using the Adjust Color Levels window, which was the case for the sample image used in this tutorial. Figure 29-10 shows the final image. Bear in mind that often when you correct a very underexposed or overexposed image, the final image can be a little grainy — basically because there was not enough image information in the original photo to give you a perfectly clear image. Incidentally, you can often make grainy images look a little better by applying a mild Gaussian Blur (Filters ⇨ Blur ⇨ Gaussian). A Gaussian Blur — using the default settings — was applied to the sample image (see Figure 29-10) to make it look less grainy.

FIGURE 29-10: The corrected image looks much better than the original in Figure 29-5.

Replacing the Background

This chapter would not be complete without a tutorial on replacing the background of a photo. Figure 29-11 is a happy snap of my little family — my wife, Rocio, and my baby daughter, Grace — and while I don't mind the photo itself, the background is pretty awful. Fortunately, with the help of GIMP, it's possible to remove and replace the background. Here is a relatively simple way of removing the background and inserting your own.

FIGURE 29-11: A happy snap with an awful background

Load the sample image (or your own image) into GIMP. Save it as a GIMP XCF image. This is necessary because you will be using layers during this process, and JPG does not support layers.

Select Dialogs ⇨ Layer. The Layer window will appear. Select Dialogs ⇨ Tool Options. The tool options window will appear. Try to arrange the windows so that you can see everything at once (as in Figure 29-12).

FIGURE 29-12: Try to arrange the windows so that you can access all the windows easily.

In the Layers window, right-click the Background layer and select duplicate layer. A new layer should appear called Background copy. Left-click the eye next to the Background layer; the eye icon should disappear. Select the Background copy layer by left-clicking "background copy."

What you're actually going to do is to cut away the foreground characters (me, my wife, and my baby) from the background using the "Select shapes from image" tool — you'll find this tool in the main Gimp tool palette. It looks like a pair of scissors with a line coming out the top.

Make sure you have the Feature Edges checkbox selected in the Tool Options menu. Set the radius to 5.0.

This tool is designed to help you trace around complex objects. Select the tool and then left-click at some point on the edge of the foreground characters. The first "control node" (a small dot) will appear.

In the case of my sample photo, I started at the bottom of my daughter's leg (bottom-left side) — see Figure 29-13. You can follow a short distance along the edge of the foreground characters and left-click again. Another control node will appear and the selection line should automatically follow the contour of the foreground characters (it works best if there is a high-contrast edge). Be patient, and try to follow the edge in small steps. Work your way all around the foreground characters. Don't worry too much if you make mistakes. These can be easily corrected. To get better results you might find it easier to zoom into your image (View ⇨ Zoom).

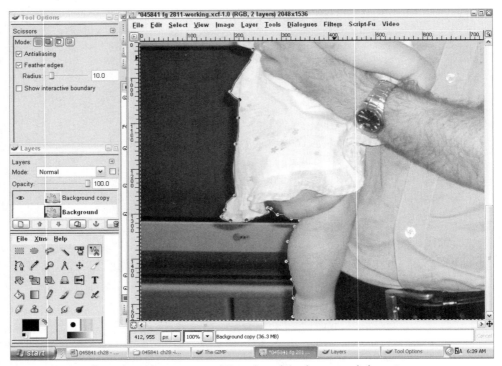

FIGURE 29-13: Follow along the contours of the edge of the foreground characters.

When you're finished, you should be back at the point you started. Left-click the first control point (the pointer icon changes when you are in the right spot). You'll probably find that you've made some mistakes, or that the auto contour hasn't quite worked, so you will need to make some adjustments to the curve. This is very easy. Simply left-click and hold down the mouse button while pointing to a control node to move it. Left-click on the curve to create a new control node. It should not take too long to create a curve that fits tightly around the foreground objects (see Figure 29-14). When you're ready, click inside the curve to make it a selection.

Now select Edit ⇨ Copy to copy the selection onto the clipboard. Right-click over the Background copy layer and from the context-sensitive menu, select New Layer. In the Layer Name text box type **Foreground** and make sure that Layer Fill Type is set to Transparent (as in Figure 29-15).

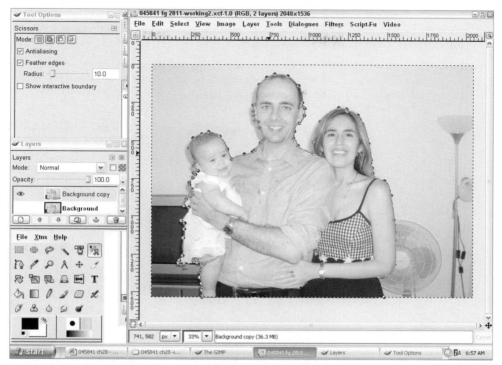

FIGURE 29-14: The curve now fully surrounds the foreground characters.

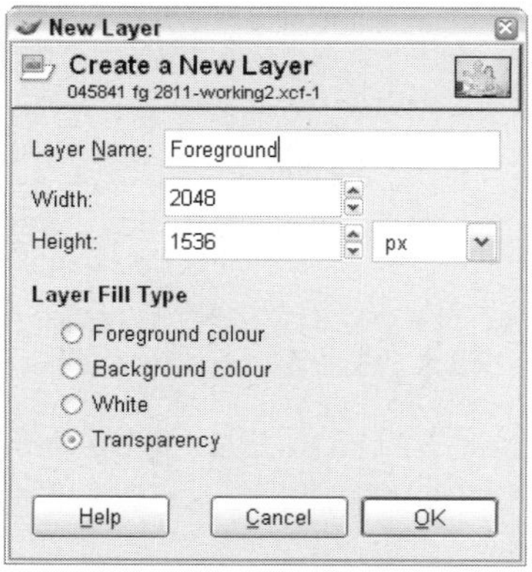

FIGURE 29-15: Creating a new layer

Select the Foreground layer by left-clicking it. Select Edit ⇨ Paste. In the Layers window, you'll see Floating Selection appear (it looks just like another layer). Right-click it, and in the context-sensitive menu, select Anchor Layer.

In the Layers window, click the eye next to the Background copy layer (so it becomes invisible) and make sure the eye is next to the Foreground layer. You should now see that the old background has been cut away (see Figure 29-16).

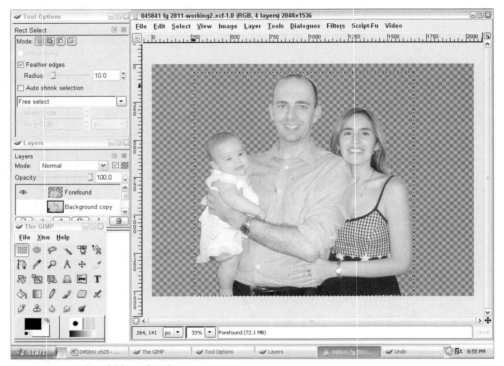

FIGURE 29-16: The old layer has been cut away.

Now it's time to put in a new background. Select File ⇨ Open As Layer. Navigate to the image file that you want as your background image and click OK. (You can use the background image supplied on the web site for this book at www.myspaceismyplace.com if you don't have your own image.) You'll need to make sure that the background is appropriately scaled before you load it, so that it properly and appropriately fills the background of the foreground image.

Chances are that when you load in the background it appears over the top of the foreground characters. Left-click the layer you have just loaded in and, holding down the left mouse button, drag it below the Foreground layer. Your foreground characters will not appear in front of your background (as in Figure 29-17). The tighter the selection of the foreground characters, the better the effect that you'll achieve. If you need to move the foreground characters, simply select the Foreground layer and use the Move Layers and Selections tool to move the layer around (this tool looks like a cross with arrows on each point).

FIGURE 29-17: The foreground now appears in front of the background image.

Make sure you save the file in the XCF format (File ⇨ Save) before saving the file as a JPG so that you can use it on your profile. Figure 29-18 shows what the final image looks like.

Tip

If you've enjoyed photo editing using GIMP and want to learn more, a good starting point is the collection of tutorials at the official GIMP web site. You'll find them here at `www.gimp.org/tutorials/`.

Figure 29-18: The final image with a new background

Wrapping Up

Even if your original image isn't up to par, chances are you can make some improvements with an image editing program, such as the open source GIMP package. A lot can be done simply by cropping, and adjusting the color and brightness. If you're a little braver, you can even put in a new background.

MySpace Music

This last part of the book looks at using MySpace to build your music career. A number of up-and-coming bands provide insights into how they use MySpace for promotion, and you may be surprised to hear just how important MySpace is becoming in this area.

The final chapter reflects on the future of MySpace and provides some ideas on where to go next to build up your skills and knowledge.

Finding Fame and Fortune on MySpace

MySpace's impact on the music industry has been amazing, and it's close to the point where all bands need to have a MySpace profile.

There's a special type of profile for musicians and bands that provides more functionality than the standard MySpace profile. It's free just as the standard profile is.

Creating a MySpace Artist's Profile

Creating a MySpace artist's profile is simply a matter of visiting www.myspace.com, clicking on the Music tab at the top of the page, and then clicking Artist Signup. Just as when you're creating a standard profile, you need to enter your details, except that with an artist signup you also need to enter your band name, music category, and whether you are signed with a record label or not.

At first glance, your home page looks very similar to a standard profile; it's only when you select Edit Profile that you can see that the control panels are very different, allowing you to add shows to your show schedule, enter your band details, enter basic information about your band, upload and manage your songs, and update your categories.

As with normal profiles, it's best to enter code through Safe Mode. Don't let the different headings fool you — placing code into an artist's profile is almost exactly the same as placing code in a regular profile, but you need to treat the Bio section as you would the About Me section, the Members section as you would treat the Who I'd like to meet section, and the Influences section as though it were the Interests section. So, for example, you'll find that the Div template you worked through in Chapter 24 works just fine, although you will need to make sure the music player is visible — which you can do by adding the following code to your style sheet:

```
td.text p object {visibility: visible; position:
absolute; left:50%; margin-left:-220px top:400px; }
```

As discussed in Chapter 25, you can also use the `margin-left` and `top` properties to position the player anywhere you like. You'll also need to remember to add back any band profile–specific links (such as the Top Artists and Music Forums links) into your Div overlays.

It's pretty easy to work out links. Just click the function you're trying to work out and the new URL is displayed in your browser when you're taken to that function. Where a token is displayed as part of the URL, simply delete everything after and including the `&`, so that:

```
collect.myspace.com/index.cfm?fuseaction=classifieds.listAds&catId=9
&Mytoken=538DF8E1-B1EB-12D0-FB0712C51C5E501070481570
```

becomes:

```
collect.myspace.com/index.cfm?fuseaction=classifieds.listAds&catId=9
```

It is theoretically possible to convert an existing regular profile into a MySpace band profile, but I recommend starting a new artist profile from scratch. I've heard of a number of people who've had problems when they tried to convert their standard profiles to band profiles.

Reality Check

Don't fool yourself into thinking you'll find fame and fortune simply by placing your band's profile on MySpace. With more than 600,000 other bands on MySpace — roughly one band for every ten regular members — that's a lot of competition.

If you want your band to be successful, obviously the first thing you need is talent. The second thing you need is perseverance, and the third thing you need is a lot of luck. That being said, MySpace can help you create your own luck by assisting you on two levels:

- **Finding fans to achieve a critical mass that helps you cut through the mass of competition:** The music industry calls this "breaking."
- **Getting a record deal:** But this is possible only if you can demonstrate your popularity on MySpace, and don't forget that there is a lot of competition.

We've covered a lot of ground in this book on hacking and design, and so we won't go over that ground again. Needless to say, it helps to have an interesting profile. I would also argue that it's important to have a number of good photographs of the band, but in the pages ahead, I will cover what you need to do to help you achieve the preceding two goals.

Using MySpace Effectively

MySpace is a great way for you to reach existing and potential fans. It's a great way for you to keep in touch with your fans, and to build your fan base.

Defining Who You Are

Before you can start selling yourself and projecting an image to the world, you need to know exactly what it is that you're selling. Ask yourself and your band members what kind of band are you? What genre do you fit into? What kind of music do you play? What kind of fans do you think you will attract? Create a profile that is consistent with what your band is about and that reflects the values your band represents.

Good Quality Sound

While you may not be able to get into a professional studio to record your songs, try to do the best you can. It's important that the sound quality of the songs you make available on your profile is at least reasonable.

Updating Regularly

Update the profile regularly — keep it fresh. Make it a place where fans can find the most up-to-date information about what the band is doing, when shows are on, whether there is a new record coming out, and so on. Use your blog to keep in touch with your fans.

Segmenting Your Market

You need to think carefully about the kinds of people you think will be interested in your music. There's no point trying to make friends with everyone on MySpace — not everyone is interested in your genre of music — and it would not be an efficient use of your time. The best approach is to try to identify a group of people that you think might be interested. In marketing, this is called *segmentation*, and basically it stems from the realization that it's very time consuming and expensive to go after everyone, and much cheaper and more effective to go after groups that you know are likely to be interested. In MySpace, you have two tools to help you segment the market: Browse and Search. Using Browse, you can target groups by age and sex, for example, or if you're in the United States, United Kingdom, or Canada by ZIP code so you can actually try to find prospective fans in your local area, which, if you're trying to get people to come to a gig, is an amazingly powerful tool. The search tool allows you to search profiles by key words, so if you put in punk, you'll get a list of profiles with a reference to that search term.

Get the Word Out

When you find someone who might be interested in your music, try to add them as a friend, putting in a short note that you think they might be interested in your music. Keep in mind that while segmentation is very important, this is also a numbers game. The more targeted approaches you make, the better your chance of collecting a number of "friends" who might be interested in your music.

Once you've identified people who might be interested in your music, what do you do? Well, really you've got two choices — you can send a friend request or send a message. The problem with a message is that there is no easy response; you can tell people what you want, but there's no quick and easy way for them to do it. From a marketing point of view, if you're asking people to do something, you want it to be as easy as possible for them to participate. That's why sending a friend request is perfect. If a would-be friend thinks she might be interested in your music she will add you as a friend. It will then be easy for her to check back on you in the future, and it also promotes your band when somebody else checks out the profile. It also means that they'll receive any bulletins you send out to your friends.

Another strategy is to leave comments on the profiles of big-name acts asking fans of that artist to come and check your music out. You could even include an image in the comment to attract attention (you can include image tags and links in your comments).

Make the Right Friends

Why are some bands so successful and others not? Sure, some bands are good, and others not so good, but as we all know, simply being good is not enough to guarantee success. So there must be something more involved.

Malcolm Gladwell, in his excellent book *The Tipping Point: How Little Things Can Make a Big Difference,* talks about the concept of social epidemics to explain, for example, the rebirth of Hush Puppy shoes, which were selling only 30,000 pairs worldwide in 1994. Gladwell's hypothesis was that a few cool kids in New York's East Village started wearing second-hand Hush Puppies. This soon caught the eye of fashion designers such as Isaac Mizrahi, which led to orders from fashion designers wanting the shoes for the catwalk, which in turn led to Hush Puppies becoming a fashion trend. In two years, more Hush Puppy shoes were sold than in the previous decade.

Obviously, you're not selling shoes, but there is something you can learn. What made the big difference for Hush Puppy was not some big advertising campaign that reached millions of people; it was just the fact that a very small number of the right people took a shining to the shoes, which caught the attraction of another small group of people (the designers), who were then in a position to promote them to the masses.

The challenge for a new band is not to reach millions of people immediately, but to find the right people, who can then, through word of mouth, spread the news. When you're searching for potential new fans, these are the kinds of people you should be looking for. This is easier said than done, and Gladwell identified a number of different types of people that can help to spread social epidemics. These included:

- **Connectors:** Those with large circles of friends who often are the hubs of these social networks. In MySpace, these would be people with large numbers of friends who receive lots of comments, and also post lots of comments.

- **Mavens:** Knowledgeable people, whom others often come to for advice. In MySpace, Mavens may be highly respected participants in groups and forums.

- **Salesmen:** Charismatic people who have the power to influence people, although it's more of a soft sell than a hard sell. You'll see them coordinating Groups and Forums on MySpace.

In real life you may find that people exhibit more than one of these traits, and many people who exhibit none of these traits. You should be able to tell from someone's profile whether he belongs to any of these categories, but remember that it is also a numbers game, so don't dwell too long on anyone's profile.

Case Studies

We can always learn from those that have come before, and in this spirit, here are the stories of five artists who currently use MySpace to promote their acts. You'll find their experiences inspirational, and the practical advice they provide very valuable. Here, then, in their own words, are their stories. You'll find links to their profiles at the companion web site, www.myspaceismyplace.com. I also plan to add some additional case studies in the future.

Jessica Mellott

Profile URL: www.myspace.com/jessicamellott

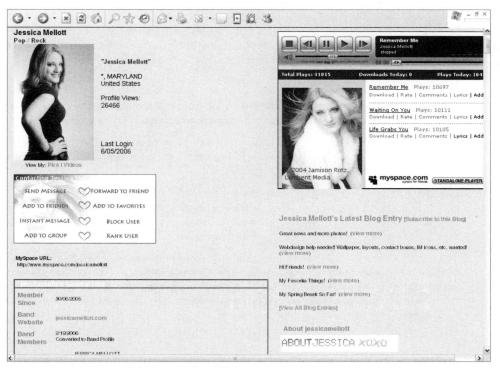

FIGURE 30-1: Jessica Mellott's MySpace profile

Jessica's Story

I have always wanted to become a professional entertainer. I started voice lessons at five.

I take lessons with a local instructor in Maryland and a coach in California via the telephone. I am a junior in high school and am enrolled in the Advanced Music Studies program so half of my day is spent singing and I love it! Throughout the years, I have been involved in a lot of musical activities including musical theater, competitions, and shows. I have performed at charities helping to raise thousands of dollars.

I cut my first demo in the fall of 2005 and one of the songs went to number one at an Internet site and stayed there for months. I cut another demo and wanted a way to expose it to a large number of people. As a high school student, I was not in a position to tour and my small hometown does not offer many singing opportunities.

I knew that many bands were on MySpace and I decided it might be a good way to reach a lot of people so I converted from a personal profile to a band profile at the end of February, 2006. At the time I converted I had about 150 friends. Within a few weeks, my songs were receiving hundreds of hits a day at my MySpace site, www.myspace.com/jessicamellott, and I had close to 5,000 friends! My MySpace profile has a link to my web site, www.jessicamellott.com, and now my web site receives hits from people all over the world!

Offers have started to come in from other MySpacers as I expand my network. Although some of these offers are just MySpace chatter, many are legitimate, including an offer to tour in Europe, have my songs remixed, sign with an Indie label, and more! As more people discover my music on MySpace, more opportunities come up to share my music!

Jessica's Tips

As an artist on MySpace, my goal is to share my music with people, and I would also like to get a record deal. I try to make my MySpace profile fun to visit and I try to keep it interesting.

I also want it to reflect my music and my personality. I love pink. So my MySpace profile is pink with a few hearts. I keep it simple so it's easy to navigate but I try to keep it interesting by adding new pictures and blogs to my MySpace.

I had banners designed that are on my profile page. People can add these to their MySpace profile and other people will see these on their page, click them, and visit my web site or my MySpace. I also have a blue button on my page. People can click it and it will post a bulletin to their friends letting them know about me and my music.

The one thing that is important is that it's not all about numbers. I could have millions of friends on MySpace but if no one is visiting my MySpace profile and listening to my music I am not accomplishing anything. So I focus on trying to get to know my friends on MySpace. I receive several hundred comments and private messages every day and I spend many hours each week answering them. I try and visit my friends and let them know I care about them. Even though I have a lot of friends I remember a lot about each and every one of them.

The Take Away

- Your profile should reflect your personality (or your band's personality).
- Keep your profile easy to navigate.
- Update your profile regularly by changing pictures and blogging.
- Get some banners designed that fans can place on their profiles to link back to your profile.
- Incidentally, if you want a blue button similar to the one that Jessica uses on her web page, you can generate it here: `http://www.chasebadkids.net/reborn/index.php?x=autobulletinpost`.

rfp

Profile URL: `http://www.myspace.com/rfp`

FIGURE 30-2: rfp's profile

rfp's story

Based out of Orillia, Ontario, rfp (radio-friendly propaganda) is a three-piece rock band striving to create its own sound while still producing a radio-friendly feel. The two founding members, Nate and Taylor, had written music together since high school and after high school found themselves performing as a two-piece rock group. The pair invested in recording a five-song demo and shortly after, Martin joined the band and the band began playing shows more often.

rfp has been together less than one year, and has made a big impression on the Orillia rock scene. Band members have won all of the band battles they have participated in, some with up to 20+ local bands, some not even in their home town. They have begun to branch out to other cities across Ontario and have found dedicated fans at each stop.

While rfp has now headlined many successful shows, the band has also shared the stage with some major-label acts, and is often found playing with notable, up-and-coming bands. The band also used its music to help others by performing many charity shows. rfp has been recognized by the Canadian Hearing Society for its fund-raising efforts, and during the 2005 Tsunami crisis, rfp organized and sponsored a charity show, raising over $1,500 that was donated to the Canadian Red Cross.

In just one year, the band has accomplished so much and the band members have met many personal goals. They are working with producer Chris Gordon (Sum 41, Our Lady Peace, Rush) on their new demo, which is set to be released summer 2006.

The band boasts a highly active MySpace profile and, as a result, has sold albums worldwide.

Nate on MySpace

MySpace will be the key to our success. I've always felt that our problem is not the product — it's the marketing, and MySpace has helped solve the problem.

Taylor came to my apartment one night and showed me a band's MySpace profile, and then told me he had signed us up. At first we had no pictures or logo or songs, but I still would browse profiles and add people. I started to use MySpace to promote our band, even though we weren't doing much at that point.

As our profile grew, I was able to ask our fans to tell their friends about us because their friends might like our music if they listened to it.

MySpace allows you to send bulletin messages to all your friends at the same time. We would send bulletins to our friends, requesting that they send a bulletin to all of their friends telling them about us. I would repeat the process as our friends list grew.

I also posted comments, with a picture banner of our band, on our friends' pages. That way, anyone who visited their page would see our band. These banners contain a link to our page that, when clicked, reveals our profile in a separate window. The code to display these banners is provided on our profile, and fans are often happy to place the banners on their own profiles.

By far, the most effective way to get attention and gain new friends is to visit the major-label bands that I have already added to our friends list, and then post a comment with our picture banner and a request that their fans check us out also. I usually post our picture on the profiles of about 50 major-label bands and artists at a time.

Persistent banner posting has resulted in thousands of plays in just hours and sometimes hundreds of friends in that same time span. The major-label bands have hundreds of thousands of friends and visits each day and by posting our picture on their profiles we are exposed to thousands of active, supportive MySpace users.

It is much more effective than just adding people randomly, or sending out mass messages using programs that aren't issued by MySpace. You are selecting your target audience, and offering yourself only to those who are interested. In the end, you end up with "friends" who actually enjoy your music and are willing to support your band.

The results have been overwhelming at times. We have been contacted by many smaller record companies offering to sign us. We also were contacted by a major record label via MySpace.

We have been able to play shows all across Ontario by networking with other bands from our area. We've sold many CDs that we personally packaged and mailed to locations around the world. All thanks to MySpace. MySpace has done so much for our careers. I can't imagine where we would be without it.

My advice to any band is to be realistic. MySpace makes it easy for a band to get exposed, but at the same time it also makes it easy for thousands of other bands. So a band that doesn't try hard won't get anywhere. Further, having an active MySpace profile doesn't necessarily bring success by any means. If you're not also playing shows like crazy, you're not much of a band. Playing shows is what makes a band a band.

We'd really like to thank John for giving us the opportunity to shed some light on what we're doing, and how MySpace has helped us reach out to thousands. In fact, it is how he found us, so again a perfect example of what MySpace is doing for not only bands and the music industry, but aspiring film makers, promoters, agencies, venues, friends, and family. We'd also like to thank you for reading, and we hope you stop by on our MySpace profile and see it for yourself.

The Take Away

- To build your fan base, post comments on your fans' profiles with banners that link back to your profile. Do same with the profiles of well-known acts. It's much better to do this than to send out mass messages.

- An active profile is not enough — you need to get out and play shows.

- MySpace is an excellent way of networking with other bands and with people in the music industry.

North of Hollywood

Profile URL: www.myspace.com/northofhollywood

North of Hollywood's Story

North of Hollywood was born when founder Chad Campbell came back to Canada after a five-year stint in Los Angeles living life, writing songs, and playing acoustic shows. He called up Matt Horvath, a childhood friend and guitarist, to begin a project that would combine his L.A. acoustic songs with a rock 'n' roll sensibility.

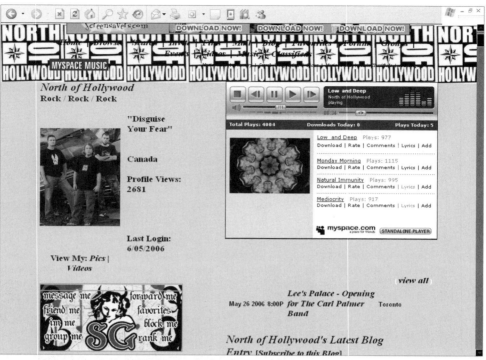

FIGURE 30-3: North of Hollywood's MySpace profile

This project saw many evolutions in terms of band members and even the style of music the band now plays. After countless members came and went the band finally settled on the well-rounded jazz/punk drummer Jay Phaby, and energetic guitarist/bass player Mike Lowry for the bass spot. With these additions, the band's music has taken on a much more driven rock 'n' roll edge, combining Chad's melodic songs with punk undertones and heavier riffs.

They are currently in pre-production for their first studio album for Bullseye and are arranging songs for an acoustic tour this summer.

Mike found out about MySpace when a friend mentioned that a band he knew set up a summer tour completely based on talking to people on the site.

From then on, Mike was constantly on the site networking and talking to bands as well as music industry and media folks.

MySpace has been a large factor in securing a fan base around Toronto and other nearby Ontario cities, but also internationally.

We find a lot of music fans are quite open-minded when it comes to music especially in countries such as Australia, Sweden, and Ireland.

And for a band that started out without the backing of a record label, MySpace has provided us with a great networking tool for setting up shows and getting the word out so that as many people as possible attend these performances.

The blogs are perfect to use for special announcements and updates.

The Take Away

- MySpace can be used to build a following both locally, as well as nationally and internationally.
- The blogging tools are a great way to keep fans up-to-date with new developments.

Joshua's Whisper

Profile URL: `http://www.myspace.com/joshuaswhisper`

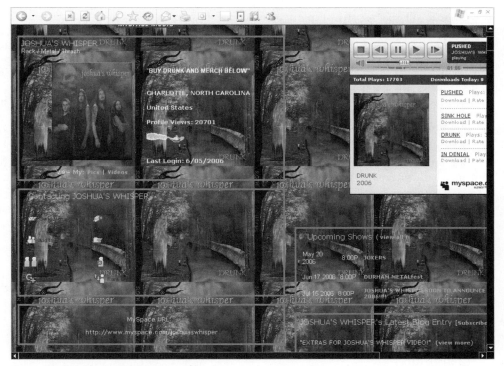

FIGURE 30-4: Joshua's Whisper's profile

Joshua's Whisper's Story

Joshua's Whisper was formed in the late 1990s by brothers Greg and Tim Bailes, bringing to life their vision of establishing a band that could incorporate a blend of heavy deep riffs and powerful vocals.

In the spring of 2001, this band was given an opportunity to introduce its demo to a panel of record executives in Atlanta, Georgia. The demo was well received by Attack Records and, soon after, Mark S. Berry, President & CEO of Attack Records, agreed to produce the band's first record, "Tempted."

Recently, Joshua's Whisper signed with Attack/Universal Records, and the band now has a new CD, "DRUNK." Their new video is being played on MUCH and a tour schedule to coincide with the new CD is planned.

Joshua's Whisper began networking on MySpace in April 2005. MySpace has definitely turned into a great source for marketing our music to the world along with selling merchandise and advertising band news. With diligent upkeep, MySpace can be a major asset for any artist interested in promoting his or her work.

Joshua's Whisper uses MySpace for promotion and advertising, as well as for direct contact with fans and possible new listeners. MySpace is a great tool for any band that wants to push its music to a wide range of listeners. As opposed to a basic web page, you have the networking system of MySpace allowing you to personally contact all MySpace clients to give them a preview of what the band sounds like and looks like, and to provide other information concerning the band. Another great attribute of MySpace is that you can monitor the demographics of your fan base.

Joshua's Whisper's Advice

My advice for bands that have been using MySpace, or are in the first stages of using it to create a profile is to be clear about what you have to offer, and what your music is about. Photos, merchandising, news, and so on will give the visitor an immediate idea of what your band is about.

The Take Away

- MySpace is a great place for keeping in touch with fans and attracting new listeners.
- Use photos, news, and merchandise on your profile to create a strong presence.

Ben Bledsoe

Profile URL: http://www.myspace.com/benbledsoe

Ben's Story

At 16, I joined the band Natural and spent the next six years recording, touring, and performing all around the world. The band received two Gold records for singles in the United States, and won awards throughout Europe and Asia.

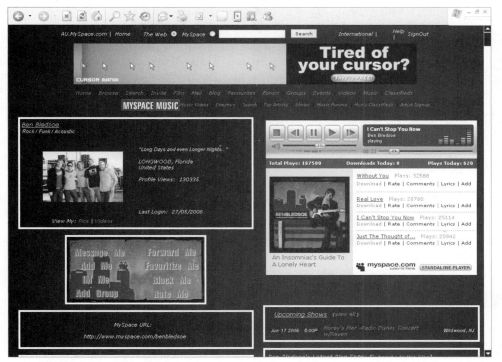

FIGURE 30-5: Ben Bledsoe's profile

I have since gone solo, and am running my own label and promotions for my new music. In August 2005, I released a new CD, "An Insomniac's Guide to a Lonely Heart."

MySpace doesn't generate a lot of sales, but it does help generate a large fan base, which helps with name and face recognition.

I signed up for MySpace because a friend of mine told me that it was a good way to get back in contact with friends from school. So I signed up . . . and in the first few days, I had a few hundred friends. A lot of the fans found out about it and jumped right in. I started to realize that it was actually set up for musicians, too, and signed up for a band account. There are a few people pretending to be me, but I'm cool with it, because usually it's pretty harmless and it's the international fans setting up pages in different languages.

So as soon as I realized that it was an easy way to reach a ton of people at one time, I started sending bulletins. I try not to con people into reading them with fake titles because I know that once I have been tricked by someone into reading something I couldn't care less about, I usually won't go back.

I just send updates and when I need help, I ask. My numbers have been going up a lot, so I get a lot of mail in response to every bulletin or blog, but it's worth it because I appreciate that everyone is even willing to listen. I like to take the time to go through everything; even though MySpace has a cap on how many mails I can send per day, I go until I can't send any more.

I think the basic trick is just keeping people interested in what you're up to. Post about your life, blog, add games or puzzles to your page, and so on. I did a chat on Valentine's Day for anyone that was single. Anything that makes people spend time on your page adds to your name and face recognition. And they get the chance to listen to your music the whole time and at least see whether they like it or not. With so much good and bad music on MySpace, your only hope is to let people hear it and judge for themselves.

MySpace has had the most significant effect at shows. I get a lot of people that come to my shows from MySpace and a lot of people who recognize me at others' shows because of my presence on MySpace.

The Take Away

- MySpace is a great way to build a fan base, and to build name and face recognition.
- Keep your fans updated with what you're doing by regularly sending bulletins and by blogging.

Wrapping Up

While MySpace doesn't eliminate the need for talent, it can provide a means to reach new fans and to network with music industry folk. If you take the time to target people who may have in interest in your music, you have a better chance of converting them into fans. The five case studies should inspire you and give you some ideas on how you can use MySpace to promote your band.

Final Thoughts

I started writing this book just after MySpace was acquired by News Limited when it had just over 40 million users. In the five months that it took me to put this book together, another 40 million users joined. It certainly seems that MySpace is well on its way to becoming a mainstream phenomenon. Here are some thoughts on the future of MySpace and also some ideas on what you can do to build on what you've learned in this book.

A Cleaner MySpace

Most people have at least heard about MySpace, although often it's in a negative context. There have been a number of stories about the dangers that young people face from Internet predators, and about the some of the risqué material that members have placed in their profiles.

Of course, with a new multinational owner, MySpace has been trying to clean up its image, with some of the more provocative MySpace profiles being deleted.

Given that what makes MySpace attractive to so many of its users is its relative openness, you've got to wonder whether a cleaner MySpace will make it less attractive to the cool, young people that have so far flocked to it. That being said, it may be that by making it more acceptable to the mainstream, News Limited will accelerate MySpace's growth — which at the time of writing, seems to be the case. It may be that MySpace turns out to be one of News Limited's more forward thinking acquisitions.

Fad or a Sign of Things to Come

Is MySpace a fad or a sign of things to come? If you're in your mid 20s or younger. you're probably too young to remember the Geocities fad in the mid 1990s, where everyone was creating their own personal web sites, which were very much "Web 1.0" in nature as opposed to the "Web 2.0" feature-rich sites we're used to today. Why did Geocities become such a fad? Well, that's the thing about fads — often they don't really have a point, and there really wasn't much of a point to Geocities (which, incidentally, was acquired by Yahoo).

Often what happened with a Geocities site (or with one of the many competitors) was that you would make up your site using the free template, and then you'd never do anything else — there really wasn't very much to do.

MySpace, on the other hand, is a very different experience — it serves to fill a fundamental human need, which is to interact with other people. Sure, you still need to create a web page, or rather a profile, but then there is so much for you do in true Web 2.0 style — publish blogs, share your photos, comment on your friend's photos, and so on.

I notice that many people use MySpace to keep in touch with friends and acquaintances that they may not otherwise be able to keep in touch with. In this way, MySpace is not only a tool for creating new social networks, but it's also a social tool for keeping existing networks alive, and for keeping lower-priority relationships bubbling away.

Thus, in the modern age of information overload, MySpace makes it possible to manage the multitude of relationships that people find themselves involved in.

For this reason, I tend to think that MySpace, from a user perspective, does solve a legitimate human need, and therefore MySpace and its competitors are more than just a flash in the pan.

The Rise of Advertainment

I was checking out the video section of MySpace, and one of the featured videos was called "Weirdo." It looked interesting, so I played it through. It was only at the end that I discovered that the video was actually an ad for an online real-estate business. The associated profile was linked to a blog that was sponsored by the same real-estate company.

A little bit of research revealed that the ad was actually part of a viral marketing campaign, and the blog was being sponsored to support the campaign. Personally, I felt a little uncomfortable that I was duped into watching an ad. In the mainstream media, it's usually made clear what is advertising and what is content, although it seems that the traditional divide between the two are less clear online. This is something you should be aware of, especially as marketers devise ever more clever strategies for "engaging" with Internet users.

Video Blogs

Video hosting has really taken off, especially with sites such as YouTube, Google Video (video.google.com), and of course MySpace making it very easy to upload video clips. And now because so many people have fast Internet connections, it's quite feasible to download video, making the Web into a true alternate video channel where people spend at least minutes, if not hours, scouring through the millions of weird and wonderful videos that are online. At the same time, it has also become very easy to produce video — anyone with a microphone and web cam can create their own video blog.

The video blogosphere has already had its overnight sensations. Take the case of Nornna, a 24-year-old Wisconsin woman, who rose to national attention because of her video blog diary on YouTube. Nornna eventually removed the video blogs from YouTube in a bid to get rid of the unwanted attention. While doing research for this book, I came across some video blogs on Youtube.com that were produced by some "emo" kids talking about all the terrible things going on in their lives, and complaining about video blogs by other emo kids. More than anything these video blogs reminded me of the characters that you see on television shows like Jerry Springer's.

In 1968 pop artist Andy Warhol famously said "In the future everyone will be world-famous for fifteen minutes." Whenever I've heard this quote I dismissed it as an artist's creative exaggeration. With the rise of blogs, and now video blogs, I can't help thinking that maybe Warhol was right after all.

Of course video blogs do require more effort to put together, and there are only so many minutes in the day. Nevertheless, video blogs, if not the next big thing, will certainly make social networking sites such as MySpace more interesting.

As with any new development, whether you're talking about the Web, podcasts, blogs, or videoblogs, in the early days everyone rushes to take part or to stake a claim (as in a gold rush). This means the level of "noise" (not very good or high quality content) is very high — while the amount of true quality content is low.

This will obviously change. People will get better — there is always consolidation — but for now, it's the Wild Wild West of the Web all over again, except that now, instead of text web sites, it's Web 2.0 feature-rich sites and digital media: text, audio, video, and combinations thereof.

Expect to see video sites continue becoming more popular, as it will likely still take some time before the true "cream" rises to the top. And because it is so easy for anyone to become a content creator, there will be a lot of noise for some time to come.

But in the end, as with everything, things will settle down, with a raft of well-known content creators at a range of levels, from the big name CNNs to the popular bloggers, video bloggers, podcasters, and so on. Overnight sensations will continue to appear — just as we have new singers appearing all the time — but to succeed, you've got to be more than a flash in the pan. Consistent quality is always going to be important if you're going to have a chance at success.

The Tipping Point

I was reading though Tom's comments (yes Tom, as in the founder of MySpace) and among the several thousand toady comments was an interesting note from a young woman who eagerly exclaimed, "Tom, you have changed society!" It was a sentiment I dismissed at first — changing society is a pretty big thing. You can certainly argue that the Internet, or the Web, or e-mail, changed society, but it's a little harder to say that a particular web site has changed society. Yet, at the same time, MySpace has had a big impact on popular culture, both in terms of what it does (especially in the case of the alternative scene and popular music) and in terms of how it has been reported on and perceived by other media (everything from being a sleazy dive to the Internet's next big thing).

One of reasons that MySpace is having such an impact is its huge membership. As I mentioned, when I started writing this book there were just over 40 million profiles. Now, five months later, there are over 80 million profiles, and there's even a cell phone company that is offering a package that includes access to MySpace, and the ability to do such things as send out blogs and bulletins.

The newest phones from Nokia and Sony Ericsson, available with 3.2 megapixel cameras and due to be released in mid-2006, have blogging software built into the phone, enabling you to instantly blog a photo you have taken by pressing a single button. No doubt the time will soon come when you can record a video podcast /blog using your phone and upload it to your blog.

The MySpace phenomenon seems to be an excellent example of a social epidemic (as described in Malcolm Gladwell's book *The Tipping Point*). Gladwell used the expression "tipping point" to describe how a social epidemic reaches critical mass, and tips over into the mainstream.

The only question is this: What will it take for MySpace to become truly mainstream? Will there ever come a time when MySpace is so popular that the majority of young people have a MySpace profile? If MySpace continues to grow, perhaps it will get to the point where if you're a young person, and you want to participate in youth culture and fit into your social network, you're going to need a MySpace account. And how soon before a true competitor to MySpace emerges, to not only challenge the dominance of MySpace, but to force MySpace to evolve into something even better and more spectacular to keep the interest and loyalty of its many millions of members? Or is MySpace really just a fad, only to be replaced by something completely different in the not too distant future?

Taking the Next Step

I hope you forgive me the indulgence of speculating about the future of MySpace. I hope this book has given you a good idea of how to create a profile that will stand out from the rest, but this is really only the first step in a journey to improve your programming and design skills. Here are my suggestions on how you can take the next step.

Improve Your CSS Skills

While many books are available on HTML and CSS, there are also many resources on the Internet. Some of the places where you can go online to learn more about CSS include:

- **World Wide Web Consortium** (`www.w3.org`): The World Wide Web Consortium (W3C) is the organization that sets the CSS standard; it has a page of resources at `www.w3.org/Style/CSS/learning` for people who want to learn more about CSS.

- **W3 Schools** (`www.w3schools.com`): W3 Schools offers free high-quality tutorials on HTML and CSS. It is a very good way to improve your skills at no cost.

- **MSDN library** (`http://msdn.microsoft.com/library/`): Microsoft has a lot of useful information in its developer's library. You can learn a lot about CSS here: `http://msdn.microsoft.com/library/default.asp?url=/workshop/author/dhtml/dhtml_node_entry.asp`.

Learn from Others

A great way to learn about creating MySpace profiles is to look at other people's profiles and try to work out how they were done. There's even a group on MySpace dedicated to outstanding layouts: Magnificent Layouts (`groups.myspace.com/magnificentlayouts`).

Join a Coder's Group

Other great resources on MySpace are groups dedicated to MySpace hacks and modifications. Here you'll find people sharing their code. Some of the sites include:

- **BBZ** (`groups.myspace.com/bbz`): A very good group that offers codes and tutorials for all sorts of customization
- **HTML Masters** (`groups.myspace.com/html`): A group that can help answer questions you might have about coding, customization, or just MySpace in general
- **DivSpace The Remix** (`groups.myspace.com/divspace2`): An "HTML Militia" offering HTML codes, Div layouts, and Flash designs

Many web sites offer MySpace codes, including the following:

- **Free Code Source** (`www.freecodesource.com`): In addition to codes and layouts, this site also has profile editors and generators.
- **Skem9.com** (`www.skem9.com`): This site has pre-made layouts, generators, and really cool graphics for your page and a great forum for help.
- **#bbz.space** (`www.bbzspace.com`): This site offers a tutorial search engine, as well as lots of great links to generators.
- **Private Pyro** (`live.privatepyro.com`): This site offers lots of MySpace codes but is well known for its Flash-based MP3 players that allow you to play a number of songs.
- **Profile Jewels** (`www.ourspace.biz/jewels/`): This site offers layouts, graphics, cursors, and codes.

Learn Flash

As you saw in Chapter 27, many of the more interesting sites use Flash movies to great effect. Many tools are available to create Flash movies, from the Flash software itself (now distributed by Adobe, `www.adobe.com`), to other commercial programs such as Swish (`www.swishzone.com`), Koolmoves (`www.koolmoves.com`), and SWF Quicker 2.2 (`www.sothink.com`). Many of these programs are available for a free trial period, so you can test out the software before you buy. This is also a good way to get a taste of whether you want to go further with Flash. MySpace is home to a number of groups dedicated to helping you learn more about Flash, including Copenhagen Flash Tutorials (`groups.myspace.com/copenhagentutorials`), which features video and written tutorials on how to create Flash-based MySpace profiles.

You'll also find a lot of resources online simply by searching for "Flash tutorials" on Google.

Final Word

Thank you for reading this book. I hope you've enjoyed it and learned a few tricks. While I hope I've given you a good foundation, the truth is that there is so much that you can do to customize your MySpace profile that I have just scratched the surface.

I would be very happy to hear from you, so please come and visit my support web site at `www.myspaceismyplace.com`. I will also be posting updates at the site as well as any corrections.

If you've read something in this book that's unclear, or you have suggestions, or if you have some code you would like to share, please come and participate in the forums on my web site. Also, there's no doubt that MySpace will change the structure of its profiles at some point, and this may affect the codes in this book. Have fun!

Color Codes

The following table shows all 143 color names that are recognized by newer browsers. It's generally better from a compatibility perspective to use the hexadecimal value given rather than the name of the color, although of course it is much more convenient to use the name of the color. Don't include the # symbol when specifying colors by their hexadecimal values.

Color Name	Hex
AliceBlue	#F0F8FF
AntiqueWhite	#FAEBD7
Aqua	#00FFFF
Aquamarine	#7FFFD4
Azure	#F0FFFF
Beige	#F5F5DC
Bisque	#FFE4C4
Black	#000000
BlanchedAlmond	#FFEBCD
Blue	#0000FF
BlueViolet	#8A2BE2
Brown	#A52A2A
BurlyWood	#DEB887
CadetBlue	#5F9EA0
Chartreuse	#7FFF00
Chocolate	#D2691E
Coral	#FF7F50
CornflowerBlue	#6495ED
Cornsilk	#FFF8DC
Crimson	#DC143C
Cyan	#00FFFF

Color Name	Hex
DarkBlue	#00008B
DarkCyan	#008B8B
DarkGoldenRod	#B8860B
DarkGray	#A9A9A9
DarkGreen	#006400
DarkKhaki	#BDB76B
DarkMagenta	#8B008B
DarkOliveGreen	#556B2F
DarkOrange	#FF8C00
DarkOrchid	#9932CC
DarkRed	#8B0000
DarkSalmon	#E9967A
DarkSeaGreen	#8FBC8F
DarkSlateBlue	#483D8B
DarkSlateGray	#2F4F4F
DarkTurquoise	#00CED1
DarkViolet	#9400D3
DeepPink	#FF1493
DeepSkyBlue	#00BFFF
DimGray	#696969
DodgerBlue	#1E90FF
Feldspar	#D19275
FireBrick	#B22222
FloralWhite	#FFFAF0
ForestGreen	#228B22
Fuchsia	#FF00FF
Gainsboro	#DCDCDC
GhostWhite	#F8F8FF
Gold	#FFD700
GoldenRod	#DAA520

Color Name	Hex
Gray	#808080
Green	#008000
GreenYellow	#ADFF2F
HoneyDew	#F0FFF0
HotPink	#FF69B4
IndianRed	#CD5C5C
Indigo	#4B0082
Ivory	#FFFFF0
Khaki	#F0E68C
Lavender	#E6E6FA
LavenderBlush	#FFF0F5
LawnGreen	#7CFC00
LemonChiffon	#FFFACD
LightBlue	#ADD8E6
LightCoral	#F08080
LightCyan	#E0FFFF
LightGoldenRodYellow	#FAFAD2
LightGrey	#D3D3D3
LightGreen	#90EE90
LightPink	#FFB6C1
LightSalmon	#FFA07A
LightSeaGreen	#20B2AA
LightSkyBlue	#87CEFA
LightSlateBlue	#8470FF
LightSlateGray	#778899
LightSteelBlue	#B0C4DE
LightYellow	#FFFFE0
Lime	#00FF00
LimeGreen	#32CD32
Linen	#FAF0E6

Color Name	Hex
Magenta	#FF00FF
Maroon	#800000
MediumAquaMarine	#66CDAA
MediumBlue	#0000CD
MediumOrchid	#BA55D3
MediumPurple	#9370D8
MediumSeaGreen	#3CB371
MediumSlateBlue	#7B68EE
MediumSpringGreen	#00FA9A
MediumTurquoise	#48D1CC
MediumVioletRed	#C71585
MidnightBlue	#191970
MintCream	#F5FFFA
MistyRose	#FFE4E1
Moccasin	#FFE4B5
NavajoWhite	#FFDEAD
Navy	#000080
OldLace	#FDF5E6
Olive	#808000
OliveDrab	#6B8E23
Orange	#FFA500
OrangeRed	#FF4500
Orchid	#DA70D6
PaleGoldenRod	#EEE8AA
PaleGreen	#98FB98
PaleTurquoise	#AFEEEE
PaleVioletRed	#D87093
PapayaWhip	#FFEFD5
PeachPuff	#FFDAB9
Peru	#CD853F
Pink	#FFC0CB

Color Name	Hex
Plum	#DDA0DD
PowderBlue	#B0E0E6
Purple	#800080
Red	#FF0000
RosyBrown	#BC8F8F
RoyalBlue	#4169E1
SaddleBrown	#8B4513
Salmon	#FA8072
SandyBrown	#F4A460
SeaGreen	#2E8B57
SeaShell	#FFF5EE
Sienna	#A0522D
Silver	#C0C0C0
SkyBlue	#87CEEB
SlateBlue	#6A5ACD
SlateGray	#708090
Snow	#FFFAFA
SpringGreen	#00FF7F
SteelBlue	#4682B4
Tan	#D2B48C
Teal	#008080
Thistle	#D8BFD8
Tomato	#FF6347
Turquoise	#40E0D0
Violet	#EE82EE
VioletRed	#D02090
Wheat	#F5DEB3
White	#FFFFFF
WhiteSmoke	#F5F5F5
Yellow	#FFFF00
YellowGreen	#9ACD32

Source: WC3 Consortium (http://www.w3.org/TR/css3-color/)

CSS Units of Measurement

There are two types of measurement units in CSS: absolute and relative. Absolute units are quite easy to understand. You specify the size (or position) and that's the size that it appears, whereas with relative units, you define the size (or position) relative to other elements or factors. The following lists provide overviews of the measurement units you'll need when working with CSS.

Relative length units:

- **px:** Pixels (the picture elements that make up images on your computer's screen)

- **%:** Percentage

- **em:** Height of the current element's fonts

- **ex:** Height of the letter x

Absolute units:

- **in:** Inches

- **cm:** Centimeters

- **mm:** Millimeters

- **pt:** Points (1 point = $\frac{1}{72}$ inches)

- **pc:** Pica (1 pica = 12 points)

At this point, you might say: Hang on. I understand that percentage is relative, but how about pixels, ems, and exs? Pixels are considered relative units because how they appear depends on the resolution and size of your screen. Obviously, 10 pixels will appear larger in an 800×600 resolution than in a 1024×768 resolution. Em and ex are relative because each is a function of the size of the surrounding font.

Glossary

attribute: In CSS, this is a value associated with a property.

AVI (Audio Video Interleave): A widely used multimedia (and, more specifically, video) format introduced by Microsoft in 1992.

class: Used in CSS to group properties so that they can be applied to HTML tags.

CSS (cascading style sheets): A computer language that allows you to define how an element will appear in a style sheet, which then allows you to apply that style as many times as you want. Used in HTML coding to customize a page's look and feel with much greater control than is possible and practical with regular HTML code.

element: In the context of web development, an element is some part of your web page, such as text, images, or tables.

Flash: A multimedia authoring program that allows the creation of web content with animation and interactivity along with audio and video capabilities if desired.

GIF (Graphics Interchange Format): An image format commonly used on the Internet with up to 256 individual colors from a possible palette of 16 million colors. The limited palette, and lossless compression, means this format is best used for logos and line illustrations. It is not suitable for photographs.

hexadecimal: A numbering system that uses the characters 0 to 9 and A to F. In the context of MySpace, this is the preferred way to specify colors.

HTML (HyperText Markup Language): A computer language designed to allow the creation of web pages through the use of tags.

JAVA: A computer programming language developed by Sun Microsystems that allows programs to run on different computers via a web browser.

JPG: A file format for photographic images that uses JPEG (Joint Photographic Experts Group) compression to minimize file size.

MP3: An audio file compression format designed to allow relatively small files that still sound like the uncompressed original to most people.

MPG: A file format that uses the MPEG (Moving Picture Experts Group) family of compression standards to compress audio and video.

property: In CSS, a property is an attribute or characteristic that can be modified by changing an associated attribute.

pseudo class: Pseudo classes are used in CSS to define behavior that cannot be defined using a standard class. For example, the pseudo class `:hover` applies only when a mouse cursor is over the element.

selector: In CSS, the selector is a class or tag that is being styled.

style sheet: A set of CSS styles that in a MySpace profile are contained within the opening and closing `<style>` tags.

tag: An instruction that appears within < > brackets that is used within HTML to define how an element in a web page appears.

Index

The best place on the Web to learn about new technologies, find new gear, discover new ways to build and modify your systems, and meet fascinating techheads...just like you.

▶ Visit www.extremetech.com.

How to take it to the Extreme.

If you enjoyed this book, there are many others like it for you. From *Podcasting* to *Hacking Firefox*, ExtremeTech books can fulfill your urge to hack, tweak and modify, providing the tech tips and tricks readers need to get the most out of their hi-tech lives.

EXTREMETECH™   Available wherever books are sold.

WILEY
Now you know.

Wiley and the Wiley logo are trademarks of John Wiley & Sons, Inc. and/or its affiliates. The ExtremeTech logo is a trademark of Ziff Davis Publishing Holdings, Inc. Used under license. All other trademarks are the property of their respective owners.